ARIS & PHILLIPS HISPANIC CLASSICS

JOSÉ LUIS ALONSO DE SANTOS

Going Down to Morocco
Bajarse al moro

Translation, Introduction and Notes by
Duncan Wheeler

Aris & Phillips
is an imprint of
Oxbow Books, Oxford, UK

Printed and bound by CPI Group (UK) Ltd, Croydon, CR0 4YY

ISBN   hardback: 978-1-90834-327-7
ISBN   paper: 978-7-90834-326-0

A CIP record for this book is available from the British Library.

This book is available direct from

Oxbow Books, Oxford, UK
Phone: 01865-241249; Fax: 01865-794449

and

The David Brown Book Company
PO Box 511, Oakville, CT 06779, USA
Phone: 860-945-9329; Fax: 860-945-9468

or from our website

www.oxbowbooks.com

*Cover image: Cover images of Madrid during the 1980s
courtesy of the private collection of Eduardo Rodríguez Merchán*

Allá donde se cruzan los caminos,
donde el mar no se puede concebir,
donde regresa siempre el fugitivo...
pongamos que hablo de Madrid.

Over there, where the paths cross,
where you can't even conceive of the sea,
where the fugitive will invariably return...
let's just say I'm talking about Madrid.

(Joaquín Sabina: excerpt from lyrics to the song
Pongamos que hablo de Madrid. Sabina 2002, 60)

Madrileños – Hemos de estar en extremo contentos y satisfechos porque Madrid se haya convertido en la fábula de Europa. Voces extranjeras la llaman la capital de la alegría y del contento de Europa. Nada puede producirnos mayor gozo, siempre ajeno a cualquier soberbia o vanidad, porque titular así a nuestra ciudad significa que es acogedora, cordial, libre, apacible y universal, todos cuyos adjetivos son muchos y muy ilustres y pocas veces se han dado reunidos en la historia de una Villa tan populosa y concurrida como es la nuestra.

People of Madrid – We should be contented and satisfied to the extreme because Madrid has become the fable of Europe. Foreign voices call it Europe's capital of happiness and contentment. Nothing could inspire in us greater joy, always distinct from any form of pride or vanity, because to label our city as such means that it is welcoming, cordial, free, pleasant and universal. All of these many adjectives are highly illustrious, and rarely have they all been applicable in the history of a town as busy and heavily populated as ours.

(Enrique Tierno Galván: edict delivered by Madrid's Mayor on
May 9 1985. Tierno Galván 1986, 111)

Y la policía buscaba en los lavabos, recortaba las puertas de los retretes (para que pudiera verse si había más de uno en ellos), sancionaba, multaba, exigía carteles a la entrada de los locales prohibiendo, en grandes letras, el uso de estupefacientes. Al principio pareció poca cosa. Pero lentamente se convirtió en una vigilancia total y severa. Claro que había drogas, sexo y brillo, pero – evidentemente – tenían que acabar. El orden jamás tolera la Felicidad.

And the police started to carry out searches in toilets, they made the doors to the cubicles smaller (so that they could see if there was more than one person in them), they penalised, fined, demanded signs on the entrances to venues prohibiting, in big letters, the use of drugs. It didn't seem a big deal at the beginning. But slowly it turned into a vigilance that was both ubiquitous and severe. Of course there were drugs, sex and wonder but – evidently – they had to come to an end. The system will never tolerate Happiness.

(Luis Antonio de Villena – excerpt from the novel
Madrid has Died. Villena 1999, 174)

CONTENTS

ACKNOWLEDGEMENTS

The preparation of this edition was enabled by a Leverhulme Research Fellowship, for which I am very grateful. Eduardo Rodríguez Merchán kindly donated the photographs shown on the cover from his personal archive.

INTRODUCTION

Madrid and La Movida

José Luis Alonso de Santos began writing *Bajarse al moro* in 1983; the play received its stage premiere in 1985, the year that marked the tenth anniversary of the death of General Franco – the unelected insurrectionist who had been in power ever since his victory in the Spanish Civil War (1936–1939) – and in which the country was courted by the international media who lauded the 'new Spain' and its ostensibly successful transition from dictatorship to monarchical democracy. *Bajarse al moro* both forms part of, and documents, *La Movida,* a catch-all phrase, which, like the 'swinging sixties', is as frequently cited as it is subject to misunderstanding and ambiguity. Broadly speaking, it is a drug-fuelled youth movement that emerged in the Spanish capital, Madrid and, to a lesser degree, in other urban centres in the late 1970s and early-mid 1980s. Franco's death provided the necessary pre-conditions for an explosion across the arts and alternative lifestyles which, although not unknown under the dictatorship, had generally been the unique preserve of either the upper-classes or those living at the margins of society.

Icons of *La Movida* such as the filmmaker Pedro Almodóvar or the singer Alaska brought the style and attitude of gay and punk sub-cultures to the general public and, in the process, revealed that there were alternative modes of living to the patriarchal nuclear family that had been the principal, and often sole, route to social inclusion during Francoism. In addition to breaking away from the regimented nature of the dictatorship, *La Movida* was equally resistant to what its chief protagonists perceived to be the earnest, almost puritanical, ideological straitjacketing of many of those who had opposed the former regime. This new generation did not want to be defined by their relationship to Franco or even by their political views. *Pepi, Luci, Bom y otras chicas del montón/Pepi, Luci, Bom and Other Girls from the Heap* (Pedro Almodóvar 1981), replete with its parody of the general elections in an *erecciones generales/general erections* contest, and its depiction of a fascist police-officer insufficiently sadistic to satisfy the desires of his masochistic wife, who instead seeks solace in a teenage lesbian punk singer, was considered an affront to those at both ends of the political

spectrum albeit for radically different reasons. Whilst, at the time of its release, Almodóvar's debut feature film was a cult classic, *La Movida* increasingly became part of the mainstream as the decade progressed. The failed coup attempt of 1981 whereby General Tejero entered the Spanish parliament and held the legally elected MPs hostage was a turning point for the nascent democracy which, somewhat paradoxically, led to the more reactionary segments of Spanish society having their power and influence diminished, whilst paving the way for the ascension of Felipe González and his centre-left Socialist government to power with a landslide victory in the 1982 general elections.

Madrid, more than anywhere else in Spain, was in desperate need of an image makeover: the legacy of the aggressively centralist Francoist state meant that the city was often seen to be inherently parasitical and reactionary (see Stapell, 2010). It would, somewhat counter-intuitively, be an ex-Marxist former university professor, Enrique Tierno Galván, who saw the solution to the Madrid ills to lie in what Joan Ramón Resina has termed 'semi-official hedonism' (2000, 95). Especially following the Socialist victory, this avuncular figure, who travelled round the city in his trusty Citroen 2CV, sought to re-open public spaces, encourage festive celebrations and subsidise pop concerts at one of which he even famously instructed the youthful public 'a colocarse y al loro', a slang phrase for becoming intoxicated on drugs. The man known as the *viejo profesor/old teacher*, whose death in 1986 was deeply mourned, was that rarest of beasts: a genuinely popular politician. He was also a canny and ruthless Machiavellian operator, fully aware of the electoral strength of a disenfranchised youth which, largely as a result of the Francoist ideal of the large family, were both huge in number, and suffering record highs in unemployment.

The Socialists had fought their national election campaign with the slogan *Por el cambio/For Change* and, in the same way that Tony Blair would later try and make New Labour chic in the UK through so-called 'Cool Britannia', *La Movida* provided a ready-made cultural accompaniment to Spain's achievements in the political realm. The policies and ideology of Spanish politicians in the 1980s secured *La Movida* a place in the (inter-)national consciousness, yet many of its chief progenitors complained that this co-option sowed the seeds of artistic decline, whilst it provided ammunition for detractors to decry it as an elaborate hoax manufactured

for political ends. There is an element of truth in both accusations, but as the singer-songwriter Joaquín Sabina writes:

> [...] lo que no me van a quitar ninguno de esos desdeñosos de la movida que dicen que nunca existió es la alegría de ocupación de espacios públicos y el estallido de libertad que vivimos durante los años de Tierno Galván. Es decir, los san Isidro, las fiestas, los conciertos, los bares y la gente. Eso pasó, simplemente pasó. Venían los turistas suecos y se bajaban en la Puerta del Sol y te preguntaban: 'Por favor, ¿me puede usted decir dónde está la movida?' [Risas.] Eso fue así.

> [...] what none of those who scorn the Movida, who say it never existed, will ever take away from me is the happiness of occupying public spaces, the explosion of freedom we lived through during the Tierno Galván years. That's to say, the celebration of Madrid's patron saint, the festivities, the concerts, the bars and the people. That happened, it happened plain and simple. The Swedish tourists came, would get off at the Puerta del Sol and would ask you: 'Would you please be so kind as to tell me where the Movida is?' [Laughter.] It was like that.

> (Sabina and Flores 2007, 89–90)

The chief achievements of *La Movida* and Tierno Galván's municipal policies were to be found in an admittedly ephemeral re-invention of city space and urban living, arguably the primary subject-matter and inspiration for *Bajarse al moro*, a play which simultaneously celebrates and laments the precariousness of the opportunities for freedom in Madrid during the early-mid-1980s. As will be discussed later, Alonso de Santos is a quintessentially urban chronicler, and much of the play's charm lies in its rootedness in a concrete socio-geographical milieu. In the same way that areas such as Brixton, Notting Hill, Harlem or Hell's Kitchen have set connotations for an Anglo-American readership, specific neighbourhoods in the Spanish capital are firmly rooted in the national consciousness, and a full appreciation of *Bajarse al moro* presupposes at least a passing awareness of Madrid's social and physical geography. The play is set in Lavapiés, an area located close to the historic centre that has long been a first stopping point for new arrivals to the city and is home to the Rastro, Madrid's historic flea market.

In the landmark neo-realist film *Surcos/Furrows* (José Antonio Nieves Conde 1951) – arguably the first example of cinematic protest during the Franco regime – the overcrowded and unsanitary development of

the ramshackle area is highlighted through the plight of a family who have moved to the city from the country in search of a better life. In spite of these conditions, the neighbourhood has always had a degree of bohemian romanticism largely as a result of the musical theatre and taverns to which it was home; this was reflected, for example, in refrains such as 'Cuando vengas a Madrid, chulapa mía, voy a hacerte emperatriz de Lavapiés'/'When you come to Madrid, my princess, I'm going to make you the empress of Lavapiés' that proliferated in the popular songbook. In other words, it conjures up a specific repertoire of sounds and images for Spaniards even if only a small percentage of the population might have had first-hand knowledge of the area. This is reflected, for example, in *Buenos días, condesita/ Good Day, Little Countess* (Luis César Amadori 1967), an anodyne star vehicle for teen sensation Rocío Durcal in which she runs a record stall on the Rastro, attracting customers by her ability to dance to both traditional Spanish and modern rock n roll songs. The market soon became a preferred destination for hippies visiting Spain, a phenomenon even reflected by the Francoist NO-DO – the official newsreel service projected in cinemas before the commencement of the main feature – which depicted, in a tone of puzzled yet benign bemusement, the colourful new foreign arrivals descending on the market en-masse in a section titled 'Trovadores del Siglo XX'/'20th century troubadours', shown as part of reel number 1443B in 1970.

The Rastro of the nascent democratic period provides a paradigmatic illustration of Sophie Watson's claim that markets allow for an 'easy sociality' thereby 'weaving complexity and difference into the texture of mundane everyday life' (2009, 1582). In addition to the presence and interaction of long-term residents, different political groups – both legal and illegal – used it as meeting ground and forum for proselytising. *La Movida* would later be associated with the more self-consciously hip and youthful Malasaña area located on the other side of Madrid's central artery, the Gran Vía, but many of the individuals who would come to constitute its core nucleus met trading comics, memorabilia or records on the Rastro's makeshift stalls. Needless to say, this melting pot provided a stimulating and instantly recognisable social backdrop for Alonso de Santos' play and was, as he discusses in my interview with him, the deciding factor for him setting the play in Lavapiés as opposed to Cuatro Caminos, the Spanish capital's other most (in)famous immigrant area

whose name – which literally translates as the four paths – is referenced in the lyrics to Sabina's *Pongamos que hablo de Madrid,* the city's unofficial anthem.

José Luis Alonso de Santos and Spanish Theatre in the 1980s

Following their first election victory, the Socialist government invested an unprecedented amount of money in culture. In terms of the dramatic arts, this was in many senses a necessary injection as the theatre was largely in disarray in the early 1980s. Whilst there was a widespread feeling that the National Theatres were a valuable asset that could be used to project a new image of Spain abroad and instil democratic values at home, they remained tainted by their associations with the previous regime whilst successive administration had failed to address very serious problems with their infrastructure and financing. Under Franco, staged performances in the burgeoning independent theatre scene were often funded by oppositional groups; at a time when the rights of assembly were severely curtailed, theatre both functioned as a rallying call for dissident politics, and a pretext and disguise for clandestine meetings. An unfortunate side-effect was that artistry was often sacrificed to an ostensibly higher cause and, post-1975, the remnants of independent theatre lost not only its economic support but, arguably, also its raison-d'être: whilst it continued to focus on the changing political climate, the speed of change meant that plays constantly seemed to lag behind what was happening in everyday life.

This is one of the reasons why a catchphrase of the more reactionary sections of Spanish society – *Bajo Franco vivíamos mejor/We lived better under Franco* – was given its own ironic variation in a pithy remark first attributed to Manuel Vázquez Montalbán: *Contra Franco vivíamos mejor/We lived better against Franco.* In other words, Spanish theatre and the former oppositional left were suffering an identity crisis in the late 1970s and early 1980s. Whilst, previously, it had been thought that Franco's death and the end of overt censorship would open the creative floodgates, practitioners and commentators could only look on in dismay as the commercial stage was dominated by the soft-porn *destape/unveiling* works that revelled in the superficial liberties afforded by the incipient democracy. State-run theatres tended to favour foreign

and national classics at the expense of new works; whether this was a symptom or cause of a dearth in new high-quality dramatic writing was a constant source of debate.

Whilst the Socialist victory and its prioritizing of the dramatic arts sought to ameliorate this situation, its success was partial at best. During the 1980s, theatre became more of a minority activity as, despite the investment in the sector by the government, the number of spectators decreased from eleven million in 1983 to just five million in 1990 (Ragué-Arías 1996, 114). On the one hand, this was the result of a pan-national trend whereby theatre, subject to an exponential inflation in costs, took on an increasingly marginal role within an ever-expanding mediascape. This was, however, exacerbated by the interventionist system of subventions set in place by the Spanish government, which arguably sought to control rather than counteract market forces. Great emphasis was placed on nurturing the existing National Theatres – the Español and María Guerrero – alongside the creation of showcase institutions such as the *Compañía Nacional de Teatro Clásico/National Classical Theatre Company* and the *Centro Dramático Nacional/National Centre for Dramatic Arts*. Priority was afforded to the performance of classic works, principal amongst which were the plays of Federico García Lorca, the martyred Andalusian poet who was one of the first victims of the Nationalist uprising led by General Franco against the legally elected Popular Front government. This attempt to recuperate alterative traditions that had often, though not always, been silenced during the dictatorship was laudable enough in itself; once again, however, this was largely done at the expense of living playwrights, and what subsidies were awarded tended to be directed towards self-consciously obtuse works that failed to attract audiences.

The major exceptions to the general pattern outlined above were *¡Ay, Carmela!, Bajarse al moro*, and *Las bicicletas son para el verano/Bicycles Are for the Summer* by José Sanchís Sinisterra, Alonso de Santos and Fernando Fernán Gómez respectively; the three best known plays of the transition period, which attracted audiences that did not habitually attend the theatre, were all subsequently made into successful films. This broad appeal and popularity has led to some charges of playing to the gallery through recourse to the lowest common denominator, a particularly loaded criticism in the context of the post-dictatorship period where popular culture was frequently equated with the manipulation of the

masses under Franco. In subsequent sections, I will suggest that *Bajarse al moro* is far more complex and multifaceted than such a critique will allow but, leaving the evaluative dimension to one side for the moment, I would like to briefly examine how and why Alonso de Santos' biography equipped him to succeed in a challenge that evaded the vast majority of his contemporaries: a well-constructed, critical yet ludic depiction of the transitional phase through which Spain was passing.

Born in Valladolid in 1942, Alonso de Santos moved to Madrid to study at university in 1959. Unlike many of his contemporaries in Spanish theatre, he was not from an artistic or intellectual family. A certain outsider status and ability to mix in a variety of milieu has always informed his writing, whilst an ear for the idiosyncrasies and characteristics of different social groups has helped render him as arguably the best writer of dialogue in post-Franco Spanish theatre. Although his degree was in Psychology, Philosophy and Information Science, he became involved in various theatre groups. Many of the great dramatists from Shakespeare to Brecht took on a variety of roles within the theatre and it is, for example, no coincidence that Lorca wrote his three most accessible and frequently staged plays, the so-called rural trilogy – *Bodas de Sangre/ Blood Wedding, La casa de Bernarda Alba/The House of Bernarda Alba* and *Yerma* – following his experiences with La Barraca, a student theatre company that sought to bring the classics of Spain's Golden Age to the rural proletariat. Alonso de Santos belongs to this tradition, and his early experiences in the independent theatre encompassed a broad range of roles including acting, directing, producing and adapting works for the contemporary stage. He also benefitted from studying with the North American William Layton who was instrumental in establishing Stansislavsky's theories in Spain and, often in collaboration with Miguel Narros, has trained and mentored many of the country's greatest actors.

The young Alonso de Santos was always a voracious reader, and he came to creative writing indirectly through adaptation. His first dramatic text, *El auto del hombre/Man Accused* with the Teatro Libre, was based on a selection of Corpus Christi plays by the great seventeenth-century Spanish playwright, Calderón de la Barca. Throughout his career, he has done versions of dramatists as diverse as Wesker, Quevedo, Molière or Aristofanes, and Margarita Piñero suggests that adaptation helped teach him the importance of linguistic economy (2005, 108), which would

instil a discipline that put him in good stead for his own writing. His debut self-penned play, *¡Viva el Duque, nuestro dueño!/Long Live the Duque, our Master* was the first dramatic work to be registered for copyright purposes following Franco's death (Amo-Sánchez 2002, 30), something of a premonition as regards the role that Alonso de Santos would play in the democratic theatrical landscape. The narrative, set in the late seventeenth-century, about the misfortunes of an acting troupe and Spain's imperial decline was a thinly disguised metaphor for the hardships endured in the present under a repressive inward-looking regime. Although the playwright was resolutely anti-Francoist, one of the keys to Alonso de Santos' longevity and continued relevance was that – unlike many of his contemporaries – neither he nor his work was defined by their opposition to the regime.

Whilst a subsequent play such as *El álbum familiar/Family Album*, premiered in 1982, make reference both to the violence committed by the Francoist state and the moral and intellectual vacuity of its rhetoric (see Alonso de Santos 1992, 57, 65–69), this is, in this case, framed within a semi-autobiographical narrative in which the emphasis is placed on the tragicomic dimensions of memory and human relationships. Similarly, *La cena de los generales/The Generals' Dinner* – premiered in 2009 and, at the time of writing, Alonso de Santos' most recent play – takes as its setting a celebratory meal that Franco wants to give in honour of his closest generals to be held in the Palace Hotel in 1939. On the one hand, it is an indictment of the violence that underpinned the Francoist regime, manifest in the genuine fear felt by the maître de and the lieutenant as to what might occur if the dinner is not a success; the play's principal appeal nevertheless lies in the comic absurdity of the situation whereby the kitchen staff remain staunch in their opposition to the dictator, combined with the pathos inherent in the depiction of human frailty and dignity common to characters from both sides of the social and political divide.

The fact that, in the interview that follows this introduction, Alonso de Santos professed his admiration to me for Pedro Muñoz Seca, a remarkably prolific and popular playwright specialising in light comedy, whose popularity far outstripped that of Lorca's in their lifetimes and who died at the hands of a Republican firing squad during the Civil War, is evidence of a certain flexibility in thought and taste. In a similar vein, Alonso de Santos may have participated in the common oppositional tactic

of puncturing the imperial rhetoric of Spain's Golden Age so beloved of Francoist mythology but he never rejected the country's great classical playwrights in the uncritical fashion that was the norm amongst many of his contemporaries (see Wheeler 2012). Despite living a somewhat anarchic existence in the 1960s and 1970s, the dramatist who would subsequently be named artistic director of the National Classical Theatre Company (2000–2004) already had a keen eye for dramatic structure, and largely abided by conventions and precepts. In one of his two books on dramatic theory and composition, he argues that:

> [...] el conocimiento de las reglas y los procesos técnicos no exige su acatamiento ni la sumisión a ningún tipo de preceptiva o norma, pero sí evita recorrer caminos trillados considerándolos originales o nuevos, y confundir la experimentación personal de épocas de aprendizaje con la experimentación real. Desgraciadamente, las buenas intenciones del creador no se corresponden siempre con los resultados que obtiene su obra.

> [...] an awareness of the rules and technical processes does not require them to be abided by or the submission to any kind of precept or regulation, but what it does do is avoid the pursuit of over-worn paths thinking them to be original or new, and the confusion of personal experimentation during an apprenticeship phase with genuine experimentation. Unfortunately, a creative person's good intentions do not always correspond to the results obtained by their work.

> (1998, 189)

This solid – his critics would argue stolid – grounding in theatrical forms not only helped to fund Alonso de Santos' increasingly sedentary existence in the 1980s when he stopped appearing on stage and complemented his creative writing with teaching at RESAD, Spain's national drama school, but also facilitated his enviable productivity,[1] and ability to communicate with a broad audience that has been reflected in him being the only prolific dramatist of his generation to have virtually all of his works staged. His rather conventional approach to dramatic form does, however, mean that some of his plays can be somewhat formulaic, and may well be driven by pragmatic rather than purely artistic motivations.

---

[1] See the author's highly informative webpage – http://www.joseluisalonsodesantos. com – for more details.

Where there can, nevertheless, be no question of his innovation or creativity is in his subject-matter. Unlike many of his contemporaries who, in spite of their ostensibly avant-garde approach, became increasingly anachronistic in their adhesion to the politics and sloganeering of yesteryear, Alonso de Santos was able to provide a compelling depiction of the modes and mores of Spain's new democratic youth culture. Although he was of an older generation than the protagonists of *La Movida*, he shared with them a desire to combine high and low art whilst his appreciation of, and immersion into, the world of popular films, songs, television programs, comics, *etc.* helped ground his characters in a recognizable milieu. A talent for compelling quotidian dialogues alongside an intuitive yet thoughtful understanding of culture in its many guises find their finest and most influential exposition in *Bajarse al moro,* a play that perfectly encapsulates Alonso de Santos' principal contribution to the contemporary Spanish stage: his capacity to imbue conventional forms with contemporary characters and concerns.

Plot Summary

Cousins Chusa and Jaimito live together in a small flat in the Lavapiés neighbourhood of Madrid, alongside Alberto – a childhood friend of the latter and casual lover of the former – who has recently joined the police force. Chusa returns to the flat with Elena, a middle-class runaway she chances upon whilst going out to buy Rizla. Much to Jaimito's initial consternation, Chusa invites her new friend to move in, and join the family business by accompanying her on a trip to Morocco where she plans to buy marihuana to then sell at a profit in Spain. Elena agrees to the plan although her initial confusion over what the trip will entail turns into concern on realising she is expected to smuggle the drugs inside her orifices; still a virgin, she fears that her vagina will be physically incapable of secreting the quantities that Chusa expects her to carry. Overcoming her embarrassment, Elena admits to her lack of sexual experience. Chusa, surprised that anyone is still a virgin in 1985, volunteers Alberto's services to resolve the situation. Elena remains non-committal; although she finds Alberto attractive, the fact that he is a policeman puts her off.

Jaimito buys alcohol and puts on music in order to create a climate ripe for sexual activity. Alberto, initially aghast on hearing Chusa's

proposal, gradually allows himself to be persuaded, and he and Elena go into the bedroom. Before anything can happen, however, Doña Antonia, Alberto's religiously pious, drink-dependent, kleptomaniac mother, bursts in on them with news that his father has been released from prison far earlier than expected. Jaimito has, by this stage, shed his initial aversion to Elena who he now clearly fancies; his attempts to flirt with her pass unnoticed, and she and Alberto are very much attracted to each other, relishing the prospect of playing their allotted parts in the plan orchestrated by Chusa, now increasingly jealous of their burgeoning relationship. A second attempt at intimacy is once again curtailed; this time due to the unexpected arrival of two knife-wielding heroin addicts, Abel and Nancho, desperate for a fix. In the ensuing fray, Jaimito uses Alberto's gun to threaten the intruders, accidentally firing a bullet that sends them running.

Alberto, maddened by what he considers to be Jaimito's irresponsibility, lectures him on the dangers of fire-arms inadvertently shooting his friend in the arm. Whilst Jaimito is recovering in hospital, Chusa heads to Morocco on her own; Elena has decided to invest financially in the venture but not to participate directly. Doña Antonia who, since their first meeting, has thought that Elena would be an ideal daughter-in-law, talks to her about Alberto's father's miraculous conversion into a respectable businessman studying for a degree; he has, she boasts, also convinced their son to ask that Jaimito pretend he shot himself so as not to place a nascent police career in jeopardy. Antonia also admits that she and Alberto have been in contact with Elena's mother; suggesting that a life of enviable respectable domesticity awaits in suburbia, she encourages the younger woman to leave the chaos of the flat and its inhabitants behind. Jaimito is discharged from hospital and, soon afterwards, Alberto and he receive news that Chusa has been arrested on her return from Morocco. Jaimito rushes to the police station to try and help her but to no avail. Tensions escalate between him and Alberto who is reluctant to get involved in fear of the potential repercussions.

Whilst Chusa continues to be held in custody, Elena and Alberto move back to her mother's place whilst they wait for their new flat to be properly furnished. Chusa, who now faces a lesser charge due to the fact that most of the drugs she was caught with have mysteriously disappeared in police custody, is released. On returning home, she is saddened by her cousin

telling her that the other two flatmates have left to set-up-house together. Elena returns to the flat to pick up some things she has left behind; the two women argue as Chusa is offended by the suggestion that she reimburse the money that Elena gave her. At the height of their argument, a bashful Alberto, accompanied by his mother, arrives. Accusations are levelled to and fro as the young couple and Doña Antonia pack. Jaimito and Chusa are left alone in the flat, feeling melancholic and angry; his aggression gradually turns to excitement on hearing that his cousin is pregnant.

Language, Dramatic Structure and Genre

Alonso de Santos has claimed that *Bajarse al moro* was partly inspired by Chejov's *Uncle Vanya* (Piñero 2005, 355), in which the arrival of an outsider to an (un)stable household propels a hyperactive narrative into motion. In a distant echo of the great Russian naturalist, his plays tend to contain what Antonia Amo Sánchez has termed, 'una expresión poética de la realidad' [a poetic expression of reality] (2004, 153). Alonso de Santos' dialogues have been painstakingly elaborated and stylised not only to paradoxically create the illusion that they replicate the way in which people speak in the street, but also to function as a privileged form of characterisation. In his own words:

> La vieja fórmula 'dime cómo hablas y te diré quién eres', es uno de los elementos constitutivos de la creación del personaje. A ella podríamos añadir las de 'dime cómo hablas y te diré hacia dónde vas, y de dónde vienes'. Es decir, las palabras definen a los personajes en cada momento del desarrollo de la acción dramática: sus conflictos, sus metas, sus emociones, sus relaciones con el entorno, su posición social, sus logros y fracasos, y su manifestación externa como seres humanos.

> The old formula 'tell me how you speak and I'll tell you who you are', is one of the constitutive elements in the creation of a character. To that, we could also add those that say 'tell me how you speak, and I'll tell you where you're heading for, and where you're coming from'. That's to say, words define characters at every stage in the development of the dramatic action: their conflicts, their goals, their emotions, their relationship with their environment, their social position, their achievements and their failures, alongside their external appearance as human beings.

> (Alonso de Santos 1996, 95)

As conventional as this realist aesthetic may appear, it was in fact something quite new within the context of Spanish theatre of the 1970s and 1980s where the prevailing norm was for actors to deliver poeticised language in a rhetorical fashion, thereby creating a distance between stage and auditorium. Alonso de Santos actively distanced himself from this tradition by, for example, creating protagonists with little social prestige operating at the margins of respectable society; even in *La sombra del Tenorio/Tenorio's Shadow* – his very personal take on a shining example of nineteenth-century romanticism, José Zorrilla's *Don Juan Tenorio* – his focus is not on the legendary lothario but on a monologue set in the present day by an ageing actor looking back on his days playing Don Juan's servant, Ciutti, and recalling its prosaic hardships ranging from hunger to the draconian actions of the Francoist censor.

A hallmark of much of Alonso de Santo's work is tragicomic realism viewed with a caustic moral eye, and often within the long-standing Spanish tradition of the picaresque. Alexander A. Parker's description of the seventeenth century literary picaroon as 'not a vicious criminal such as a gangster or a murderer, but someone who is dishonourable and anti-social in a much less violent way' (1967, 4), also provides a perfect fit for many of Alonso de Santos' most memorable characters who, in typical picaresque fashion, generally turn out to be far more honest, or at least less dishonest, than the individuals and society that implicitly or explicitly accuses them of moral licentiousness. Hence, for example, there is the clear implication that Chusa only receives a lesser charge because the police have stolen most of the drugs she was carrying for their own purposes.

A more politicised and idiosyncratic revival of the picaresque mode in Spanish theatre occurred at the end of dictatorship when Alfonso Sastre wrote *Ahola no es de leíl/No Laughing Mattter* – an updated version of Miguel de Cervantes' satirical seventeenth-century short story, *Rinconete y Cortadillo/Rinconete and Cortadillo*, now set during the War of Independence in nineteenth-century Cuba – whilst in prison between October 1974 and June 1975 on suspicion of terrorist activities with Basque terrorist group ETA. The dialogue, memorably revived and updated for the stage by Philip Swanson and Stuart Green at the Universities of Sheffield and Leeds in 2012, was originally written using prison slang and also drawing on Sastre's various trips to Cuba from the

mid-1960s onwards as part of the then-illegal Spanish Communist Party.
In a subsequent semi-parodic treatise, he used his first-hand experience
of the language used by the oppressed to argue that he was providing
the first literary testament to the experiences and language of a section
of Spanish society who 'no han tenido, después de la guerra civil, sino
remedos populistas (Cela) o superficialmente hiperpolíticos' [since
the Civil War, have only had populist mimicries (Cela) or been hyper-
politicised in a superficial manner] (1980, 17).

   This politicised backdrop helps to contextualise the difficulties Alonso
de Santos discusses in the interview that follows this introduction in
finding an actress willing to take the lead role in *La estanquera de Vallecas/
The Tobacconist Woman from Vallecas*. The play, about a robbery and
subsequent hostage situation set in a working class district on the edges
of Madrid, was first staged at the small local theatre El Goyo Vallecano
on 11 Dec 1981 (Piñero 2005, 338), but it was only when it was re-
staged in 1985 that it triumphed at the box-office (2005, 237), concurrent
with *Bajarse al moro*'s success. Alonso de Santos' plays were part of
a general integration of the marginal into mainstream culture reflected
when, for example, Las Vulpes, performed *Me gusta ser una zorra/I like
being a whore* – an adaptation of Iggy and the Stooges' 1969 song *I
Wanna be Your Dog* – on the national state television channel in 1983;
in the ensuing scandal, future Nobel-prize winning novelist, Camilo José
Cela, openly supported the all-female punk band. We have testimony
to these changing mores in a number of texts that emerged around this
time. The iconoclastic prose-writer and journalist, Francisco Umbral,
published the most famous – the *Diccionario cheli/Cheli Dictionary*
(1983), a somewhat idiosyncratic guide to *Movida*-speak – but it was in
fact predated by Juan Villarín's *Diccionario de argot/Dictionary of Slang*
in which he spoke of how:

> El código secreto de claves y de gestos de 'la canalla', hasta ayer soterrado,
> abandona sus purezas ocultas y, a la par que establece niveles más
> superficiales de expresión, gana en adeptos. Ésta es la era de lo fácil. Así,
> el argot de ahora mismo, fecundado en la mezcolanza y el amasijo, admite
> todo tipo de innovaciones. [...] En efecto, abunda el adolescente que se
> adhiere a los sistemas de defensa de sus predecesores más 'antisociales'
> y cunde el joven que se abraza al estatuto oral del argot, por aquello de
> alimentarse en humores contestatarios o de pose.

The 'rogue's' secret code of words and gestures, completely underground until very recently, has abandoned its hidden purities and established itself with a more superficial form of expression at the same time that it's been adopted by a much greater number of people. This is the age of whatever's easiest. Thus, the slang of right now, originating in a hodgepodge jumble of this and that, permits all manner of innovations. [...] In effect, what's happened is that there are an abundance of adolescents who use the defence mechanisms of their more 'anti-social' predecessors, and the phenomenon of the young person who embraces slang as an oral statement of intent, either to feed their rebellious mood or adopt a pose is spreading.

(1979, 10)

In the Spain of the late 1970s and early 1980s, even the manners and activities of the criminal underclass were, for better or worse, becoming more democratic. It is from this new generation of young people, living on the fringes of society but hardly hard-boiled criminals, that Alonso de Santos found his inspiration and thereby introduced a new kind of character and form of speech onto the Spanish stage. If *Bajarse al moro* was more readily accepted by Spanish audiences than *La estanquera*, it was partly due to the fact that the time-lapse between their respective premieres allowed for a certain degree of social and linguistic normalization; it was, however, also because the protagonists of the latter spoke in a denser argot befitting the highly-politicised working-class area of Vallecas situated on the edges of Madrid, whilst the former featured characters who, without relinquishing their status as social outcasts, nevertheless spoke and behaved in a way that had become the norm across an increasingly broad spectrum of Spanish youth.

It is no coincidence that Alonso de Santos, like Jaimito with his pet hamster named after Humphrey Bogart, is something of a film buff, and *Bajarse al moro*, like many of his plays, has far more in common with the cinema than the theatre of the time. On the one hand, it shares an appreciation of the tragicomic psychological wit of classic Hollywood comedians from Billy Wilder to Woody Allen with a new sub-genre, the so-called *Nueva Comedia Madrileño/New Madrid Comedy* (see Ibáñez and Iglesias 2011), that emerged in the early 1980s in Spain with films such as *Ópera prima* (Fernando Trueba, 1980) whose narratives focussed on the amorous adventures of young middle-class students or professionals. The difference was that Alonso de Santos' protagonists were

less respectable. In this regard, the plays were closer to the *cine quinqui* in which filmmakers such as Eloy de la Iglesias – whose filmography includes the cinematic adaptation of *La estanquera* (1987), for which Joaquín Sabina provided the music – and Carlos Saura depicted youthful anti-heroes destined to live fast and dangerously, on the edges of the city and the law to the soundtrack of bands such as Los Chingutos (see CCCB 2009; and Whittaker 2012), the flamenco-rock band from Vallecas whose rumbas Jaimito enjoys singing along to. In the same way that the Rastro would have been one of the few places where the characters of these two very different urban cinematic traditions might have had any interaction, *Bajarse al moro* offered a hybrid of these two very different urban cinematic traditions: less nihilistic than the latter but more gritty than the former.

Whilst Alonso de Santos' engagement with the present might have distanced him from contemporary dramatists, it paradoxically led him to engage with Spain's theatrical tradition, most noticeably the *sainete*, 'la forma casticista y popular de teatro opuesta al gusto neoclásico, que hicieron valer autores como don Ramón de la Cruz y Juan Ignacio González del Castillo, entre otros muchos' [the form of popular theatre typical of Madrid, opposed to neo-classical taste, whose mettle was shown by writers such as don Ramón de la Cruz, Juan Ignacio González del Castillo, amongst many others] (Huerta Calvo, Peral Vega and Urzáiz Tortajada 2005, 635). The brevity and psychological simplicity of this genre of short-plays, a descendent of the *entremeses* used to entertain theatre audiences in the interval between the acts of the main play from the sixteenth-century onwards, ensured that they were as rumbustious as they were simplistic. Alonso de Santos appropriates the underlying conceit of marginal but never purposefully malicious protagonist(s) struggling with circumstances in an often hostile albeit charming urban setting, but imbues it with a hitherto unknown degree of moral and psychological complexity. In the words of Huw Aled Lewis, the dramatist 'constantly challenges preconceptions and subverts our expectations, defying us to rely on easy generalisations about the world in which we live, and provoking us to question all that we see around us, all that we have traditionally accepted as being "true"' (2007, 109–10).

Characters in the Play

Bajarse al moro portrays the ways in which human-beings, however absurd their situation or actions, are able to treat their way of life as natural and justifiable. One of Alonso de Santos' principal talents is to make extreme scenarios and characters credible. Much of the play's humour and moral complexity derives from the ironic disparity between how remarkably un-self-aware individuals view themselves, and how they are seen from the outside. In an early comic scenario, Alberto, for example, cannot understand why Elena is asking what he considers to be silly questions about his uniform not realising that she, quite reasonably, cannot imagine that someone living in a drug-infested flat could be an agent of the law. In a later scene, the priest who lives next-door complains about the noise they are making at midnight; the inhabitants of the flat are able to convince themselves that it is, in fact, the clerical lifestyle that is disreputable. In this section, I would like to offer a brief description of the five principal characters before returning to the question of how they impact on the audience, and their role in the play's narrative structure and moral message(s).

Chusa, described as being twenty-five years old, having a chubby face and glasses, may not be a conventional beauty but her lust for life and good-heartedness serve to make her the play's most consistently attractive and sympathetic character. Although she does have the cynical motivation of having her as a companion for a trip to Morocco, the audience and Jaimito – who complains about the number of waifs and strays she picks up – sense that a maternal protectiveness and inherent generosity are her primary motivations in inviting Elena to stay at their flat. It is fitting that Chusa's subsequent arrest on her return from Morocco is a result of her selflessly sharing some of her drugs with an undercover police officer. There are implicit suggestions throughout the play that her outward bonhomie shields a tender interior, and that her generosity might be the result of her desire to be loved and needed. Although the audience is not made privy to many details about her past, she makes occasional negative comments about her own upbringing, suggesting that it is an advantage, as in the case of Elena, not to know one's father. She may flaunt her modernity, and takes pride in her open sexual relationship with Alberto, but it is evident that she would like a more stable partnership

with him. She makes it clear to Elena that she is only lending him to her out of practical necessity, and that she would not like it if they were to have sex more than once; her admission to loneliness at the end of the play when Alberto has left, alongside her certainty over the identity of her unborn child's father, suggests that, in spite of her public image, she is monogamous. Whilst our appreciation of her personality develops as the play progresses, she is the character whose speech patterns and modes of address change the least; she may not be completely honest, either to herself or others, but a candid mixture of wide-eyed innocence and street smarts is central to her appeal.

Jaimito, described as having a glass-eye and the look of someone who does not have many friends, is at least as vulnerable and sensitive as Chusa, but his self-defence mechanism is outward hostility rather than friendly gregariousness. He does not accompany his cousin on her trips to Morocco due to his physical appearance that would immediately arouse suspicion but, instead, stays at home raising what money he can mending sandals and dabbling in petty crime; one suspects, however, that he is effectively subsidised by Chusa. From a humble background – he lived in Vallecas before moving to Lavapiés – and lacking his childhood friend Alberto's good looks, Jaimito becomes an increasingly sympathetic character over the course of the play as both his frustrations and capacity for kindness come to the fore. Hence, for example, we see how his initial rudeness to Elena was, at least in part, the result of his awkwardness around attractive women. When Alberto suggests that Jaimito take the newcomer's virginity in his place, Chusa dismisses the idea claiming her cousin is useless at such things, and that Elena's not stupid; this is later borne out in a scene where Jaimito wants to volunteer himself in Alberto's absence, but is clueless as to how to pursue his goal, awkwardly attempting to flirt with her by telling a completely inopportune yarn about his ex-girlfriend leaving him for a leather-jacketed rocker. He does, however, have his own idiosyncratic charm, at least for the audience, and his enthusiasm for life and popular culture is a key element in creating the flat's unique atmosphere. Another attractive quality is his generosity: he automatically offers, for example, to either pay for Chusa to have an abortion or help raise her unborn child. In spite of his outward appearance and criminal tendencies, he, like his cousin, has an underlying innocence which allows him to be taken advantage of such as when Alberto persuades him to tell

the police that he shot himself. At the end of the play, Jaimito has two parallel fantasies that bear testimony to his defining character traits. In the first, he imagines himself as a pirate gunning down those pillars of society who have turned him into a pariah; then, more poignantly, he optimistically imagines a different, better world in which Chusa's child will be raised: 'You're born and, right away, some money to study, or to travel or to live how you want, without having to be there like some loser all your life; because everything will be organised the reverse of how it is now, and people will finally be able to be happy and well.' Jaimito's tragedy is that he is aware enough to realise his personal and social limitations, but lacks the skills or resources to transform them.

When discussing Elena with my students, the invariable reference point is the young woman described in Pulp's 1995 hit, *Common People*, a well-off art-student wanting to leave her sheltered upbringing behind to experience, albeit vicariously, the lives of the poor and bohemian. Whilst Elena clearly enjoys the happy-go-lucky atmosphere of the flat, willingly joining the others in taunting the priest next-door for example, it is immediately obvious to both the on-stage characters and audience that she speaks a very different language: one that is grammatically correct and well-mannered, albeit with the occasional incursion into the kind of *chelí* that could well have been learnt from a dictionary. The appearance of Abel and Nancho, two desperate high-class heroin addicts, suggests that social marginalisation is not the exclusive preserve of the working classes, but this twenty-one year old student's upbringing has clearly shielded her from life's cruel vicissitudes. Ostensibly naive, this virginal runaway is hardly a victim and is strategically passive from the outset; witness, for example, how she absolves herself from the discussion between Jaimito and Chusa as to whether she can stay, and simply waits to have a cup of tea made for her. She later claims to be pretty clueless about drugs, just knowing that she likes to smoke marihuana, but is quick to spot the investment possibilities of the premium 'double zero' variety. Elena might initially be coy about sleeping with a policeman but, it is she, not Alberto, who subsequently takes the initiative in pursuing a sexual relationship, whilst she has no qualms about subsequently becoming romantically involved with a man that her friend has made clear to her is on loan for one night, and one night only. In a manner akin to her half-hearted attempts to run away from her over-bearing religious mother

and petty-bourgeois lifestyle, Elena's flirtation with alternative lifestyles and belief-systems is clearly selfish, superficial and temporary; her very selective reading of an Umberto Eco text allows her to justify not going to her university lectures, yet she is still willing to take her classmates' notes and return home in order to sit the exams. These latent self-serving hypocrisies come to the fore when she decides not to accompany Chusa to Morocco, but still expects her to return the money she invested in the failed escapade to help fund her and Alberto's escape to the suburbs.

The character who is discussed in most detail before he is ever seen on-stage is Alberto. Chusa speaks of how good-looking he is but, less positively, we are already given a hint of his nascent distance from the others, and possible selfishness, when Chusa tells Elena not to touch his things because it makes him annoyed. Although he tends to act in his own self-interest, Alberto always endeavours to maintain the moral high ground. This is used for great comic effect when, for example, he convinces himself that taking Elena's virginity is the right thing to do because it is a public service and the police are there to serve the public; a more unpleasant side is, however, later manifest when, fearful of the repercussions, he refuses to intervene on Chusa's behalf when she is arrested claiming that she has to take responsibility for her actions. An important strand of the play's narrative is the growing divide between him and his flatmates, who attribute this change to Alberto becoming a policeman and, in Jaimito's sardonic words, not even taking his uniform off to piss; what had begun as a means to an end, a collective albeit expedient joke, mutates into a lifestyle choice exemplified in his decision to move to Móstoles. Chusa and Jaimito's attitude to this new town is almost identical to Jah Wobble's view of Essex in the 1960s. The bassist of PIL, the band Johnny Rotton formed after punk-group the Sex Pistols split, recalls how, after a family-member moved there, he and his sister made a pact to never leave London's East-End: 'At that time I viewed Essex as a sort of Siberia. I saw it as a conformist suburban hell, where people lived in quiet desperation. I thought that moving there was "taking the path of least resistance", and therefore cowardly, and to be avoided' (2009, 18). Alberto's defining characteristics are, in fact, conformism and moral cowardice. He allows his father to persuade him to ask Jaimito to pretend that he shot himself in order to safeguard his career, whilst subsequently attempting, albeit unsuccessfully, to avoid a showdown with

his former best friend by moving out of the flat whilst Jaimito is visiting Chusa in police custody. Unlike Elena, he clearly feels guilty for much of Act Two but, rather than act on his moral conscience, he uses pompous rationales – both his own and those of his parents – to safeguard his own interests. Less in-control of his external self-image than Elena, Alberto is the character whose speech patterns and vocabulary unwittingly change the most as he tends to allow himself to be moulded by the demands of other characters and the situations in which he finds himself.

One of the explanations for Alberto having something of a nondescript personality would appear to be his dominating mother, Doña Antonia, first seen hitting him with her handbag and described in the stage directions as 'fat and foul-mouthed'. This rotund middle-aged woman is a judgemental socially aspiring snob, manifest in throwaway comments about the clientele at the bingo or her obsession with having a university student as a daughter-in-law. Her limited social horizons are, however, shown by how ridiculously impressed she is by Elena's mother living and having an electrical appliances store near Quevedo, a respectable but hardly aristocratic area of Madrid. Although Elena's mother never appears on stage, she is similarly religious and hypocritical, spinning a series of improbable yarns – impregnation via an errant sperm in a council swimming pool, and a job in Czechoslovakia – to avoid telling the truth about whatever happened with her father. Much of the play's light relief derives from the hollowness of Antonia's pious rhetoric; she may claim respectability but she is a brandy-swigging shop-lifter whose husband has been in prison for many years. Reminiscent of many of the mothers in Almodóvar's films, Alonso de Santos taps into a comic tradition which, though hardly unique to Spain, is nevertheless particularly popular and prevalent there: that of the demonic mother. Certain running gags involving gin and brandy, which lend themselves to being over-played on stage, may be facile and tedious but Antonia does have some genuinely amusing set-pieces. Audiences tend to react with uproarious laughter when she relishes in the salacious gossip she hears at group confessions at her Neocatechumenate meetings whilst lamenting that some people are just too honest: an unemployed builder and a mechanic should not, for example, confess, at least in so much detail, to their homosexual escapades! Antonia elsewhere voices the typical hysterical laments for a society in decline – permissive nudity and sexual relations;

six-year-olds shooting up at school – which suggest a nostalgia for the Francoist past, and yet she is enthused by her husband's rhetoric of a new society in which they can also benefit under Socialist rule; the irony is that he is only saying this because he has found a lucrative banking job through a contact he met in prison who is, in turn, good friends with a minister. In addition to the comic dimension, there is a socio-political correlative to Antonia's mode of discourse used to parody the opportune fickleness of large sections of Spanish society at the time, who spent more time bemoaning scandalous occurrences amongst the young than focussing on issues of genuine concerns such as the corruption which was rife amongst successive Socialist governments in the 1980s and 1990s.

If the play's comic elements derive principally from the contradictions and absurdities that characters accept as normal in their lives, *Bajarse al moro* in its entirety is, I would suggest, a tragicomedy because characters are sometimes forced to recognise the reality behind the façade, and the consequences, both material and emotional, that this entails. Chusa and Jaimito come face-to-face with the solitude of their marginality when Elena and Alberto choose to conform, thereby revealing that the hermetic universe of the flat was neither normal nor natural. In line with the picaresque mode, the loveable law-breakers are shown to be more honest than those who make and perpetuate the law. The play thereby suggests that their lifestyle is, if anything, less ridiculous and more ethical than those of ostensibly normal people. In spite or perhaps because of the fact that they might be considered 'losers' by society at large, Chusa and Jaimito are clearly the play's most attractive characters. Alonso de Santos has recognised the romantic appeal but cautioned against its applicability or relevance outside of the theatre:

> [...] te puedes imaginar la cantidad de conferencias que he dado sobre *Bajarse al moro*. Todos los chicos jóvenes adoran a Jaimito y siempre me preguntan '¿y usted a quién cree que se parece?' 'Pues yo al otro. Si no, no estaría aquí dando una conferencia.' Jaimito no da conferencias. Jaimito es un pobrecillo, no le dejan entrar. '¡Ah no, usted tiene que ser como Jaimito!'. Pues no nos engañemos, Jaimito no da conferencias, yo soy Alberto. El profesor, el escritor, siempre es un integrado en cierto sentido.

[...] you can well imagine the number of talks I've given on *Going Down to Morocco*. All the young kids adore Jaimito and they always ask me, 'and who do you think you're like?' 'Well, I'm like the other one. If not, I wouldn't be here giving a talk.' Jaimito doesn't give talks. Jaimito's a poor soul, they wouldn't let him in. 'Ah no, you've got to be like Jaimito!' Let's not kid ourselves, Jaimito doesn't give talks, I'm Alberto. In a certain sense, the teacher, the writer, is always part of the system.

(cited in Amo-Sánchez 2002, 18).

Even taking into account the denouement's tragic pathos, *Bajarse al moro* remains primarily a comedy for as long as audiences identify, as they generally do, with the loveable cousins. Whilst it could be argued that this helped foster a much-needed tolerant antidote to the inflexibility of Francoist ideology, this effect is, however, largely based on an act of collective (self-)deceit; the play's tragic subtext is capable of revealing to us the absurdity and ethical hollowness of our own lives. In the interview that follows, Alonso de Santos is remarkably candid about his somewhat selfish dealings with the woman on whose story he drew for the trip to Morocco. Although he identifies himself with Alberto, the character that both he and we as spectators or readers have most in common with is Elena. We take a vicarious pleasure following the exploits of those who operate, to an extent that the vast majority of us never will, on the margins of society yet nevertheless assume that the lyrics sung by Pulp's Jarvis Cocker – 'everybody hates a tourist, especially one who thinks it's all such a laugh' – somehow do not apply to us.

Critical and Commercial Reaction

Bajarse al moro has enjoyed incredible success on the page, stage and screen. Eduardo Haro Tecglen, the chief theatre critic at *El País* – Spain's most important daily newspaper – was on the panel that awarded the play-text the Tirso de Molina prize in 1984, and subsequently wrote a very enthusiastic prologue for the play-text which has gone on to sell nearly a million copies. In the theatre, the play debuted on 6 April 1985 at the Teatro Principal in Zaragoza though it only really began to grab the public imagination when it was staged later that same year with a different cast at the Teatro de Bellas Artes in Madrid under the direction of Gerardo Malla. Adverts taken out in newspapers boasted, '¡Por fin! Un autor conecta con

nuestro tiempo'/'At last! A writer relates to our time'. Verónica Forqué, who headed the cast as Chusa, recalls the production and the complicity it was able to establish between stage and auditorium with fondness:

> El público se identificaba de algún modo con todos los personajes que vivían en esa buhardilla, y lo pasaba tan bien que cuando la obra acababa estábamos llenos de energía, y aunque hacíamos dos funciones diarias, no nos quejábamos.

> The audience somehow identified with all those characters who lived in that attic apartment, and they had such a good time that we were full of energy at the end of the play and, even though we did two performances a day, we didn't complain.

(cited in Piñero 2005, 375)

In line with Alonso de Santos' careful balance of the old and the new, the action takes place in one room and the staging echoes that of the traditional drawing-room drama albeit with a poster of Dr Frankenstein and cultural paraphernalia of a similar ilk. The production was broadcast on national television, staged over a thousand times and toured Spain for nearly four consecutive years (Piñero 2005, 399). It received nearly universal critical acclaim apart from in Barcelona where it was met with a mixed reaction. Joaquim Vilà I Folch, for example, accused the play of crass populism, and complained about importing a big success from Madrid to re-open the emblematic Teatro Goya (1986). It is somewhat ironic, therefore, that the initial idea for the cinematic adaptation (Fernando Colomo 1989) came from Catalonia via film producer, Carlos Durán, and its premiere took place in Barcelona with the cast and crew arriving by train from Madrid, an event given extensive media coverage.

One of the film's major advantages over the stage production is that it is able to show Chusa's adventures in Morocco and, given that the play is set in such a specific socio-geographic milieu, Colomo makes good use of location shooting in and around the Rastro alongside performances by the real-life musical formation, Pata Negra, who are shown living in the flat opposite. In comparison with many cinematic adaptations – see, for example, *Salvajes/Savages* (Carlos Molinero 2001) based on the homonymous play by Alonso de Santos about immigration and Neo-Nazis – *Bajarse al moro* is relatively faithful to the original. The director, well-known for his outlandish comedies, does nevertheless adopt a lighter

Figure 1. Still from the film adaptation of Bajarse al moro *(Fernando Colomo, 1989). Courtesy of Video Mercury.*

tone; indicative of this is the unequivocally happy ending with Chusa and Jaimito walking around Madrid at Christmas with a baby in tow. The inclusion of Alberto's father and Elena's mother, characters only alluded to in the play-text, contribute to the film's slapstick nature; the former is shown chasing her daughter around Madrid in a car with a model of a shark, designed to advertise her store, protruding out of the roof.

Although Jesús Bonilla, the actor who played Jaimito in the Bellas Artes production, had been relatively thin, the chubby Juan Echanove took on the role in the film and turns the character into a comic fool. In a marked departure from the play-text, Elena – played by the very slim Aitana Sánchez Gijón – initially agrees to lose her virginity to Jaimito; she changes her mind not, as we might expect, when he first removes his Sex Pistols T-Shirt to reveal a hefty paunch, but when he subsequently discusses the fact he has crabs. Forqué is the only member of the original cast to reprise her role on screen although she had aged in the interim, and lacks some of her on-stage vibrancy. The film's star turns come with Antonio Banderas and Chus Lampreave as Alberto and Doña Antonia revisiting, albeit in a more comic guise, their pairing as a phallic mother and emasculated son in *Matador* (Pedro Almodóvar 1986). The presence of Banderas, just prior to his departure to Hollywood, clearly did nothing

Figure 2. Still from theatrical production of Bajarse al moro *staged at the Teatro de Bellas Artes (1985).*

to harm box-office takings – it was seen by over 400,000 spectators on its initial release in cinemas[2] – but, I would suggest, it has been more important retrospectively. In the same way that the legend surrounding the stage production has only grown over the years due to the renown of actors such as Forqué, Emma Suárez, or Natalia Dicenta who appeared in it, the film remains a television staple partly because it features a youthful Banderas and some of the best-loved actors of the 1980s alongside early appearances by Carmelo Gómez (Abel) and Sánchez Gijón who would subsequently become major stars in Spain in the 1990s.

Whilst the play does not exactly have Banderas's international profile, it has been translated into multiple languages and performed around the world. In the only major translation into English (Zatlin 1992), *Going Down to Marrakesh*, the translator's decision to allude to a famous song by Crosby, Steels, Nash and Young – Marrakesh Express – in the title is indicative of a relatively free approach, endorsed by Alonso de Santos, which draws on slang from the Metropolitan area of New York (see Zatlin 2002). This version in English was staged by students from the Theatre Department at the University of Missouri-Kansas City; the

---

[2]	Figures taken from the Ministry of Culture database. See www.mcu.es/cinema.

production was generally well-received (see Espejo-Saavedra 1993), although the department apparently received multiple complaints from audience-members offended by the reference to female orifices and what they construed as the condoning of drug-taking (see Zatlin 2002, 37). In demonstrable proof that Spain is not the only country to suffer from censorship, Zatlin then tried to have *Bajarse al moro* staged at a Hispanic theatre in New York; the director told her that he very much liked the play, but that he could not risk staging it for it could potentially jeopardise future subsidies upon which the theatre was dependent, but which were conditional on not offending the church establishment (Zatlin 2002, 37). Somewhat less controversially, the play is a very popular part of the second-year undergraduate module I run at the University of Leeds, whilst students from the Department of Spanish at the University of Edinburgh staged it in 2012.

Contemporary Relevance

In addition to the play's not inconsiderable merits, and the actors who brought it to life, *Bajarse al moro* is guaranteed a privileged place in Spain's cultural and theatrical history by virtue of the fact that it so perfectly encapsulates a pivotal socio-historical moment in the life of the country and its capital. There has, in recent years, been a surge in nostalgia for *La Movida* with, for example, *Hoy no me puedo levantar/Today, I Can't Get Up,* a musical based on the songs of pop group Mecano, that recounts its own version of the story of Madrid in the 1980s (see Fouz Hernández 2009); the production out-performed Abba's *Mamma Mia* musical at the box-office, and has become the most profitable Spanish play of all time. Although *Bajarse al moro* had continued to be performed by amateur and professional groups ever since its premiere, it has also benefitted from this renewal of interest in the 1980s; its highest-profile revival to date taking place in a production, directed by Alonso de Santos himself, which toured the country in 2007–2008 including an extended residency at the Muñoz Seca theatre in Madrid.

What the revival demonstrated was that the human drama and love-stories at the heart of the play had withstood the test of time and remained both entertaining and moving. The only time where I felt that it was showing the signs of age was in the lack of any apparent censure on the

part of the playwright or audience in relation to Chusa's casual racism which is particularly offensive given the fact that Chaouen is a holy shrine for all Muslims in Morocco, a symbolic worth probably lost on Spanish drug-smugglers but that had been exploited by earlier generations in the ill-fated Morocco War where the Spanish army planned to take the town and stage a triumphant entry for King Alfonso XII (Balfour 2002, 61); the offensive was not successful and the retreat, let by General Franco, was so disastrous and bloody that the then-dictator, Primo de Rivera, forbade any officers to speak of the campaign upon pain of death (2002, 103). Ethical qualms aside, the production's major weaknesses stemmed from inappropriate casting – Charo Reina (Doña Antonia) was the most famous actress and her scenes were needlessly extended, whilst it was difficult to distinguish the slim Raquel Guerrero (Chusa) in physical attractiveness from Cristina Vergel (Elena), a former 'Miss Spain' contestant – whilst I was not altogether convinced that setting the play in the present-day was a good idea. Updated references such as a poster of Johnny Depp from *Pirates of the Caribbean* (Gore Verbinski 2003) reflected the increased globalisation of youth tastes, but seemed less precise than in the original. What, I think, this might suggest is that characters such as Chusa and Jaimito alongside the counter-cultural lifestyles and tastes they embody are a thing of the past.

La Movida cannot be properly understood, as it often mistakenly is, purely in terms of Francoism; the freedom it enveloped was primarily a result of it taking place in a period of transition where one set of rules had disappeared, and a new set had yet to be put firmly into place. Even though the space allotted to Chusa and Jaimito was a marginal one, it has been further reduced in the intervening years. As Spain became an increasingly market-driven economy over the course of the 1980s and 1990s, it would more likely have been them, not Elena and Alberto, who would have gone to live on the outskirts on Madrid, forced out of Lavapiés by exponentially rising rents and increased police surveillance. Seen in this light, *Bajarse al moro* is less a document of the here and now than a lament for what has been lost along the wayside. Over the course of the 1980s and 1990s, successive municipal and national governments increasingly clamped down on the consumption of illegal substances, whilst the often mortal casualties from drug-use and the advent of AIDS began to cast a sizeable shadow over the ludic dimension of freedom.

In one sense, *Bajarse al moro* is remarkably prescient in that the gulf which develops in the play between the upwardly mobile and social drop-outs at the individual level anticipates what would subsequently occur at a wider social level. There is, however, a residual optimism in the play which was conspicuously absent from the social-realist plays that Alonso de Santos would go on to write in the 1990s. In *Salvajes,* set on the outskirts of Madrid, we are presented with the harsh realities of drug dependency, seen as the cause and consequence of long-term unemployment which also contextualizes, whilst not justifying, racist skinhead violence. Arguably even more despondent is *Younquís and Yanquis/Junkies and Yankees*, set to the backdrop of the Gulf War in the peripheral region of Las Fronteras where prostitution, long-term unemployment, violence, drugs and AIDS are rife. When talking about the play, Alonso de Santos commented:

En *Bajarse al moro* hay todavía un canto a la esperanza. Era una broma; la droga era simpática. La marginalidad era graciosa; tenía ternura. Ahora sólo hay muerte y destrucción, porque digamos que la esperanza de la redención, de la droga, de las capas marginales, de un mundo especial para todos, ha decaído. Pero eso también en los Estados Unidos. Cada mundo se ha vuelto económicamente más duro; no hay porción para los que no tienen empleo.

In *Going Down to Morocco,* there is still a hope for the future. It was a joke; the drugs were nice. Social exclusion was funny; it had tenderness. Now there is just death and destruction, because let us say that the hope for redemption, from drugs, from the socially excluded, for a world that is special for all, has reduced. But this is also the case in the United States. Every world has become tougher economically; there's no slice left for the unemployed.

(cited in Doll 1999, 13)

Whilst conservative sections of Spanish society would suggest – with some justification – that the problems of latter years were largely the hangover from the permissiveness of the 1980s, *La Movida* continues to resonate amongst audiences nostalgic for a time in which Jaimito's dream for Chusa's unborn child might have seemed idealistic, but not an absolute impossibility. My original plan had been to prepare a dual-language edition of the 2008 production, thereby providing an up-to-date

translation. On comparing the two versions, I was, however, surprised to discover that, although some specific references had been changed, they were linguistically almost identical. Following some further research, I came to the conclusion that the language of the street, which became more mainstream in Spain during the transition, has remained far more static than its equivalent in say the UK or the US. Although we may not encounter the characters that populate *Bajarse al moro* on a daily basis, their speech patterns and the vocabulary they employ has become part of everyday conversation in Spain where, I would suggest, popular and youth culture(s) continue to be children of the 1980s.

Notes on My Translation

In line with the remit of a dual-language critical edition as a tool of language-acquisition, my translation remains relatively close to the original play-text in Spanish, with footnotes indicating major changes that took place in the 2008 revival. Practical considerations aside, I favoured this approach for a number of interrelated reasons. Firstly, *Bajarse al moro* is of socio-historical value for anyone interested in Spain's transition to democracy. Secondly, by setting the play in Madrid, I avoided the temptation to exoticise the language and mores of a different sub-culture. As I hope to have convinced the reader, Alonso de Santos' use of language is both naturalistic and economical. In the interview that follows, he discusses what he perceives to be the dangers of an author using characters as a pretext to exhibit their own poetic voice and linguistic virtuosity; needless to say, translators are hardly immune from this danger, which is equally if not more applicable to the colloquial form of address as it is to language that would more traditionally be conceived as literary. The only time that I break this general rule of socio-geographical specificity is when there are local references that would not be understood by non-Spanish audiences. Hence, for example, I refer to 'Thomas Cook' travel agents although, even here, I have purposefully chosen a business that has operated in Spain for many years and is likely, therefore, to be familiar to at least some Spaniards. Thirdly, modernised translations have a tendency to age quicker than the texts they ostensibly update. In addition, as noted, everyday Spanish slang has changed substantially less over the course of the last three decades than its

Anglophone equivalents. This raised the question of whether to employ English slang from the 1980s or the present-day; I opted for a halfway solution by which I prohibited myself from using diction that would not have been around in the 1980s but, in an attempt to avoid a specific 'period' feel, restricted myself to using words and expressions still used by young people in the twenty-first century. I am, in this regard, very much indebted to my students with whom I carried out a staged reading of an earlier draft, during the course of which they identified anything that they felt to be anachronistic. Fourthly, and finally, this translation in no way prohibits – quite the opposite in fact – it being used as what I hope to be a reliable starting-point from which to prepare versions set in a different time and/or place.

BIBLIOGRAPHY

Alonso de Santos, J. L. (1992) *El álbum familiar/Bajarse al moro*, ed. A. Amorós. Madrid: Espasa-Calpe.

Alonso de Santos, J. L. (1996) Autor dramático y sociedad actual, *ADE Teatro*, 50–51, 94–95.

Alonso de Santos, J. L. (1998) *La escritura dramática*. Madrid: Castalia.

Amo Sánchez, A. (2002) José Luis Alonso de Santos, dramaturgo: escoger la escritura, *Quimera*, 213, 27–33.

Amo Sánchez, A. (2004) La fauna urbana en el teatro de José Luis Alonso de Santos: del 'moro' a la moralidad. In *Teatro y sociedad en la España actual*, eds W. Floeck and M. F. Vilches de Frutos. Madrid and Frankfurt: Iberoamericana and Vervuert, 151–160.

Balfour, S. (2002) *Deadly Embraces: Morocco and the Road to the Spanish Civil War*. Oxford: Oxford University Press.

CCCB (2009) *Quinquis dels 80: Cinema, premsa i carrer*. Barcelona: CCCB i Direcció de Comunicació de la Diputació de Barcelona.

Doll, E. J. (1999) El teatro madrileño de los 90: una encuesta, *Estreno*, 25.2, 12–19, 47.

Espejo-Saavedra, R. (1993) *Bajarse al moro* en Kansas City, *Estreno*, 19.1, 3–4.

Fouz-Hernández, S. (2009) Me cuesta tanto olvidarte: Mecano and the Movida remixed, revisited and repackaged, *Journal of Spanish Cultural Studies*, 10.2, 167–87.

Huerta Calvo, J., Peral Vega, E. and Urzáiz Tortajada, H. (2005) *Teatro Español de la A a la Z*. Madrid: Espasa Calpe.

Ibáñez, J. C. and Iglesias, P. (2011) Comedia sentimental y posmodernidad en el cine español de la transición a la democracia. In *El cine y la transición en España (1975–1982)*, ed. M. Palacio. Madrid: Biblioteca Nueva, 103–25.

Lewis, H. A. (2007) Subversion in the theatre of José Luis Alonso de Santos. In *Nuevas aportaciones a los estudios teatrales: del Siglo de Oro a nuestros días*, eds H. Brioso and J. V. Saval. Alcalá: Servicio de Publicaciones, Universidad de Alcalá, 109–19.

Parker, A. A. (1967) *Literature and the Delinquent: The Picaresque Novel in Spain and Europe, 1599–1753*. Edinburgh: Edinburgh University Press.

Piñero, M. (2005) *La creación teatral en José Luis Alonso de Santos*. Madrid: Fundamentos.

Ragué-Arias, M.-J. (1996) *El teatro de fin de milenio en España: de 1975 hasta hoy*. Barcelona: Editorial Ariel.

Resina, J. R. (2000) Short of memory: the reclamation of the past since the Spanish transition to democracy. In *Disremembering the Dictatorship: The*

Politics of Memory in the Spanish Transition to Democracy, ed. J. Ramón Resina. Amsterdam: Editions Rodopi B.V., 83–126.

Sabina, J. (2002) *Con buena letra: Edición actualizada*. Madrid: Temas de hoy.

Sabina, J. and Menéndez Flores, J. (2007) *Sabina en carne viva: Yo también sé jugarme la boca*. Barcelona: Random House Mondadori.

Sastre, A. (1980) *Lumpen, marginación y jerigonça*. Madrid: Editorial Legasa.

Stapell, H. M. (2010) *Remaking Madrid: Culture, Politics and Identity after Franco*. New York: Palgrave Macmillan.

Tierno Galván, E. (1986) *Bandos del alcalde*. Madrid: Editorial Tecnos.

Umbral, F. (1983) *Diccionario Chelí*. Madrid: Ediciones Grijalbo.

Vilà i Folch, J. (1986) Un escenari recobrat, *Avui*, 24 Oct., 31.

Villarín, J. (1979) *Diccionario de argot*. Madrid: Ediciones Nova.

Villena, L. A. de (1999) *Madrid ha muerto: esplendor, ruido y caos de una ciudad feliz de los ochenta*. Barcelona: Planeta.

Watson, S. (2009) The magic of the marketplace: sociality in a neglected public space, *Urban Studies*, 46.8, 1577–91.

Wheeler, D. (2012) *Golden Age Drama in Contemporary Spain: The Comedia on Page, Stage and Screen*. Cardiff: University of Wales Press.

Whittaker, T. (2012) Mobile soundscapes in the quinqui film. In *Screening Songs in Hispanic and Lusophone Cinema*, eds L. Shaw and R. Stone. Manchester: Manchester University Press, 98–113.

Wobble, J. (2009) *Memoirs of a Geezer. The Autobiography of Jah Wobble: Music, Mayhem, Life* (London: Serpent's Tale).

Zatlin, P. (1992) *Going Down to Marrakesh/Bajarse al moro*. In *Plays of the New Democratic Spain (1975–1990)*, ed. P. W. O'Connor. Lanham, New York: University Press of America, 313–79.

Zatlin, P. (2002) Traducción o adaptación? Cómo llevar el teatro de Alonso de Santos al escenario norteamericano, *Quimera*, 213, 34–8.

Further Reading

Background Reading on Contemporary Spanish Theatre

Cabal, F. and Alonso de Santos, J. L. (1985) *Teatro español de los 80*. Madrid: Editorial Fundamentos.

Delgado, M. M. and Gies, D. T. (eds) (2012) *A History of Theatre in Spain*. Cambridge: Cambridge University Press.

Huerta Calvo, J. (ed.) (2003) *Historia del teatro español*. Madrid: Gredos.

O'Connor, P. W. (1992) *Plays of the New Democratic Spain (1975–1990)*. Lanham, New York: University Press of America.

Oliva, C. (2004) *Teatro español del siglo XX*. Madrid: Editorial Síntesis.

Pörtl, K. (1986) *Reflexiones sobre el nuevo teatro español.* Tübingen: Max Niemeyer Verlag.

El Público (1985) Mesa redonda: Escribir en España, *Cuadernos El Público*, 9, 15–39.

Ruíz Ramón, F. (2005) *Historia del teatro español: Siglo XX.* Madrid: Cátedra.

On José Luis Alonso de Santos

Alonso de Santos, J. L. (1998) *La escritura dramática.* Madrid: Castalia.

Alonso de Santos, J. L. (2007) *Manuel de teoría y práctica teatral.* Madrid: Castalia.

Alonso de Santos, J. L. and Amorós, A. (1998) Del manuscrito al escenario, del escenario a la publicación. In *Conversaciones con el autor teatral de hoy, I*, ed. P. González. Madrid: Fundación PRO-RESAD, 18–45.

Amo Sánchez, A. (2004) La fauna urbana en el teatro de José Luis Alonso de Santos: del 'moro' a la moralidad. In *Teatro y sociedad en la España actual*, eds W. Floeck and M. F. Vilches de Frutos. Madrid and Frankfurt: Iberoamericana and Vervuert, 151–60.

Conde Guerri, M.-J. (2003) El teatro de José Luis Alonso de Santos: contra la puerta cerrada. In *La comedia española: entre el realismo, la provocación y las nuevas formas (1950–2000))*, eds M. Cantos Casenave and A. Romero Ferrer. Cádiz: Servicio de Publicaciones de la Universidad de Cádiz y Fundación Pedro Muñoz Seca, 113–21.

Doménech, F. (1996) Entrevista, José Luis Alonso de Santos: 'No sé dirigir si no encuentro un marginado', *ADE Teatro*, 52–3, 84–91.

Leonard, C. (1985) Entrevista con José Luis Alonso de Santos, *Estreno*, 11.2, 7–12.

Medino Vicario, M. (1994) *Los géneros dramáticos en la obra de José Luis Alonso de Santos.* Madrid Ediciones Libertarias.

Operé, F. (2010) Una España para ser narrada: los cronistas de la transición, *Hispanic Journal*, 31.2, 39–52.

Piñero, M. (2005) *La creación teatral en José Luis Alonso de Santos.* Madrid: Fundamentos.

Rodríguez Richart, J. (2004) Temas sociales conflictivos en el teatro de José Luis Alonso de Santos. In *Teatro y sociedad en la España actual*, eds W. Floeck and M. F. Vilches de Frutos. Madrid and Frankfurt: Iberoamericana and Vervuert, 161–73.

Santolaria Solano, C. (1998) José Luis Alonso de Santos y el teatro independiente: veinte años de vinculación (1960–1980), *ALEC*, 23.3, 791–810.

Santolaria Solano, C. (1998) Recepción del teatro de José Luis Alonso de Santos, *Rivista di Filologia e Letterature Ispaniche*, 1, 178–94.

Wood, G. H. (2003–4) Una entrevista con José Luis Alonso de Santos, *Letras peninsulares*, 16.3, 521–30.

Zatlin, P. (1985) Three playwrights in search of their youth, *Estreno*, 11.2, 4–6.

Recommended Editions of Bajarse al moro

Alonso de Santos, J. L. (1985) *Bajarse al moro*, prologue by E. Haro Tecglen. Madrid: Ediciones Cultura Hispana e Instituto de Cooperación Iberoamericana.

Alonso de Santos, J. L. (1992) *El álbum familiar/Bajarse al moro*, ed. A. Amorós. Madrid: Espasa-Calpe.

Alonso de Santos, J. L. (2001) *Bajarse al moro*, ed. J. L. Sánchez Ferrer. Madrid: Anaya, Nueva Biblioteca Didáctica.

Alonso de Santos, J. L. (2009) *Bajarse al moro*, ed. F. Tamayo and E. Popeanga. Madrid: Cátedra.

On Bajarse al moro

Álvaro, F. (ed.) (1986) *Bajarse al moro*. In *El espectador y la crítica: el teatro en España en 1985*, ed. F. Álvaro. Valladolid: Edicion del autor, 48–51.

Cuesta, S. de la (1996) *Bajarse al moro*, de José Luis Alonso de Santos. In *Veinte años de teatro y democracia en España (1975–1995)*, ed. M. Aznar Soler. Barcelona: CITEC y Cup D'Idees, 131–36,

Cueto, E. (1995) *La estanquera de Vallecas* y *Bajarse al moro*: Alonso de Santos y el público español de los 80, *Romance Languages Annual*, 7, 436–40.

Gutiérrez Carbajo, F. (2001) Versiones fílmicas de *Bajarse al moro*, de José Luis Alonso de Santos, y de *La mirada del hombre oscuro*, de Ignacio del Moral, *ALEC*, 26.1, 213–37.

Hart, P. (1998) Things are looking up for Chusa: editing the postmodern in Fernando Colomo's film adaptation of *Bajarse al moro* by José Luis Alonso de Santos. In *Cine-Lit, III: Essays on Hispanic Film and Fiction*, eds G. Cabello-Castellet, J. Martí-Olivella and G. H. Wood. Carvallis: Oregon State University, 90–99.

Hernando Cuadrado, L. A. (2001) El registro coloquial en *Bajarse al moro* de J. L. Alonso de Santos, *Cuadernos para investigación de la literatura hispánica*, 26, 145–54.

Lewis, H. A. (2007) Subversion in the theatre of José Luis Alonso de Santos. In *Nuevas aportaciones a los estudios teatrales: del Siglo de Oro a nuestros días*, eds H. Brioso and J. V. Saval. Alcalá: Servicio de Publicaciones, Universidad de Alcalá, 109–19.

Luque Toro, L. (2008) ¿Cómo evaluar una obra de teatro? El caso de *Bajarse al moro* de José Luis Alonso de Santos. In *La evaluación en el aprendizaje y la enseñanza del español como lengua externa/segunda lengua, XIII congreso internacional de la Asociación para la Enseñanza del Español como Lengua Externa/Segunda Lengua*, eds S. Pastor Cesteros and S. Roca Marín. Universidad de Alicante: Servicio de Publicaciones, 396–401.

Thompson, P. (1998) *Bajarse al moro*: a socio-political examination of the 'family' and contemporary Spain, *ALEC*, 23.3, 811–19.

Walkoviak, M. (2009) La lengua renovadora del teatro: el mundo como una fiesta bajtinesca en *La llamada de Lauren*, de Paloma Pedrero, y *Bajarse al moro*, de José Luis Alonso de Santos. In *Comedia, fiesta y orgía en la cultura hispánica*, eds R. de la Fuente Ballesteros and J. Pérez Magallón. Valladolid: Universitas Castallae, 279–83.

Wood, G. H. (2003) Lo cinematográfico en el teatro de José Luis Alonso de Santos. In *La comedia española: entre el realismo, la provocación y las nuevas formas (1950–2000)*, eds M. Cantos Casenave and A. R. Ferrer. Cádiz: Servicio de Publicaciones de la Universidad de Cádiz y Fundación Pedro Muñoz Seca, 225–42.

Ynduráin, D. (1989) *Bajarse al moro*. In *Teatro en democracia, vol. 2*, ed. J. Monleón. Madrid: Primer Acto, 241–49.

ENTREVISTA A JOSÉ LUIS ALONSO DE SANTOS

Duncan Wheeler entrevista a José Luis Alonso de Santos
en la casa del escritor, el 29 de septiembre de 2011.

DW: ¿Cuáles fueron sus primeras experiencias teatrales y artísticas en Valladolid, su ciudad natal?

JLAS: En Valladolid, existe la tradición de *Don Juan Tenorio* y de Zorrilla. Mis primeras experiencias fueron el contacto con la poesía y con el teatro romántico – cosa que luego yo no he seguido en general salvo una obra que he escrito que se llama *La sombra del Tenorio* que hace un juego con el romanticismo. Pero, en general, Valladolid me sirvió para empaparme de la poesía y del romanticismo pero no llegué a entrar en esa estética y entré en otra estética más madrileña.

DW: Y empezó en el teatro universitario e independiente.

JLAS: Bueno, la historia de cómo empiezas en el teatro es siempre muy complicada. Hay un estudio que ha hecho una profesora estupenda [Marga Piñero], la que más sabe de mis orígenes porque además es mi mujer, que fue su tesis doctoral y luego lo publicó: *La creación teatral en José Luis Alonso de Santos*. En ello va explicando la relación mía en mi época de estudiante – lo que yo estudiaba, el teatro que hacía – y, bueno, ni yo mismo soy consciente; cuando ella busca material, sí que he sido consciente. Es un poco el resultado de por un lado alguien que vivía la vida callejera y, por otro lado, que vivía la vida universitaria. Es que soy un hombre de la calle, de los grupos, de escuchar a los gitanos, a los otros, a los de las cárceles y tal pero también de escuchar a Cervantes y a Calderón y a Lope desde muy pequeño. Y yo con mis hijos, y con los filólogos, pregúntame tal y cual y yo me sé capítulos enteros del Quijote o de Lope de Vega u obras de Calderón. Soy un hombre de cultura muy clásica. Entonces, yo estaba metido en muchos movimientos universitarios y muchos movimientos culturales y la mezcla de todo eso fue luego cuajando en el teatro.

DW: Trabajaba y estudiaba con William Layton, el norteamericano afincado en Madrid. ¿Qué supuso para usted esta relación?

INTERVIEW WITH JOSÉ LUIS ALONSO DE SANTOS

Duncan Wheeler interviews José Luis Alonso de Santos
in the playwright's Madrid home on September 29 2011.

DW: What were your first theatrical and artistic experiences in Valladolid, your city of birth?

JLAS: In Valladolid, there is the tradition of *Don Juan Tenorio* and of Zorrilla. My first experiences were the contact with romantic theatre and poetry – something that I have not generally built upon apart from a play that I wrote called *Tenorio's Shadow*, which plays with romanticism. But, in general, Valladolid served to imbue me with poetry and romanticism although this wasn't an aesthetic that I then followed, as I pursued an aesthetic from Madrid.

DW: And you started out in independent and university theatre.

JLAS: Well, the story of how you begin in the theatre is always very complicated. There is a study by an excellent academic [Marga Piñero], who knows more about my origins than anyone because she is also my wife, which was originally her doctoral thesis that she subsequently published: *José Luis Alonso de Santos's Theatrical Creativity*. In it, she details my connections during my student days – what I was studying, the theatre I was involved in – and, well, not even I was aware; when she looked for the material, I became conscious. It's kind of the result of someone whose life was, on the one hand, very much in the street and, on the other, was in the university. The thing is that I'm a man of the street, of groups, of listening to gypsies, to the marginalised, to prisoners and so on; but also of listening to Cervantes, Calderón and Lope from a very young age. And when I am with my children or literary scholars, ask me this or that and I know whole chapters of *Don Quixote*, or Lope or Calderón plays off by heart. I am very much a classical culture kind of guy. In those days, I was also involved in many university and cultural movements, and it is the mixture of all that which then began to take form in the theatre.

DW: You worked and studied with William Layton, the North American resident in Madrid. What did that relationship mean to you?

JLAS: Él fue un poco mi maestro primero, mi maestro de referencia, el que me acercó a las formas teatrales. No es un maestro de tipo filosófico – que he tenido otros – o de tipo cultural. Es un maestro de tipo teatral; aprendí desde el principio con él a buscar lo que los americanos llaman la verdad del teatro, el alma, la veracidad y este tipo de cosas.

DW: Ha trabajado como director, escritor, actor y gestor. ¿Sus experiencias en el teatro universitario e independiente le ayudaron a ser tan polifacético?

JLAS: Bueno, ¿sabes qué pasa? A mí, se me dan pocas cosas bien – para la mayoría de las cosas, soy un inútil. Así que, no me considero útil para todo, ni listo para todo pero yo, desde que llegué al teatro muy jovencito, la verdad es que en el teatro todo se me da bien. Me parece fácil. Hay gente que conduce coches de carreras – que yo me mataría antes de sentarme en el coche – y conduce el coche muy rápido y muy bien porque son muy buenos para eso. Han aprendido pero, además, es que tenían condiciones. Quiero decirte que yo cuando llegué al teatro inmediatamente cualquier trabajo que hice en el teatro – la escenografía o dirigir o puestos de importancia en los Teatros Nacionales o ser director de empresa – todo eso siempre se me ha ido bien. Porque ha sido fácil. Era fácil para mí. Fíjate que cuando he intentado hacer eso en el cine o en la televisión, me ha resultado mucho más difícil. O en la poesía, ya me es más difícil. Luego es que realmente no sé por qué – por este milagro de la vida – pues, entré en el teatro y resulta que todo ha sido fácil.

DW: ¿Se siente como un pez en el agua?

JLAS: Eso es. Entonces, aprendía con facilidad, lo hacía con facilidad y después de llevar cuarenta, cincuenta años en el teatro, todo lo que tiene que ver con el teatro lo sigo haciendo con facilidad. Eso no quiere decir que todo me salga bien. A veces, me salen cosas mejor. A veces, me salen cosas peor. Pero me salen fácil. Mientras que hay otras cosas en la vida que me salen fatal.

DW: He leído una entrevista suya en la que decía que, cuando era joven, le parecía fatal que la gente se lo pasara bien viendo un partido de fútbol, pero después llegó a pensar que se equivocaba y que está muy bien que la gente se divierta haciendo las cosas que les gusten. A mí, esa me parece una actitud muy típica de la oposición durante la dictadura: la idea de

JLAS: He was kind of my first teacher, the one I always referred back to, who introduced me to theatrical forms. He is not a philosophical teacher – I've had others – or a cultural one. He is a specifically theatrical teacher; I learned with him from the outset to look for what the Americans call the truth of the theatre, the soul, the veracity and these kinds of things.

DW: You have worked as a director, as a writer, as an actor and in management. Did your experiences in independent and university theatre help you to turn your hands to so many different tasks?

JLAS: Well, you know what happens? There are very few things I can do well – I am useless at most things. As such, I do not consider myself apt or clever at everything but, ever since I entered the theatre world at a very young age, the truth is that everything came easily to me. It seems simple to me. There are people who drive racing cars – I'd kill myself before sitting in the car – and they drive the car very quickly and very well because that's what they are meant to do that. What I want to say to you is that as soon as I began in the theatre, any kind of job that I have had there – set-design, directing, important roles in the National Theatres, running a business – it's all come easily to me. Because it has been simple. It was simple for me. Go figure, mind, I have found it much more difficult when I have tried to do that in cinema or in television. Or, with poetry, I've found it even harder. But then, and I really don't know why – because of this miraculous thing that is life – I began in the theatre and everything has been very simple.

DW: You took to it like a duck to water?

JLAS: That's it. Then, I learnt easily, I did things easily and after spending forty, fifty years in the theatre, I continue to be able to do anything relating to the theatre with ease. That's not to say that everything I do turns out well. Sometimes, things turn out better; sometimes, they turn out worse. But they come with ease. Whilst in other aspects of life, I struggle dreadfully.

DW: I have read an interview with you where you say that, when you were young, you were very disapproving of the fact that people had a good time watching a football match, but that you subsequently came to think that you had been wrong and that it's great that people enjoy themselves doing the things they like. The former attitude seems to me to be very typical of the opposition during the dictatorship years: the vision

la cultura popular como algo negativo como si fuera el opio del pueblo. Llegó antes que muchos otros escritores a la conclusión de que el hecho de que una obra fuera divertida para enganchar al público no constituía en sí ni un pecado ni una traición.

JLAS: Claro. No solo eso, sino que yo respeto mucho el entretenimiento. La gente odia las palabras "entretener" y "divertir". La gente que quiere quedar como muy brillante. Cuando un joven quiere quedar como brillante, dice que el arte no es para divertir, el arte no es para entretener, es para revolver, para decir cosas muy sorprendentes. El arte ha servido para todo a lo largo de la historia. Ha habido creadores que han revuelto, ha habido creadores que han entretenido y cado uno ha aportado algo si ha sido bueno en su decisión. Respeto muchísimo a algo que siempre están criticando: la televisión. Todo el mundo critica la televisión y toda la gente la ve. Creo que la televisión es estupenda y que es un medio de entretenimiento. Que a veces milagrosamente puede haber una cosa artística o de calidad pero todo lo que nos rodea no tiene que ser arte, calidad y de primera categoría. Nos volveríamos locos. Creo que la rutina, el entretenimiento, la diversión, la fiesta forman parte del componente de la humanidad y el teatro; una gran parte del teatro desde que nació, se ha desarrollado para entretener, para gustar, para disfrutar y para liberarse los que lo hacían.

DW: Y que también existe la famosa idea de Horacio: que se debe deleitar enseñando.

JLAS: Pero, incluso, aunque no enseñaran. Incluso los cómicos que desde los comienzos de los tiempos que no han tenido como objetivo enseñar a nadie sino únicamente divertir y sacar para comer son muy respetables. Porque lo que importa no es tanta la intención primaria sino lo que han conseguido después. Hay gente que dice, "yo hago teatro para cambiar el mundo, para cambiar el arte" – y luego lo ves y aquello no es nada. Y hay gente que dice, "yo hago teatro únicamente para ganar dinero" – pongamos que es lo peor que se puede decir. Y luego lo ves y dices, "es estupendo". La intención que diga el creador carece de interés. Lo que importa es el cuadro.

DW: Sí, estoy de acuerdo, pero muchos, digamos, intelectuales españoles, todavía son muy reacios a la hora de hablar y apreciar la dimensión lúdica de la cultura. Por poner un ejemplo concreto, a la mayoría de los

of popular culture as being automatically negative as if it were the opium of the people. You came to the conclusion long before many other writers that the fact a play was fun so as draw an audience in was not in itself a sin or a betrayal.

JLAS: Of course. It's not just that; I have a great respect for entertainment. People hate the words "to entertain" and "to have fun". People, that is, who want to be seen as brilliant. When a youngster wants to be seen as brilliant, they say art is not about having fun, art is not about entertaining, but is rather to shake things up, to say the unexpected. Art has covered all the bases throughout history. There have been writers who have shaken things up, there have been creative people who have entertained, and each and every one of them has brought something to the table if they have made the right decision. I have a huge respect for what I always hear people criticising: the television. Everyone criticises television and everyone watches it. I think the television is great and that it is a medium of entertainment. That, miraculously, there might sometimes be something of artistic worth, of quality, but everything around us does not have to be art, first-rate and of high quality. It'd drive us mad. I think that routine, entertainment, the fun and the festive have formed a part of what constitutes humanity and the theatre; a grand part of the theatre since its very beginnings has been about giving pleasure, having fun and liberating those who did it.

DW: And there's also Horace's famous adage: that one should delight and teach at the same time.

JLAS: But even if they don't teach. Even the actors that since time and memoriam have not set out to teach anyone, but rather to entertain and put food on the table, are worthy of our respect. Because what is important is not so much the first intention but rather what they subsequently achieve. There are people who say, "I work in theatre to change the world, to change art" – and then you see it and it's nothing. And there are people who, to cite the worst you can say, claim, "I work in theatre to make money". And then you see it and you say, "it's brilliant". The intention the artist claims for their work is of no interest. The proof is in the pudding.

DW: Yes, I agree but there are many, for want of a better word, intellectuals in Spain who are still very reluctant to speak of and appreciate the fun side of culture. To give a concrete example, it seems to surprise most

profesores españoles les choca que pueda dar clases sobre La Movida y sobre Alaska en una universidad británica.

JLAS: Sí, es por una razón. En España, ha habido, durante muchos años una relación – y sobre todo en los poderes de la izquierda – una relación tonta, entre diversión, entretenimiento, artes populares y la derecha, y el dinero. Entonces, ellos rápidamente se han puesto del otro lado y han dicho: "¿Cómo somos? Cultos, exquisitos, no nos importa el dinero, y hacemos un arte como el alemán el cual no tiene que entender la gente." Es absurdo porque la cultura española precisamente está basada en una comunicación que entiende la gente; el *Quijote* lo entiende la gente. Es absurdo. El español es una lengua que está inventada a partir de Nebrija para que escrito y hablado tengan una comunicación real, no como el alemán. Los alemanes hace muchos años que distinguieron las clases populares de las clases cultas pero no en España ni en Italia ni en Inglaterra. Que no, la gente en España, en Inglaterra, o en Italia goza, es popular y es culto. Es alucinante, tal vez *Las Valkirias* no, porque la cultura alemana es otra cosa. Pero Mozart, ¿qué es? ¿Popular o culto? Es una tontería, como los Beatles o Alaska. Pero en España, eso que tú dices ha sido muy exagerado por una tendencia hacia la izquierda y porque las subvenciones eran de la izquierda y te lo digo yo, que yo he estado en sus comités muchos años, se han dado siempre al que ha ido contra el mercado, contra la diversión, contra todo eso, contra la masa, y se ha revestido un poco de esa cola de mandarines que dan a lo que va contracorriente y a lo que no entiende la mayoría. Bueno, eso crea un espejismo porque luego la gente o se divierte o no se divierte. Y la gente acaba yendo a lo que es divertido. Divertido no es sólo el más elemental. Divertido también es Shakespeare. O sea divertido en un amplio sentido. De repente, yo te digo Shakespeare y dirían, "ah bueno", pero si digo Muñoz Seca, ya muchísima gente española diría, "¡Qué vergüenza!". Y a mí, me parece graciosísimo.

DW: Pero es también porque Muñoz Seca es una figura muy politizada.

JLAS: Bueno, te he dado un ejemplo muy exagerado. A mí, me parece que Muñoz Seca lo que hace – que no es gran arte – lo hace muy bien. Y el que hace algo, y lo hace muy bien, es merecedor de nuestro respeto. Que cada vez que veo una película, no tiene que ser la película que cambia la historia del cine, con que sea entretenida y dicen, "ya, pero es mejor *El Padrino*". Hombre, pues claro.

Spanish academics that I am able to give classes on *La Movida* and about Alaska in a British university.

JLAS: Yes, and there's a reason for that. In Spain, there has, for many years, been an association – and, above all, amongst the left-wing establishment – a stupid association between fun, entertainment, popular arts, and the right and money. Then they have quickly gone the other way and have said, "What are we like? Cultured, refined, indifferent to money and we make art like the Germans that people don't have to understand". It's absurd. Spanish, unlike German, is a language which has been designed since Nebrija to be genuinely communicable in both written and spoken forms. The Germans made a division many years ago between the popular and the cultured classes, but this hasn't happened in Spain or, for that matter, in Italy or England. It just hasn't; people in Spain or in England or in Italy simply take pleasure, it is both popular and cultured. It's remarkable; perhaps it doesn't happen with *The Valkyries* because German culture is something else. But Mozart, what is he? Popular or cultural? It's a ridiculous way of looking at things; the same goes for the Beatles or for Alaska. But, in Spain, what you're saying has been very exaggerated because of a drift towards the left, and the fact that subsidies have come from the left; I can tell you, because I was on their committees for many years, that they have always been awarded to that which has flown in the face of the market, of fun, of all of that, of the masses and they have become very inward-looking giving to that which goes against the tide and that most people don't understand. Well, this distorts things because then people either enjoy themselves or they don't. And they will end up going to what is fun. Fun isn't just the lowest common denominator. Shakespeare is also fun. In other words, fun in the broadest sense of the word. Now, if I say Shakespeare people say, "well, fine" but, if I say Muñoz Seca, many Spaniards instinctually react by saying "What a disgrace!" And I, personally, find him really amusing.

DW: But that's also because Muñoz Seca is such a politicised figure.

JLAS: Okay, I've given you an exaggerated example. Personally I think that what Muñoz Seca does – which isn't great art, – he does very well. And someone who does something, and does it well, is worthy of our respect. Every time I see a film, as long as it's entertaining, it doesn't have to be the film that changed cinema history – they'll say, "alright, but *The Godfather* is better". Okay, granted.

DW: Y supongo que es por esa postura que se atrevió a dirigir un montaje con la Compañía Nacional de Teatro Clásico de *Peribáñez y el Comendador de Ocaña* de Lope de Vega, una obra muy divertida pero politizada a la vez, debido a ese aire festivo y lúdico de la vida campesina que trae recuerdos de los Festivales de España y la ideologización de la cultura popular durante la dictadura.

JLAS: Sí, sí y eso da pavor. Esas obras de tipo rural no las quiere hacer nadie nunca. Es algo que no se ha hecho nunca porque son un poco "la cultura popular". Que salga gente cantando y bailando y tal, parece que son Festivales de España todavía. Y a mí, ¿qué me importa? Puede parecer lo que sea, es la cultura popular española.

DW: Así que, ¿no le molesta ser ni popular ni populista?

JLAS: No, no, no. Perdóname. No es solamente que no me moleste, sino que al fin y al cabo quiero ser popular. Toda mi vida he intentado escribir y hacer teatro para la mayoría partiendo de que estoy trabajando en un medio de minorías. Porque si ya trabajo en un medio como es el teatro que trabaja para minorías y luego tengo dos filas, es un sufrimiento. Todo el que dice que trabaja para minorías, es que no ha tenido dos filas. Yo he tenido teatros llenos y he tenido teatros con dos filas y te aseguro que, metas el rollo que metas, y digas lo que digas, cuando van dos filas, es un sufrimiento y cuando está el teatro lleno aquello es una alegría. Luego, tienes que justificarte y decir que haces un teatro de minorías. Es a posteriori. Yo, desde luego, lo que he pretendido siempre y siempre pretenderé es tener mayorías. No tener minorías. A veces, desgraciadamente, he tenido minorías.

DW: Y cuando estaba escribiendo *Bajarse al moro*, ¿pensó que iba a arrasar?

JLAS: Bueno, ahora te explico la segunda parte. Cuando escribes, cuando intentas hacer un trabajo, solo intentas hacerlo bien. Pues, yo de joven, tenía mucha confianza en mí mismo, en lo que hacía era lo que tenía que hacer. Y yo lo hacía porque *Bajarse al moro*, como otras muchas obras, la leí a mis amigos y me dijeron que la cambiara, que la tirara y tal y no les he hecho caso y les he dicho: "Esto no lo voy a hacer". Yo era muy

DW: I suppose it was this attitude that made you brave enough to direct for the National Classical Theatre Company a version of Lope's *Peribáñez and the Commander of Ocaña*, a very fun play that has also been heavily politicised due to that festive and playful depiction of rural life that recalls the Festivals of Spain and the instrumentalisation of popular culture during the dictatorship.

JLAS: Yes, yes and that scares peoples. Nobody ever wants to do those rural plays. It's something that's never been done because they resemble 'popular culture' somewhat. People coming out singing, dancing and the like; it looks as if the Festivals of Spain live on. But why should that bother me? It can resemble whatever, it's Spanish popular culture.

DW: It doesn't, therefore, bother you to be either popular or populist?

JLAS: No, no. Wait a minute. It's not just that it doesn't bother me but rather that, at the end of the day, I want to be popular. All of my life, I've tried to write and stage theatre for the majority knowing that I am working in a minority medium. Because, if I am already working in a medium such as the theatre that is aimed at a minority audience, and I then only have two rows, that is a painful experience. Whoever claims to be working for a minority audience has never had two rows. I've had full houses and I've had theatres with two rows, and I can assure you that whatever you may get mixed up in, or whatever you may say, it makes you suffer when there are two rows and it makes you happy when the theatre is full. Later, you have to justify yourself and say that the theatre you do is for a minority audience. But that comes after the event. What I, of course, have always and will always set out to do is to reach a mass audience. Not a minority one. On occasion, unfortunately, I've had a minority one.

DW: And when you were writing *Going Down to Morocco,* did you think that it'd go on to be so successful?

JLAS: Right, now I'll explain the second part to you. When you write, when you're trying to get a job done, you just want to do it well. Well, as a young man, I was very self-confident and had faith in the fact that I was doing what I ought to be doing. And I did it; with *Going Down to Morocco*, I did what I often do with my plays and read it to friends. They told me I should change this and that, that I should get rid of things and whatever, but I never paid them any attention and said: "I'm not going to

cabezón y creía en lo que hacía, porque si no, ¿por qué lo hacía? Vamos a ver. Tenía, digamos, confianza en mí mismo pero no seguridad en el éxito, que eso es siempre una cosa muy rara. Cuando estás haciendo algo, como autor, como director o tal, no tienes que estar pendiente de gustarles a todos. Y mis obras, mis montajes, a algunos les han gustado y a otros no. En general, les gustaban porque si no, no estaría aquí con cincuenta años de teatro, pero hay personas que no les gusta en absoluto lo que hago y me parece muy respetable igual que a mí, no me gustan cosas de mucha gente. Mis hijos han visto la de Almodóvar [*La piel que habito*] – que yo todavía no – y a uno la ha gustado mucho y otro no la ha podido soportar. Bueno, porque el gusto también está metido dentro de la historia del arte. A mí, me gusta mucho más Velázquez que El Greco. Veo El Greco y digo, "exagerado", pero a otra gente le gusta mucho más El Greco que Velázquez. No pasa nada. Son gustos.

DW: He leído que siempre borra los diálogos que al principio le gustan más de las obras. ¿Es un proceso de depuración?

JLAS: Hay que tener cuidado con no entusiasmarse con la parte poética juvenil que tiene uno. Vamos a ver, por ejemplo a mí no me gusta Antonio Gala, un escritor que para mí es detestable. Y no me gusta porque Antonio Gala se entusiasma más con su parte juvenil y dice frases un poco cursis, que si quitaran, quedaría mejor.

DW: Pero en el caso de Gala, eso tiene mucho que ver con el hecho de que ha trabajado mucho en el periodismo y tiene ese tipo de retórica, esa manera de expresarse.

JLAS: Eso te estaba diciendo. Yo soy un castellano de Valladolid. Que Valladolid y Castilla, aunque tienen la parte romántica, tienen la parte de la economía del lenguaje, de decir las cosas con pocos adjetivos, de no ser pesado, de no ponerse estupendo. Yo en mis obras no quiero que la gente diga cada minuto, "oh, qué obra más bonita ha hecho el autor". Yo no estoy allí; tiene que ser de los personajes. Si los personajes dicen cosas que son del autor, lo hemos estropeado.

do that". I was very pig-headed and believed in what I was doing because why else do it? Now, having said that, I had, shall we say, faith in myself but not in success which is always a very strange thing. When you are working on something as an author, director, or whatever, you shouldn't fret about appealing to everyone.

Some people have liked the plays I've written, the productions I've staged, others haven't. On the whole, more people have liked them than not, because otherwise I wouldn't be here with fifty years in the theatre behind me but there are those who don't like what I do in the least, and that's fine by me in the same way there are things many people do which I don't like. My kids have been to see the latest Almodóvar [*The Skin I Live In*] – I still haven't – and one really liked it, and the other couldn't stand it. Fine, because taste also forms parts of the history of the arts. I, personally, much prefer Velázquez to El Greco. I see an El Greco and I say, "over-the-top" but other people much prefer El Greco to Velázquez. It's not a problem. They are tastes.

DW: I have read that you always dispense with those dialogues you started out liking the most from your plays. Is this a process of distillation?

JLAS: One has to be careful with not getting too enthused by one's adolescent poetic side. Let's see; I, for example, don't like Antonio Gala, a writer that I find detestable. And I don't like Antonio Gala because he is primarily enthused by his most adolescent side, and he utters somewhat pretentious phrases. If they were cut, the end result would be much better.

DW: But, in the case of Gala, this has a lot to do with the fact that he has worked extensively in journalism and he has that kind of rhetoric, that way of expressing himself.

JLAS: That's what I was saying to you. I am a Castilian from Valladolid. Valladolid and Castile, although they have their romantic side, also have a side which is about the economy of language, of saying things with very few adjectives, of not being a bore, or not trying to shine. I, in my plays, don't want people to be saying every minute, "Oh what a beautiful play the dramatist has done". I'm not there; it has to come from the characters. If the characters say things that belong to the author, then we've mucked it up.

DW: En consonancia con esta estética, *La estanquera de Vallecas*, la obra anterior de *Bajarse al moro*, supuso un gran cambio en la escena española en el sentido de romper con el decoro escénico. Incluso después del destape y todo eso, los personajes no hablaban en el teatro serio entrecomillas, o en el teatro respetable, de la misma manera que la gente hablaba en la calle.

JLAS: Hombre, yo no soy quien para presumir y la palabra "nuevo" siempre es delicada pero sí que hay estudiosos y mucha gente que habla de que yo fui el primero que hice esa aportación. Hasta entonces, parece que el sainete, el teatro popular eran unos serenos y unos no sé qué, que salían allí y hacían unos pequeños *sketch*. Y digamos que a la gente que me ha defendido menos las llaman sainetes largos, pero la gente que me ha defendido más dice que como mucho trasciende el sainete, y que son comedias modernas.

DW: Y son personajes de carne y hueso también.

JLAS: Ya no pertenecen al esquema de sainete sino que pego un brinco y pueden tener algo de Arniches o de Ramón de la Cruz pero, claro, también pasado por el cine americano. *Bajarse al moro* lo han catalogado como sainete, lo han catalogado como comedia moderna, y lo han catalogado casi como vanguardia cultural. Por un lado, estaba el teatro como culto. Por otro lado, el teatro popular. Por un lado, el teatro como culto importante de palabras y por otro lado, el teatro de la calle. Y que yo, de alguna manera, lo he mezclado. Eso siempre ha sido un poquito mi intención porque también es mi formación. Hay una tesis en América muy bonita que es el octosílabo y el endecasílabo en *Bajarse al moro*; la obra que vas a hacer está llena de octosílabos y endecasílabos. Pues, claro, y eso lo descubrió un profesor con sus alumnos. No digo que estén rimados, digo que son frases de ocho sílabas con una acentuación muy buscada y son chicos de la calle hablando en argot pero con una endecasílaba clásica de Garcilaso de la Vega. Ese intento de mezclar lo clásico con lo popular es lo característico de mi obra. Y en *La estanquera* pasa igual. En *La estanquera* hay una mezcla de cultura y de natura, del pulso de la calle y del pulso de la cultura española.

DW: Parece que la gente ya se ha acostumbrado más a esta mezcla. Pero imagino que fue algo muy chocante en aquella época. ¿Es verdad que tuvo problemas a la hora de encontrar actores para representar *La estanquera* sobre las tablas?

DW: In line with this aesthetic, *The Tobacconist Woman from Vallecas*, the play before *Going Down to Morocco*, constituted a great change in Spanish theatre in the sense that it broke with stage decorum. Even after the *destape* and all of that, characters in, inverted commas, serious or respectable theatre didn't speak like the man or woman in the street.

JLAS: Well, it's not for me to show off and the word 'new' is always delicate but, yes, there are scholars and many people who have spoken of how I was the first to make this contribution. Up until then, it seemed as if the *sainete*, popular theatre, was a few serene figures that, I don't even know, came out and did some small sketches. And, let us say, those who have defended me the least have called my works extended *sainetes* and those who have defended me the most have said they go far beyond the *sainete* and are modern comedies.

DW: And they are also flesh-and-blood characters.

JLAS: They no longer belong to the scheme of the *sainete*; rather I've made a jump and, although there might be something of Arniches or Ramón de la Cruz in there, they've also clearly been filtered through American cinema. *Going Down to Morocco* has been variously categorised as a *sainete*, as a modern comedy and as being almost at the vanguard of culture. On the one hand, there is the idea of theatre as the veneration of words and, on the other, theatre from the street. And I, somehow, have mixed them up together. That has always kind of been my intention because it's also the way I've grown up. There is a beautiful thesis in America on the octo- and hendecasyllable in *Going Down to Morocco*; the play you are going to do is full of octo- and hendecasyllables. Well, of course, and a lecturer discovered this with their students. I'm not saying they rhyme, but there are phrases with eight syllables on which the pattern of the stresses has been carefully elaborated. They are street kids speaking in slang but with a classical hendecasyllable straight out of Garcilaso de la Vega. That attempt to mix the classical with the popular is what characterises my work. In *The Tobacconist Woman*, there is the same mixture of nature and culture, the pulse of the street and of Spanish culture.

DW: People now seem to have become accustomed to this combination. But I imagine it was quite shocking at the time. Is it true that you had problems finding actors to stage *The Tobacconist Woman*?

JLAS: En *La estanquera* más que en *Bajarse al moro*. En *Bajarse al moro*, son jóvenes. Y además habían pasado algunos años. Pero *La estanquera* fue muy difícil. En los años ochenta cuando yo buscaba las actrices que tenían la edad y eran famosas me decían, "Me encanta, me encantaría". Porque además había un buen empresario, un contrato bueno: tuvimos un tiempo en el Teatro de la Comedia que entonces era el teatro número uno; el empresario Tirso Escudero que era el número uno – ponía dinero, lo que hiciera falta y no la encontramos. Íbamos una por una y se echaban atrás. Alguna me decía que ella tenía su camerino lleno de vírgenes y que no iba a defender una obra que, en la segunda escena, le está metiendo mano el chico a la chica. Ninguna actriz popular española quería hacer ese personaje y decir esos tacos en escena. Alguna incluso me dijo que si ella lo hiciera, ellos dirían que era comunista. En aquella época, una actriz que hacía eso podría ser considerada como tal. Y acaba haciendo el personaje en Madrid Conchita Montes, que era una conocida actriz de la derecha, lo cual era una contradicción de esas inverosímiles. A ella le daba igual. Y, entonces, acaba haciendo el papel en ese montaje. Había muchos montajes hechos por jóvenes, pero cuando quise una actriz de categoría, de peso, hablé con muchas y ninguna se atrevía en aquella época. Bueno, hoy es ingenuo todo eso, porque se ha visto hacer durante mucho tiempo y ya la obra se ha hecho en distintos mundos, pero en aquella época *La estanquera* fue un paso complicado. Es que de la España de los ochenta a la de ahora…, estamos hablando de dos mundos.

DW: Casi todas las críticas tanto de *La estanquera* como de *Bajarse al moro* coincidieron en llamarle un "autor joven". Con todo el respeto, no era tan joven en aquel momento: ya había cumplido los cuarenta. ¿Ese desfase indica que faltó una generación de nuevos autores, nuevas voces?

JLAS: Pocos autores saltan directamente al teatro normal. Los autores suelen tener un camino – escuelas, salas alternativas, teatros oficiales. Que un autor en los cuarenta, cincuenta años que yo he trabajado, he visto autores que se han acercado el público de pago, de llegar y llenar el teatro, te contaría con los dedos de la mano. En cuarenta años. Otra

JLAS: More with *The Tobacconist Woman* than with *Going Down to Morocco*. In *Going Down to Morocco*, it's young people. But *The Tobacconist Woman* was very difficult. When, in the 1980s, I was looking for actresses of the right age who were famous, they all said to me, "I love it, I'd love to do it". Because there was also a good promoter behind it, a good contract: we had a run at the Comedia Theatre which was at the time the number one theatre; the promoter, Tirso Escudero, was second to none – he put the money up front, whatever was necessary but we still couldn't find an actress to do it. We went through them one by one and they all backed off. One of them told me her dressing room was full of images of the virgin, and that she wasn't going to stand up for a play in which the lad is groping the girl in the second scene. No popular Spanish actress wanted to play that character and say those curses on stage. One even said to me that if she did it, they would say she was a communist. At that time, all sorts might have been thought of an actress who did that. Conchita Montes, a famous actress known for being a right-winger, ended up taking the role in one of those contradictions that seem unreal. She wasn't bothered in the least. So she ended up taking the role in that production. There had been numerous productions done before by youngsters but when I wanted a well-renowned actress with credentials, I spoke with loads of them and none of them dared take it on at that time. Well, this all seems very quaint now because it has been the norm for a long time and the play has been staged in different worlds but, in that era, *The Tobacconist Woman* was a difficult step to make. The thing is that between the Spain of the 1980s and that of now … we are speaking of two different worlds.

DW: Almost all of the reviews of both *The Tobacconist Woman* and *Going Down to Morocco* coincide in referring to you as a "young author". With all due respect, you weren't that young at that stage: you were over forty. Do you think this anomaly is indicative of an absence of a new generation of writers, of new voices?

JLAS: Very few writers enter the commercial stage directly. Writers tend to have a set trajectory – schools, fringe theatre, official theatres. In the forty, fifty years that I've worked in theatre, I could count on the fingers of one hand the number of writers that have made it as a result of the general public coming and filling the theatre. In forty years. That's not

cosa es que hayan vivido muy buenos autores que se han estrenado en el Teatro Nacional, unas subvenciones, pero que te pague el público es como un novelista nuevo. Que el público simplemente a un novelista nuevo, le compre la novela es muy difícil. Tuve, en aquel momento, dos o tres obras que se pusieron en los teatros comerciales normales y llenaron, llenaron a tope. Y eso, claro, tenía cierto boom porque no es normal. Y en este sentido, era nuevo porque había vivido del teatro. Vivir como autor del teatro normal, del público tal vez Antonio Buero Vallejo, Antonio Gala en aquella época y Paco Nieva a medias, y no sé quién más. Cinco o cuatro autores que eran todos mayores. Entonces, yo era muy joven – llegué y además en unos años, en cuatro o cinco años, me llegan treinta o cuarenta premios. Hay como un reconocimiento y ya pasé a ser autor más reconocido.

DW: Entonces, ¿fue como un relevo generacional?

JLAS: Sí, ya había tenido algunas obras en otro tipo de teatro como *El álbum familiar.* Y mientras tanto, desarrollaba un teatro más trágico, más poético que siguen haciendo en Teatros Nacionales y por grupos. Pero si te digo la verdad esas obras que se han puesto por el mundo entero y tal nunca tuvieron la aceptación popular que tuvieron mis comedias. Mis comedias fueron un boom.

DW: A mí, me parece que *Bajarse al moro* está a caballo entre el cine quinqui y la nueva comedia madrileña. Hay más terreno común con unas películas de los ochenta o incluso con la música de, por ejemplo, Joaquín Sabina que con los dramaturgos coetáneos.

JLAS: Sí, porque el teatro español ha arrastrado siempre un poco de lo retórico de las grandes épocas del teatro y de los grandes autores – Valle-Inclán y Lorca – que no dejan de tener un teatro muy literario. Mejor, el de Lorca que el de Benavente pero no deja de estar lleno de imágenes de la luna; es un teatro culto. Que el autor desde la primera frase está recordándole al espectador, "Oiga, éste es un teatro culto, yo soy muy culto y usted me tiene que"; eso que dice Valle-Inclán del espectador: "usted me tiene que ver a mí por encima de usted y tal". No tengo nada que ver con eso. He tenido una relación con el espectador de igual a igual, y por eso es más del cine y mis personajes son más del cine. No hago

to say there haven't been very good writers who have premiered in the National Theatre, some subsidies, but that the general public pays you is akin to a new novelist. That the public simply buys a novel by a young novelist is very tricky. At that point, I had two or three plays that were put on in commercial theatres and they were full, they were filled to the rafters. And that, of course, was something of a *boom* because it's not the norm. In that sense, I was new, because I was making a living out of the theatre. The only writers to make a living from the paying public were perhaps Antonio Buero Vallejo, Antonio Gala at that stage, Paco Nieva kind of, and I don't know who else. Four or five writers, all of whom were old. I was very young then – I arrived on the scene and, in the space of a few years, thirty or forty prizes came my way. There is a form of recognition, and then I became a better known writer.

DW: So it was something of a generation shift?

JLAS: Yes, I had already had some plays from a very different kind of theatre such as *Family Album.* And, at the same time, I was developing a more tragic, more poetic kind of theatre, which continues to be staged in National Theatres and by groups. But, to tell you the truth, those plays that have been staged all around the world and so on, have never had the popular approval that my comedies had. My comedies were a boom.

DW: And it seems to me that *Going Down to Morocco* is halfway between the new Madrid comedies and the 'delinquent' cinema being made at the time. There is more common ground with films of the 1980s or even with the music of, for example, Joaquín Sabina, than with contemporary dramatists.

JLAS: Yes, because Spanish theatre has always kind of carried with it the rhetorical baggage of the great theatrical periods, and of the great writers – Valle-Inclán and Lorca – which is invariably a very literary kind of theatre. Lorca's is better than Benavente's but they never cease to be filled with images of the moon; it's a cultural form of theatre. From the first phrase onwards, the writer is reminding his audience, "listen, this is a very cultured form of theatre, I am very cultured and you need to esteem me"; what Valle-Inclán says about the spectator, "you have to see me as being your better and the like". I have nothing to do with that. My relationship with the spectator has been one of equals and, because of that, both the relationship and my characters are more cinematic. I don't

teatro de grandes señores ni de príncipes; hago teatro de camareros o de tal; igual que el cine. Así son herencias del cine que convierte a cualquier personaje en un príncipe. Evidentemente, luego el tipo de lenguaje y el dialecto y tal tiene mucho que ver con el cine. Con el cine americano por un lado y con el cine español de toda aquella época por otro, seguro.

DW: Usted mismo es un gran aficionado del cine, ¿verdad?

JLAS: Sí, y sobre todo, tienes tú razón que en aquel momento salió un gran nuevo cine español que luego ha costado mucho. Luego el cine en España se ha perdido pero hubo, en aquella época, grandes películas que cambiaron también el estado del cine.

DW: He leído que la anécdota, el argumento de *Bajarse al moro*, viene de una historia que le contó una estudiante.

JLAS: A ver, sí. En las relaciones con gente joven y tal, alguien me había hablado del viaje al moro. Y una chica me habló un día de que ella no había ido al moro – estaba yo mucho con la historia en la cabeza – pero que había ido su hermana. Y eso me interesó mucho. Y quedé con la hermana. E incluso grabé cosas que me contó y tal. Pero esto lo he hecho muchas veces. En *Yonquis y Yanquis* con presos o en *Salvajes* con los nazis. Y, entonces, bueno, a veces quedo con alguien, les grabo o les pregunto cosas, hablamos. Ella me dio muchos datos, sobre todo de la parte del viaje.

DW: Y ¿a dónde iba ella para comprar las drogas? ¿A Marrakech?

JLAS: No, a Chaouen. El mismo viaje que yo conté. Eso suelen cambiar mucho las versiones actuales porque se hablaba de un tren muy largo – antes los trenes eran muy largos – y después un barco y ahora la gente va en un tren muy corto y en un ferri. Que yo no tenía idea. Que nunca había ido a Chaouen; fui después. Pero mucho me lo contaron, ella sobre todo, y otros que habían ido. Y de alguna lectura, de algún reportaje. Lo hice un poco de oídas pero luego, cuando fui, pensé, pues coincide muchísimo con lo que había leído.

DW: ¿Y sabe lo que ha sido de ella?

JLAS: No, no. Nunca la vi tan particular. Era la hermana de una amiga y me contó su viaje; que había ido varias veces. Me lo contó y la cosa se borró en el tiempo. Te diré que generalmente los creadores somos

do theatre about noblemen or princes, I do theatre about waiters and the like; the same as in the cinema. These traits, that turn any character into a prince, are inherited from the cinema. Evidently the type of language, the dialect and the like have much to do with the cinema. With American cinema on the one hand, and with Spanish cinema of all that period for sure.

DW: And you are a great cinema fan, aren't you?

JLAS: Yes, and above all, you are right when you say that a great new kind of Spanish cinema emerged at that time which was then difficult to sustain. Spanish cinema has subsequently lost its way, but there were great films which changed the state of cinema at that time.

DW: I've read that the anecdote, the plot of *Going Down to Morocco*, came from a story told to you by a student.

JLAS: Let's see, yes. In my relations with young people and the like, somebody had spoken to me about the trip to Morocco. And a girl said to me one day that she had never gone to Morocco – I'd already got the story running around my head, – but that her sister had. That really interested me. And I met up with the sister. And I even recorded the things she had to tell me. But I've done this many times. With prisoners in *Junkies and Yankees*, or with Nazis in *Savages*. And then, well, sometimes I meet with someone, I record them or ask them things, we chat. She gave me a lot of information above all about the trip itself.

DW: And where did she go to buy drugs? To Marrakesh?

JLAS: No, to Chaouen. The same trip I depict. They tend to have to change that a lot in modern-day versions because it spoke of a very long train – trains used to be very long – and then a boat, but now people go in a short train and a ferry. I had no idea. I'd never been to Chaouen; I went later. But they told me a lot about this, her more than anyone, and others who had gone. And from some reading, the odd report. I kind of did it based on what I'd heard but then, when I went, I saw how similar it was to what I had read about.

DW: And do you know what happened to her?

JLAS: No, no. I never saw anything particularly special in her. She was a friend's sister and she described her trip to me; she had gone a number of times. She told me, and then the thing got lost in the passage of time. What I will say to you is that us creative types are generally very selfish

muy egoístas en el sentido de las relaciones. Entonces, cuando estamos creando un libro de pájaros, nos interesan mucho los pájaros. Vamos a ver pájaros, hablamos con los de los pájaros. Teniendo el libro, adiós pájaros. ¿Por qué? Porque acabas un poco harto. Digamos que te puedes imaginar que me han propuesto hacer series de *Bajarse al moro* desde entonces para televisión, escribir la segunda parte y tal, y siempre dije que no. No quiero saber nada más de *Bajarse al moro*. Yo ya no podría escribir *Bajarse al moro* porque tengo otra edad, otras circunstancias, otras vivencias.

DW: Y es otro país también.

JLAS: Es otro país. Lo escribí en aquel momento que se daban todas esas circunstancias. Ahora escribo otras obras. O sea, que cuando estás con una cosa, la trabajas, la estudias, la preparas y tal, y cuando termina – eso lo dice mucha gente – el libro es historia terminada y hasta los recuerdos. Por eso, a veces los estudiosos que han hablado de *Bajarse al moro* han contado mejor las cosas que yo porque han buscado en mis papeles y cosas que yo dije – cosas que yo mismo he olvidado – porque digamos que cada obra es como un amor. Pero, y si te preguntan ahora, "¿te acuerdas de que hace cuarenta años que tuviste una novia?" No me acuerdo de casi nada. Ni de cómo se llama. Tú me entiendes. Así cada obra es un amor en su momento. Y luego ya, pues pasa que a veces tal vez dices tú, "pues vamos a hablar", y hablamos un rato pero de alguna manera pertenece a una época mía que murió. Y entonces los recuerdos, los de aquellas chicas, de aquellos pisos; he vivido en pisos sin puerta muchos años con gente así y tal, pero ahora no tiene nada que ver con mi vida. Evidentemente todo aquello me sirvió para escribir *Bajarse al moro*.

DW: Pero aún así, veo una continuidad en su obra. Ya hemos hablado de su contacto con el mundo de la calle. Es algo muy evidente que alguien como Pedro Almodóvar, o incluso Joaquín Sabina, son ahora figuras muy públicas y tienen experiencias y vidas muy distintas que las de hace treinta años. Hay como un "antes" y "después" en su trayectoria. Que se nota en las películas de Almodóvar que no vive en el mundo de la calle – que las obras, para bien o para mal, son cada vez más herméticas. Pero en su caso, aunque sus obras son muy famosas, no es una figura pública

in terms of our relationships. Hence, when we are preparing a book about birds, we are very interested in birds. We go and see birds, we speak with bird specialists. When the book's done, bye, bye birds. Why? Because you end up a bit fed up. Let's put it this way, as you can imagine, they've suggested that I do a television series based on *Going Down to Morocco*, that I write a second part and whatever; and I've always said no. I don't want to know anything else about *Going Down to Morocco*. I would no longer be capable of writing *Going Down to Morocco* because I'm at a different age with different circumstances and experiences.

DW: And it's also a different country.

JLAS: It's a different country. I wrote it at that moment due to all those circumstances. Now I write different plays. Or, to put it another way, when you're with a project, you work on it, you study it, you prepare it and the like and – many people say this – when you finish it, the book is finished business, and even the memories. This is why scholars who have talked about *Going Down to Morocco* have been better in their descriptions than I have, because they have looked amongst my correspondence and things I've said – things that I myself have forgotten – and, let us say, every play is like a love affair. And if someone asks you now, "do you remember the girlfriend you had forty years ago?" I can hardly remember anything. Not even her name. You get me. So every play is a love affair at the time. And then what happens is that, from time to time, someone such as yourself says, "let's talk", and we talk for a while but, in one sense, it belongs to a period of my life that has died. And then, the memories, of those girls, of those flats; I lived in flats without doors with those kind of people for many years but that does not have anything to do with my life now. Obviously all of that helped me to write *Going Down to Morocco*.

DW: But, even so, I see a level of continuity in your work. We have already spoken about your contact with the real world. It's very evident that someone like Pedro Almodóvar, or even Joaquín Sabina, are now very public figures, and they have very different experiences and lives than those they had thirty years ago. There is something of a 'before' and 'after' in their careers. You can see in Almodóvar's films that he no longer has so much contact with the outside world – that, for better or worse, his films are increasingly hermetic. But, in your case, although your plays are very famous, you are not a public figure in the same way,

en el mismo sentido e imagino que esto le da cierta libertad para seguir observando al mundo. Además, ha trabajado muchos años como profesor y sospecho que esto ayuda a mantener este contacto con el mundo joven. La primera obra suya que vi fue el montaje de *Peribáñez* que dirigió en 2002. Yo trabajaba entonces para el Instituto Británico dando clases en Vallecas. Fui con los chavales del instituto y había algo en la producción que era muy juvenil; era como un canto al primer amor.

JLAS: Esto está muy bien visto. Quise que *Peribáñez* fuera eso. Y también está muy bien visto lo segundo que has dicho. Uno de los elementos clave del teatro es los jóvenes tirando para adelante en un mundo muy difícil. Es como *Titanic*; los chicos en la quilla del barco allí en la primera parte y hay siempre estas historias. Y yo siempre quiero que en mis obras nazca una historia de amor entre jóvenes, claro. Hace poco se estrenó *La cena de los generales* y ahora va a empezar la película. Para mí, en el montaje, el director no había potenciado suficientemente. Yo iré insistiendo al guionista que va a hacer ahora la película, "por favor, potencia mucho la historia del amor entre los jóvenes", porque es muy importante. Pasa aquí una historia de amor que a lo mejor ni siquiera son ellos estupendos. Son regulares como en *Bajarse al moro*. Porque la historia de amor es entre estos dos que se van y son gente que ni siquiera nos caen bien de todo.

DW: No son héroes convencionales ni mucho menos.

JLAS: Pero están creando esa historia de amor, y su piso, su nido, su esperanza y tal, y eso es muy bonito.

DW: Tanto en *Bajarse al moro* como en *La estanquera de Vallecas*, Madrid es como un personaje más en la obra. Hay dos dimensiones. En primer lugar, es una obra sobre los jóvenes y, en segundo lugar, una obra sobre una ciudad joven. O sea que el Madrid de los ochenta fue en cierto modo como un adolescente y, sin caer en la nostalgia, se puede decir que ha perdido parte de su inocencia.

JLAS: Sí, fíjate que yo, es que eso lo he dicho pocas veces si es que lo he dicho. Estoy recordando ahora, yo dudaba mucho si situarlo en Lavapiés o en Cuatro Caminos. Porque Lavapiés me gustaba por el mundo andaluz y por el mundo de las canciones. Por eso iba mejor. Lavapiés es un barrio

and I imagine this gives you a certain freedom to continue observing the world. Furthermore, you have been a lecturer for many years and I suspect that this allows you to maintain in contact with the world of young people. The first play of yours I saw was the production of *Peribáñez* you directed in 2002. At that time, I was working for the British Council giving classes in Vallecas. I went with the kids from the school and there was something very youthful about the production; it was like a paean to first love.

JLAS: That is very astute on your part. It's what I wanted *Peribáñez* to be. And the second thing you say is also very well observed. One of the fundamental keys to theatre is young people struggling to keep afloat in a difficult world. It's like in *Titanic*; the kids there in the keel in the first part, and there are always these stories. And I, of course, always want two youngsters to fall in love in my plays. They premiered *The Generals' Dinner* recently and they are about to start making the film. In my opinion, the director didn't stress this vein enough in the stage production. With the screenwriter who is now going to do the film, I'm going to insist, "please emphasise the love story between the two youngsters", because it is very important. Perhaps they are not brilliant people but there is a love story here. They are average people like in *Going Down to Morocco*. Because the love story is between the two of them that go off and they are not people we altogether warm to.

DW: They are far from being conventional heroes.

JLAS: But they are creating a love story, and their flat, their nest, their hope and whatever, and that is very beautiful.

DW: In both *The Tobacconist Woman* and *Going Down to Morocco*, Madrid is like an additional character in the play. There are two dimensions. Firstly, it is a play about young people and, secondly, a play about a young city. To put it another way, Madrid in the 1980s was, in a certain sense, an adolescent and, without wanting to wallow in nostalgia, one could say that it has lost some of its innocence.

JLAS: Yes, go figure, I have said this very few times if I have said it at all. I'm remembering now that I spent a lot of time deliberating between setting it in Lavapiés or in Cuatro Caminos. Because I liked Lavapiés because of the Andalusian air and world of song that are there. That's why it worked best. Lavapiés is an edgy area that continues to be

marginal que sigue siendo marginal. Que está metido en el corazón de Madrid pero allí van los marginados. Si son turcos o son moros – o son rumanos o son andaluces – van a Lavapiés. Pero hay otra imagen de Madrid que me gustaba mucho para la obra que es Cuatro Caminos. Incluso lo pensé al principio cuando no tenía el titulo, que estaba en mi cabeza; no me gustaba como título sino la idea: Cuatro Caminos. Madrid es un sitio donde se cruzaban los caminos y eso – la canción de Sabina – cruzan los caminos. Porque Madrid era en aquella época "llega alguien con la maleta"; siempre pero en aquella época era gente rural, gente moderna, gente antigua, y un poco de Cuatro Caminos. Y de eso hay también en la obra, un poco. Lavapiés y Cuatro Caminos.

DW: Cuando hicieron la versión cinematográfica, originalmente querían rodarla en Malasaña pero dijo que no. ¿Por qué estaba en contra de la idea de rodarla allí?

JLAS: Bueno, Malasaña con el tiempo se ve que también tenía algo de moderno, de chicos jóvenes y tal pero a mí, me gustaba Lavapiés por dos razones. Primero, porque era más marginal y segundo porque estaba cerca del Rastro. Y el Rastro es muy importante. Roban las ruedas de coche; y las venden en el Rastro. El Rastro es un lugar, sigue siendo un lugar de supervivencia. Tú pasas por el Rastro e igual que hace treinta años hay alguien que te vende un bolígrafo. Y dices, "coño, ¿cómo vendes un bolígrafo?". Y hay quien te vende el reloj que acaba de robar en la calle de al lado. Esas cosas que son El Rastro y la marginación.

DW: Sí, ese lado picaresco. Dicho todo eso, es curioso que una obra tan madrileña se estrenara en Zaragoza.

JLAS: Iba a ir de gira y empezó la gira en Zaragoza como podía haber empezado en, no sé, en Huesca. Empezó de gira; primero hizo una gira y luego ya vino a Madrid. Y la gira cayó en Zaragoza por casualidad. No tiene ningún valor.

DW: Hemos hablado de su deseo de comunicarse con el público. En el fondo, ¿qué quería transmitir con *Bajarse al moro*?

JLAS: Primero, quería hacer un acto de fiesta y de comedia, lo primero de todo. Una comedia divertida donde nos riéramos un poco de nuestros problemas y tal. Luego ya viene la capa filosófica. Explico en mis

edgy. It's right there in the heart of Madrid but it's where those on the fringes of society go. Be they Turks or North Africans – or Romanians or Andalusians – they all go to Lavapiés. But there is another image of Madrid that I also liked for the play which is Cuatro Caminos. At the outset, when I didn't even have a title, I had it in my head; I liked the idea rather than the title: Cuatro Caminos, the Four Paths. Madrid is a place where the paths cross – like in Sabina's song – the paths cross. Because Madrid at that time was "someone arrives with their suitcase"; that's always been the case but at that time there were country folk, hip folk, old-fashioned people and something of those four paths. And something of that mixture is in the play. Lavapiés and Cuatro Caminos.

DW: And when they did the film adaptation, they originally wanted to shoot it in Malasaña but you said no. Why were you against the idea of shooting it there?

JLAS: Well, with hindsight, it is clear that Malasaña had something of that hipness, of youngsters and all that jazz, but I liked Lavapiés for two reasons. Firstly, because it was more edgy and, secondly, because it was near the Rastro. And the Rastro is very important. They steal car wheels; they sell them in the Rastro. The Rastro was a place, and it continues to be a place, of survival. You pass by the Rastro and there will be somebody, same as thirty years ago, who will sell you a Biro. And you say, "Christ, how can you sell a biro?" And someone will sell you a watch they've just stolen in the adjacent street. That's the Rastro and social exclusion for you.

DW: Yes, the picaresque side. Having said all of that, it is strange that such a quintessentially Madrid play was premiered in Zaragoza.

JLAS: It was going on tour and that tour began in Zaragoza in the same way it could have begun, I don't know, in Huesca. The tour began; it did a tour first and then came to Madrid. And, by coincidence, the tour began in Zaragoza. There's nothing to be read into it.

DW: We have already spoken of your desire to communicate with the audience. What, basically, did you want to transmit with *Going Down to Morocco*?

JLAS: First and foremost, I wanted to create a festive and comic event. A fun comedy, where we could laugh a bit at our problems and the like. Then, there is the philosophical layer. In my manuals, I speak of how,

manuales que, consciente o inconscientemente, en las obras siempre hay una carga filosófica. En aquella época, *Apocalípticos e integrados* de Umberto Eco tuvo una real importancia. Fue un libro muy, muy bueno porque él recogía también una tradición; es que Umberto Eco no era un filósofo, era un comunicador. En *Apocalípticos e integrados* explica las dos posturas frente al mundo de la juventud: o integrarse, tener un piso y vivir; o ser un apocalíptico, ir contra el sistema y tal. Y durante mucho tiempo ha sido el gran debate social de la juventud. El chico siempre llega a algún momento cuando tiene dieciocho, diecinueve, veinte años y se siente atrapado entre la necesidad de construir una familia, ser como su padre, tener una casa, integrarse en el sistema y vivir por otro "yo" que de pirata que tiene, lo que quiere que mande todo. Y yo, desde luego, estoy más al lado del pirata de Jaimito. Los llevo allí en la lucha entre el descaro de querer ser marinero y el descaro de querer ser familiar. Y ese descaro, que es muy típico de los jóvenes está en *Bajarse al moro*.

DW: ¿Cómo recuerda el trabajo con los actores y con el director?

JLAS: Hubo muchas dificultades porque el director no entendía la obra; él me decía, y los actores también, que, ¿por qué si la obra era filosófica e importante, hablaban de una forma tan tonta? Esto siempre ha sido difícil de entender porque por un lado parece una obra muy sencilla, muy elemental, de unos chicos y un piso, ese aire de sainete y de cuatro palomas y por otro lado está hablando del sentido de la vida y juntar estas dos cosas es muy difícil. De tal manera que empezó la gira y el reparto que se hizo no era el adecuado. La escenografía que se hizo, como era como del Rastro y tal, que era miserable y aquello era muy feo. Ni el montaje acababa de acertar ni estuve a gusto ni los actores que fueron elegidos funcionaban y la escenografía no me gustaba nada. Era cutre. La idea que tiene uno bien instalada de que la gente que vive en El Rastro es cutre, miserable. Era como vulgar. Y afortunadamente José Tamayo quien lo trajo a su Teatro de Bellas Artes se enganchó mucho con mi idea. Cuando lo vio, le gustó mucho la obra pero no le gustó nada lo que había allí. Y dijo una cosa maravillosa: que eso iba a su teatro pero si se cambiaba todo. Y, yo, encantado. En el Teatro de Bellas Artes, se hizo un reparto completamente diferente; que yo decía que era importante que fueran marginales, pero con encanto.

consciously or unconsciously, plays always have a philosophical charge. At that time, Umberto Eco's *Apocalyptic and Integrated Intellectuals* was really important. It was a very, very good book because he also picked up on a tradition; the thing is that Umberto Eco wasn't a philosopher, he was a communicator. In *Apocalyptic and Integrated Intellectuals*, he explains young people's two approaches to the world: they either conform, have a flat and live; or they are an apocalyptic, going against the system and the like. And, for a long time, it has been youth's major social debate. A young man always reaches a point when he is eighteen, nineteen or twenty years old when he feels split between the need to build a family, to be like his father, to have a home, to become part of the system and to live; and then, another 'I', the pirate he carries inside him who wants to have complete control. I am, of course, more in tune with Jaimito's pirate. I present this battle between the nerve required to be a sailor or to form a family. And that nerve, very typical of young people, is in *Going Down to Morocco*.

DW: How do you recall the work with the actors and the director?
JLAS: There were many problems because the director didn't understand the play; he, and the actors as well, said to me why, if the play was philosophically important, did the characters speak in such a stupid manner? This has always been difficult to understand because, on the one hand, it appears to be a very simple play about some youngsters and a flat with this air of a *sainete* and a folkloric tune but, on the other, it talks about the meaning of life, and combining these two aspects is very difficult. So, the play began to tour and the cast assembled was unsuitable. The set they did, because it was from the Rastro or whatever, was miserable and it was all very ugly. The production didn't come together; I wasn't happy; the actors who were cast didn't work and I didn't like the set design at all. It was shabby. The idea a well-to-do person has that people who live in El Rastro are shabby, down-at the heel. It was kind of vulgar. And, fortunately, José Tamayo who brought it to his Bellas Artes theatre really got hooked on my idea. When he saw it, he really liked the play but didn't like what was there at all. And he said something wonderful: it could go to his theatre but if everything was changed. This was great as far as I was concerned. They put together a completely different cast in the Bellas Artes theatre; I said it was important they were social outcasts, but with charm.

DW: Y incluso El Corte Inglés se encargó de los muebles y los decorados. Es una puesta en escena acogedora.

JLAS: Claro. Tiene que ser un sitio marginal pero con encanto, que dé gusto llegar allí. No es un sitio cutre. Y la escenografía encontró la poesía, los actores se encontraron y a partir de ahí ya fue un gran éxito. Pero había que encontrárselo y en el primer montaje que fue de gira no se encontró.

DW: Casi todas las críticas eran muy positivas con la excepción de las de Barcelona, donde la obra reinauguró el Teatro Goya con la idea de promover un nuevo tipo de programación comercial en castellano. Pero el montaje de *Bajarse al moro* no tuvo la calurosa acogida crítica que había recibida en el resto de España.

JLAS: Pero nunca he enganchado ni con el público ni con la crítica de Barcelona. Mis obras se han puesto allí con cierta normalidad y tal, pero el debate Cataluña y España y no sé qué y el castellano. Fíjate que en el País Vasco, que es el otro punto delicado de España, siempre ha sido entendido mi teatro y ven todas mis obras. Tú vas a San Sebastián o a Bilbao y haces una obra y, curiosamente, la gente no te está mirando con la prepotencia de los catalanes a pesar de que luego los vascos han sido más extremistas con la independencia. Digamos que el espíritu catalán, de ese del "yo", lo suyo, el desprecio al castellano y a España y tal, siempre me ha tocado las narices. Los catalanes me han tocado las narices toda la vida. Los catalanes, esta cosa mía de mi teatro que era por un lado popular y por otro lado y tal, ellos que querían ser tan europeos nunca acaban de, nunca acabé de ser aceptado en Cataluña. Lo cual también me parece muy bien. Me han aceptado en muchos otros sitios. Pero en Cataluña, digamos que Cataluña y yo, yo y Cataluña, nunca hemos llegado a un acuerdo. Hasta cuando era director de la Compañía Nacional, allí con mis montajes he tenido muchos problemas.

DW: ¿Y tiene alguna idea sobre cuál fue el público para *Bajarse al moro*? Imagino que fue una mezcla, ¿verdad? Gente que veía sus vidas reflejadas en el escenario y otros que tenían curiosidad, que habían oído de cómo vivía la gente en Lavapiés.

JLAS: Cuando tienes un éxito, precisamente lo que pasa con ese éxito si es muy grande es que borran ya los niveles del público. He tenido muchas obras que han fracasado, que no ha ido nadie por lo que sea.

DW: And the Corte Inglés department store even provided the furniture and sets. It's a very welcoming stage design.

JLAS. Of course. It has to be a marginal place but with charm, that is pleasurable to go to. It's not a shabby place. And the set-design found its poetry, the actors got a hold on it, and from that point onwards it was a great success. But that had to be found, and it wasn't found on the tour.

DW. Almost all of the reviews were very positive apart from those from Barcelona, where the play was the first to be staged at the re-opened Teatro Goya with the idea of promoting a new kind of commercial programming in Castilian. But the production of *Going Down to Morocco* didn't have the warm critical response it'd had in the rest of Spain.

JLAS. But I've never appealed to either audiences or critics in Barcelona. My plays have been staged there with a certain regularity and whatever, but with the debate between Catalonia and Spain and I don't know what and Castilian. Go figure that in the Basque Country, which is the other sensitive point of Spain, my theatre has always been understood and they see all my plays. You go to San Sebastian or Bilbao and curiously, in spite of the Basques then being more extreme in relation to their independence, you put on a play there and they don't look at you with the arrogant disdain of the Catalans. Let us say that the Catalan spirit, all that 'I am', getting their own way, contempt for Castilian and Spain, and the like, has always got on my wick. The Catalans have got of my wick all through my life. The Catalans, with them wanting to be so European, and this thing of mine of having a popular theatre on the one hand and whatever on the other, they have never, I have never really been accepted in Catalonia. Which is also fine by me. I've been accepted in many other places. But Catalonia and me, let us say, me and Catalonia, have never come to an understanding. Even when I was the director of the National Company, I had a lot of problems with my productions there.

DW: And do you have any idea about who the audience for *Going Down to Morocco* were? I imagine it was a mixture, wasn't it? People who saw their lives reflected on the stage, and others who were curious, who had heard about how people lived in Lavapiés.

JLAS: When you have a success, what a success means if it is big enough is that the distinctions between audiences disappear. I've had a lot of plays that have failed, that nobody's gone to see for whatever reason.

Otras que han funcionado para un público. Son para un público. Y otras que han entrado en esa categoría de no sé, como *Tres sombreros de copa*, esa categoría donde ya la gente va a verla y ya está y se acabó. Entonces *Bajarse al moro* es una de las obras que entró en esa categoría y que iban a verla jóvenes, mayores, de derechas, de izquierdas, y yo que sé. En general, iba a verla todo el mundo. Luego, ya te digo ha habido zonas donde ha gustado más y otras donde ha gustado menos. Eso es normal. Pero ha pasado igual cuando la he visto en Méjico, la he visto en Japón, la he visto en Estados Unidos. Y ya ha pasado, esas obras que se escapan del autor y forman parte de historia de la cultura. Y representa un momento determinado o representa tal. Entonces, ¿de qué público son? Pues, ya son de todos. ¿Sabes? Ya están en los manuales de los institutos, la gente las estudia y ya son del todo del público.

DW: ¿Y qué pensó de la película que se rodó basada de la obra?

JLAS: Las películas siempre tienen ventajas e inconvenientes. Yo creo que tenía mucho estilo y hubo momentos muy bonitos y tal. Y, luego, hago comedia divertida pero siempre con elementos dramáticos, y creo que *Bajarse al moro* tiene unos elementos dramáticos muy duros que hay que respetar. Esa mezcla de lo cómico y lo trágico es muy importante en mi obra. Y creo que en la película eso patinaba un poco. Tuvo éxito, funcionó, se ha visto millones de veces. La gente me conoce más por la película que por la obra. No hay ninguna duda. En cuanto a los actores – alguno, por ejemplo, Antonio Banderas estaba estupendo – pero a mí, no me gustaba y era muy importante, Juan Echanove de Jaimito. Porque hacía un Jaimito Jesús Cristo tonto. Era como muy bueno y muy tonto. Y a mí, me parece que Jaimito es marginal. Y que Jaimito tiene que tener cosas de bueno y cosas de malvado porque un marginal sufre y como no le aceptan a él, tampoco él ha aceptado. El monólogo del pirata y tal es de alguien que está intentando agredir al mundo desde su forma de ser. Y a mí me parece que lo que hacía este chico…

DW: Hacía de gracioso, ¿no?

JLAS: Hacía de tontón. Yo cuando veía la película, veía a ese hombre y no me gustaba el tontón. Y el final, que era Navidad, y ellos habían tenido el niño y todo eso, y ya me repateaba. Bueno, pero esto pasa siempre con las películas que se hacen sobre obras, que hay cosas que les gustan y otras

Others have worked for a specific audience. They are for a specific audience. And others that have joined that category of, I don't know, *Three Top Hats*, that category where people just go and see it and that's that. Thus, *Going Down to Morocco* is one of those plays that entered into that category and young people, old people, those on the left, those on the right, and God knows who went to see it. In general, people from all walks of life went to see it. Then, as I say, there were places people liked it more or less. That's normal. But the same happened when I saw it in Mexico, Japan or the United States. And that's already taken place; it's one of those plays that no longer belongs to the author and now forms part of cultural history. And it represents a specific moment or whatever. Thus, who were the audience? Well, everyone. You see? It's now in school textbooks, people study it, and it belongs to everyone.

DW: And what did you think of the film they shot based on the play?

JLAS: Films always have their pros and cons. I think it had a lot of style and there were some very nice moments and so on. But, then, I do fun comedies but always with dramatic elements, and I think that *Going Down to Morocco* has some dramatic elements that need to be respected. That mix of the tragic and the comic is very important in my work. And I think the film went a bit amiss in this regard. It was successful, it did well, it's been seen a million times. People know me more for the film than the play. Without a shadow of a doubt. As for the actors, some – for example, Antonia Banderas – were superb but, personally, I didn't like, and it was very important, Juan Echanove as Jaimito. Because he played Jaimito as if he were Jesus Christ but stupid. He was very good and very stupid. And, personally, I think that Jaimito is a social outcast. And that Jaimito must have good and evil things about him because he is an outcast who suffers; because he's not accepted, neither is he very accepting. The monologue about the pirate comes from someone who is trying to attack the world through their way of being. And, for me, what that lad did...

DW: He made him a clown, didn't he?

JLAS: He made him an idiot. When I saw the film, I saw that man and I didn't like that idiot. And the ending, it's Christmas, and they've had the kid and all that, that really got my back up. But, well, this always happens with films they do based on your plays; there are things you like

que no. Pero, luego, a cambio, tenía escenas muy graciosas, tenía el aire muy bien, tenía el aire de comedia madrileña de época muy simpática, y tenía cosas que estaban bien. Y luego tenía a Antonio Banderas – que he visto muchos Albertos de *Bajarse al moro* en teatro, la he dirigido yo muchas veces, y no he visto ninguno que esté tan bien como Antonio Banderas. Esa cosa que tiene de canalla, de guapo, de gracioso, marginal y a la vez que se ve que se deja a todos y todo. Para mí, eso lo hace Antonio Banderas maravillosamente bien.

DW: Por lo general, parece que está mucho menos defensivo con su obra que muchos otros dramaturgos y que no le molesta que la gente cambie cosas, etc.

JLAS: Es imposible ser el policía que va por todos sitios vigilando a quien te cambie y quien no te cambie. El problema no es si te cambian o no te cambian; el problema es el nivel de talento que tienen. El arte nunca es un problema de fidelidad; si lo hacen en el escenario, ya no es igual que está escrito. Si hacen una obra, imagínate que hacen *Hamlet* una compañía pero al pie de la letra. La hace perfecta y larga como *Hamlet*. Un rollo. Lo que importa es que lo que hagan, sea más corto o cambiado y tal, esté bien. A mí, me han llamado muchas veces y me han dicho: "¿podemos cortar una parte del texto suyo largo? Que lo hace un actor que es muy malo." Y digo: "sí, claro; que si lo hace un actor que es muy malo, mejor cortarlo". Porque, imagínate que, por respeto a mí, un actor muy malo, muy malo – porque no tenían otro, los pobres, – tiene que hacer el monólogo muy largo, muy largo, ese de Doña Antonia. Eso lo aconsejo siempre: si tienes una actriz buena, pues cuanto más largo mejor; si tienes una actriz mala, por favor, córtalo. Pues, el respeto al autor luego en el escenario puede cargarse al autor. La gente lista hace montajes listos; la gente torpe hace montajes torpes. No es un problema de fidelidad. He visto muchísimos montajes en mi vida de obras mías; unos están mejor y otros están peor. Siempre lo han querido hacer bien pero algunos están preparados y otros no. Luego, ya tienen que tener categoría escénica, tiene que ser arte y para que sea arte, es que es muy difícil. El teatro lo hacen cien compañías. Tú vas a ver cien obras de teatro. Bien. Cincuenta o sesenta que son ridículas. De gente que está aprendiendo solo. Está bien. Veinte o treinta que son buenas intenciones.

and things you don't. But, then, in contrast, there were very funny scenes, it had a very good feel, it had the nice feel of the Madrid comedies of the time, and some things were really well done. And then it had Antonio Banderas – I've seen many Albertos from *Going Down to Morocco* in theatre, I've directed them many times, and I've not seen anyone do it as well as Antonio Banderas. That thing he's got of being a cad, a looker, a clown, an outcast and, at the same time, letting us see that he'd be capable of leaving everyone and everything behind. Personally, I think Antonio Banderas did that brilliantly.

DW: In general, you seem far less defensive with your work that many other dramatists, and it doesn't seem to bother you if people change things etc.

JLAS: It's impossible to spend your life as a policeman keeping guard everywhere on who changes you and who doesn't. The problem isn't if people do or don't make changes; the problem is their level of talent. Art is never a fidelity issue; if it's put on a stage, it's already different to how it was on the page. If they stage a play, imagine a company stages *Hamlet* following the text word-by-word. It's done as perfectly and lengthily as *Hamlet*. A drag. What's important is that what they do, be that shorter or adapted or whatever, is well-done. I've been phoned many times and been asked: "can we cut a part of your long text. A really bad actor is doing it". And, I say: "yes, of course; if a really bad actor's doing it, it's best to cut it". Because, imagine that, out of respect for me, a really really bad actor – because, the poor things don't have anyone else – has to do that really really long monologue, the one by Doña Antonia. My advice is always, if you've got a good actress, the longer the better; if you've got a bad actress, please, cut it. Respect for the author can then screw the author over on stage. Clever people do clever productions; and clumsy people do clumsy productions. It's not an issue of fidelity. In my life, I've seen many productions of my plays; some are better and some are worse. They've always wanted to do them well but some have been in a position to do so and others haven't. Then, they have to have a stage presence, it has to be art and, in order to be art, it's very difficult. A hundred companies do some theatre. You go and see a hundred plays in the theatre. Alright. Fifty or sixty that are ridiculous. By people who are just learning. That's fine. Twenty or thirty with good intentions. Ten that

Diez que son interesantes y habrá seis a diez que estén bien, y uno o dos que están estupendas. Esa es la proporción.

DW: Ya ha dicho que ha visto muchos montajes de *Bajarse al moro*. ¿Hay uno que le haya gustado mucho por algún motivo especial?

JLAS: Hombre, para mí, el montaje primero: el estreno en las Bellas Artes. Había una actriz que arrasaba que era Verónica Forqué. Luego la obra duró muchos años, se fue Verónica y pasaron muchas otras: Natalia Dicenta y un largo etcétera. Ninguna la hizo como Verónica; hacía una marginal encantadora. Era como de cuento. Ella vivía en un cuento. Y ese era el momento brillantísimo de Verónica Forqué. Y así como en la película es Antonio Banderas, en la obra de teatro ella está impresionante. Tú vuelves a ver el vídeo ahora mismo y cómo dice ella las frases, cómo anda por casa, cómo arregla el mundo, cómo llora, cómo ríe; está maravillosa. Representa esa movida, ese Rastro, ese mundo con pocos medios pero lleno de belleza y de ilusiones. Representa algo sin saberlo.

DW: Vi ese montaje en vídeo pero vi el montaje que hicieron hace dos o tres años en el Teatro Muñoz Seca. Y la actriz...

JLAS: Es que la actriz que hacía el papel de Verónica no tenía eso.

DW: Y era demasiado guapa; no había tanta diferencia ni físicamente ni en su manera de ser entre ella y el personaje de Elena.

JLAS: Es que encontrar a una Chusa que dé lo que daba Verónica Forqué en el teatro es que no había forma. Elena, se encuentra a muchas Elenas. La ha hecho Emma Suárez. La han hecho muchas y la han hecho muy bien. Pero Chusa solamente la ha hecho una persona maravillosamente bien – y le debo el cincuenta por ciento del éxito – de captar el sentido de la obra, de captar la vida, de ser ella; Verónica era más la obra que yo.

DW: Cuando publiquemos la traducción esperamos que algunos grupos de profesionales, de aficionados, de estudiantes o quienes sean hagan sus propios montajes en inglés. ¿Tiene algún consejo para ellos?

JLAS: Nada. A la gente que hace teatro solo le doy un consejo: que se divierta. Que se lo pase bien. No que le salga bien, porque eso no es un

are interesting, and there will be between six and ten that are well-done, and one or two that are brilliant. That's the proportion.

DW: You've already mentioned that you've seen many productions of *Going Down to Morocco*. Is there one that you've particularly liked for any special reason?

JLAS: Personally, the first production: the premiere in the Bellas Artes theatre. There was an actress who triumphed, and that was Verónica Forqué. Then, the play went on for many years, Verónica left and many others took on the role: Natalia Dicenta and a long list. None of them did it like Verónica; she played it as a charming outcast. She was straight out of a fairytale. She lived in a fairytale. Verónica Forqué was, at that point, at her most brilliant peak. And, in the same way that the film is Antonio Banderas, she is incredible in the theatrical staging. You go back and watch the video right now, and how she says the phrases, how she walks about the flat, how she puts the world to rights, how she cries, how she laughs; she's marvellous. She represents that *Movida*, that Rastro, that world with few resources but full of beauty and hope. She represents something without even being aware.

DW: I saw that production on video, but I saw the production they did two or three years ago in the Muñoz Seca theatre. And the actress…

JLAS. The thing is that the actress who took on Verónica's role didn't have that.

DW: And she was too pretty; there wasn't much difference either physically or in her way of being between her and Elena's character.

JLAS. The thing is that finding a Chusa who gives what Verónica Forqué gave in the theatre; there's no way. Elena, you can find a lot of Elenas. Emma Suárez played her. Many actresses have played her, and they've done it very well. But only one person has played Chusa marvellously well – and I owe her fifty percent of the success – of capturing the play's meaning, of capturing life, of being her; Verónica represented the play more than I did.

DW: When we publish the translation, we hope that some professional groups, or amateurs or students, or whoever, stage their own productions in English. Do you have any advice for them?

JLAS: None. To people who are going to do theatre, I only give them one piece of advice: that they have a good time. Not that they do it well,

consejo – que todo el mundo quiere que le salga bien –, sino que se lo pase bien. Todos tienen buena voluntad pero, hombre, si el arte fuera fácil, ello no tendría mérito. Lo mismo pasa pintando cuadros, tocando la guitarra – el arte es difícil. Y pocas veces se consiguen objetivos importantes. Cuando me siento a ver obras mías, o traducciones mías, o cosas que hacen los demás, me doy cuenta que el arte es difícil. Si lo sacara todo el mundo, no tendría mérito.

DW: Entonces, ¿es casi una postura pragmática?

JLAS: Soy comprensivo. Todo el mundo tiene fallos, yo también. Hombre, yo soy menos comprensivo con la falta de trabajo. Si voy a ver una obra mía, que alguien me invita y voy y ni se saben el texto, y aquello está muy mal hecho por falta de tiempo, me siento ofendido.

DW: Es como una falta de respeto.

JLAS: Falta de respeto, sí. Pero si hay un respeto, pues la calidad, mira, ¿qué quieres que te diga? Que se lo haga con rigor, con tiempo porque medios no tiene todo el mundo – hay gente que tiene millones y gente que no tiene ni para comer – ni talento, ¿pero tiempo? Si lo pudieras organizar en tu universidad, yo vendría encantado a dirigir la obra en Leeds con tus estudiantes.

DW: Perfecto, muchas gracias. Quedamos en eso; ahí tenemos una meta en común.

because that's not advice – everyone wants to do it well – but rather that they have a good time. They're all doing it in good faith but, if art were easy, then it wouldn't have any merit. The same happens in the painting of a picture or the playing of the guitar – art is difficult. And it's very rare that important objectives are achieved. When I sit down to see my plays, or translations of my work, or things that other people have done, I realise that art is difficult. If everyone could do it, it wouldn't be of any merit.

DW: It is, then, almost a pragmatic attitude?

JLAS: I'm understanding. Everyone has faults, me included. I'm less understanding about a bad work ethic. If I go and see a play of mine, someone invites me and I go, and they don't even know the text, and it's very badly done because of a lack of preparation, I feel offended.

DW: It's like a lack of respect.

JLAS: A lack of respect, yes. But if there's respect, look what do you want me to say about the quality? It should be done with rigour, with ample time because not everyone has resources – there are people with millions and people who don't even have enough to eat – or talent, but time? If you can organise it in your university, it'd be my pleasure to come and direct the play with your students in Leeds.

DW: Perfect, many thanks. Let's leave it there; we've now got a common goal.

BAJARSE AL MORO

GOING DOWN TO MOROCCO

Estrenada en el Teatro Principal de Zaragoza, el 6 de abril de 1985 en una producción de Justo Alonso

Reparto

(POR ORDEN DE INTERVENCIÓN)
CHUSA
ELENA
JAIMITO
ALBERTO
DOÑA ANTONIA
ABEL
NANCHO

ACTO PRIMERO

Escena Primera

Habitación destartalada en una calle céntrica del Madrid antiguo. Posters por las paredes y un colchón en el suelo cubierto de almohadones. Sobre una mesa, revistas pop, como «Víbora», «Tótem» y otras. En un rincón una señal de tráfico, y en el otro una jardinera municipal. Sobre ella una jaula con un hámster. En el centro una mesita con aire moruno y unos sillones de mimbre de antes de la guerra. Además hay tiestos y otros cachivaches inesperados, como una cabeza de esclavo egipcio con una gorra puesta, y cosas por el estilo encontradas en el Rastro. A la derecha, formando un recodo se ve la puerta que da a las escaleras de salida a la calle. A la izquierda, una ventana por la que entran los ruidos de la ciudad. Y al fondo, una cocinilla, una puerta que da al lavabo, y otra que da a un cuarto pequeño. Por las paredes anda una flauta, un mantón de manila, unos bafles que no suenan, un armario, una colección de llaves, la cara de Lennon, el espejo de la Cenicienta y un horóscopo chino. Y sin embargo, a pesar del aparente desorden, hay algo acogedor, relajante y bueno para los que están mal de los nervios; porque es un lugar tranquilo y pacífico donde el caos que uno lleva dentro se encuentra lógico y con ganas de tomar asiento. Al comenzar nuestra historia, en escena está JAIMITO, un muchacho delgaducho de

ACT ONE

Scene One

A ramshackle room in a city centre street in Madrid's old town. Posters on the walls and a mattress on the floor covered with cushions. On the table, pop magazines including Víbora and Tótem.[i] In one corner, there is a traffic light and, in the other, a city council window box. On top of it, a cage with a hamster. In the middle of the room, a Moorish-style small table and some pre-Civil-War wicker chairs. There are also flowerpots and other unexpected bits and bobs, such as the head of an Egyptian slave wearing a cap, and the kind of things you find in the Rastro. One can see, on the right hand side, in the shape of a bend, the door which opens onto the stairs which lead down to the street. On the left hand side, a window through which the city noises enters. And, at the far end, a small kitchen, and one door that leads into the bathroom, and another into a small bedroom. A flute, an embroidered silk shawl, some loudspeakers incapable of emitting a sound, a wardrobe, a collection of keys, Lennon's face,[ii] Cinderella's mirror and a Chinese horoscope are all strewn around the walls. In spite of the apparent disorder, it has something that is welcoming, relaxing and good for those who suffer from their nerves; it is a quiet and peaceful place where the chaos that one harbours inside makes sense and feels at home. At the beginning of our story, we have JAIMITO, a scrawny lad of an indeterminable age, on

edad indefinida, haciendo sandalias de cuero. Suena «Chick Corea» en un casette. Es la una de la tarde y entra el sol por la ventana de la habitación.

(Se abre la puerta de la calle, y aparece la cabeza de CHUSA, *veinticinco años, gordita, con cara de pan y gafas de aro.)*

CHUSA   ¿Se puede pasar? ¿Estás visible? Que mira, ésta es Elena, una amiga muy maja. Pasa, pasa, Elena.

(Entra, y detrás ELENA *con una bolsa en la mano, guapa, de unos veintiún años, la cabeza a pájaros y buena ropa.)*

                Éste es Jaimito, mi primo. Tiene un ojo de cristal y hace sandalias.

ELENA   *(Tímidamente.)* ¿Qué tal?

JAIMITO   ¿Quieres también mi número de carnet de identidad? ¡No te digo! ¿Se puede saber dónde has estado? No viene en toda la noche, y ahora tan pirada como siempre.

CHUSA   He estado en casa de ésta. ¿A que sí, tú? No se atrevía a ir sola a por sus cosas por si estaba su madre, y ya nos quedamos allí a dormir. *(Saca cosas de comer de los bolsillos.)* ¿Quieres un bocata?

JAIMITO   *(Levantándose del asiento muy enfadado, con la sandalia en la mano.)* Ni bocata ni leches. Te llevas las pelas, y la llave, y me dejas aquí colgao, sin un duro… ¿No dijiste que ibas a por papelillo?

CHUSA   Iba a por papelillo, pero me encontré a ésta, ya te lo he dicho. Y como estaba sola…

JAIMITO   ¿Y ésta quién es?

CHUSA   Es Elena.

ELENA   Soy Elena.

JAIMITO   Eso ya lo he oído, que no soy sordo. Elena.

ELENA   Sí, Elena.

JAIMITO   Que quién es, de qué va, de qué la conoces…

CHUSA   De nada. Nos hemos conocido anoche, ya te lo he dicho.

stage, making leather sandals. Chick Corea is on the cassette player.[iii] *It is one in the afternoon and the sun comes in through the room's window.*

(The front door opens and CHUSA *– twenty-five years old, overweight with a chubby face and round glasses – pokes her head round it.)*

CHUSA   Is it okay to come in? Are you decent? Look, this is Elena, a nice new friend. Elena, come in, come in.

(She enters with ELENA, *bag in hand, behind her; roughly twenty-one years old, she wears good clothes and has her head in the clouds.)*

This is little Jaime, my cousin. He's got a glass eye and makes sandals.

ELENA   *(Shyly.)* How are you?

JAIMITO   Do you also want the number of my ID card?[iv] I'm not going to tell you. Where, might I ask, have you been? You haven't been here all night, and now as away with the fairies as ever.

CHUSA   I've been in this one's house. Oy, you, isn't that so? She didn't dare go to pick up her stuff alone in case her mum was there, and we ended up crashing the night there. *(She takes stuff to eat out of her pockets.)* You want a bap?

JAIMITO   *(Getting up out of the seat very annoyed, with sandal in hand.)* To hell with the bap and everything. You take the dosh, and the keys, leaving me here in the lurch without a penny to my name… Didn't you say you were going out for Rizla?

CHUSA   I was heading out for Rizla but then I came across this girl, like I told you. And as she was on her own.

JAIMITO   And this girl, who is she?

CHUSA   She's Elena

ELENA   Hi, I'm Elena.

JAIMITO   I've already heard that, I'm not deaf. Elena.

ELENA   Yes, Elena.

JAIMITO   But who is she? What's she up to? How do you know her?

CHUSA.   I don't know her at all. We met last night, I've already told you.

JAIMITO	¿Otra vez? ¿Qué me has dicho tú a mí, a ver?
CHUSA	Que es Elena, y que nos conocimos anoche. Eso es lo que te he dicho. Y que estaba sola.
ELENA	(*Se acerca a* JAIMITO *y le tunde la mano, presentándose.*) Mucho gusto.

(JAIMITO *la mira con cara de pocos amigos, y le da la sandalia que lleva en la mano; ella la estrecha educadamente.*)

JAIMITO	¡Anda que…! Lo que yo te diga.
CHUSA	(*A* ELENA.) Pon tus cosas por ahí. Mira, ese es el baño, ahí está el colchón. Tenemos «maría» plantada en ese tiesto, pero casi no crece, hay poca luz. (*Al ver la cara que está poniendo* JAIMITO.) Se va a quedar a vívir aquí.
JAIMITO	Sí, encima de mí. Si no cabemos, tía, no cabemos. A todo el que encuentra lo mete aquí. El otro día al mudo, hoy a ésta. ¿Tú te has creído que esto es el refugio El Buen Pastor, o qué?
CHUSA	No seas borde.
ELENA	No quiero molestar. Si no queréis, no me quedo y me voy.
JAIMITO	Eso es, no queremos.
CHUSA	(*Enfrentándose con él.*) No tiene casa. ¿Entiendes? Se ha escapado. Si la cogen por ahí tirada… No seas facha. ¿Dónde va a ir? No ves que no sabe, además.
JAIMITO	Pues que haga un cursillo, no te jode. Yo lo que digo es que no cabemos. Y no digo más.
CHUSA	Sólo es por unos días hasta que se baje al moro conmigo.
JAIMITO	¿Que se va a bajar al moro contigo? Tú desde luego tienes mal la caja.
CHUSA	¡Bueno! (*Se desentiende de él y va hacia la cocina.*) ¿Quieres un té, Elena?
ELENA	Sí, gracias; con dos terrones.

JAIMITO	Not again? Let's see, what did you say to me?
CHUSA	That she's Elena, and that we met last night. That's what I said to you. And she was on her own.
ELENA	(*Moving towards* JAIMITO, *she holds out her hand to introduce herself.*) It's a pleasure to meet you.

(*JAIMITO looks at her with the air of someone who doesn't have many friends, holding out the sandal he has in his hand; she shakes it politely.*)

JAIMITO	Get away. What can I say.
CHUSA	(*To* ELENA.) Put your things there. Look, that's the bathroom, there's the mattress. We've got the 'ganja' planted in that flower pot though there's so little light that it hardly grows. (*Seeing the expression on* JAIMITO'S *face.*) She's going to come and live here.
JAIMITO	Yes, on top of me. There's no room, love, there's no room. Let all the waifs and strays come here. The other day, the mute guy, now this one. Do you think this is the Sally Doodle, or what?
CHUSA	Don't be so pig ignorant.
ELENA	I don't want to be a bother. If you don't want me, I won't stay and I'll clear off.
JAIMITO	You've got it in one, we don't want you.
CHUSA	(*Squaring up to him.*) She doesn't have a home. Get it? She's run away. If they find her, left to fend for herself… Don't be fascist 'bout it. Where's she gonna go? Anyway, can't you see she's clueless.
JAIMITO	Well, for fuck's sake, let her do an evening class. What I'm saying is there's no room. I say no more.
CHUSA	Only for a few days until she comes down to Morocco with me.
JAIMITO	She's going down to Morocco with you! You must have a screw loose!
CHUSA	Fine! (*She leaves him be, and heads towards the kitchen.*) Would you like a tea, Elena?
ELENA	Yes, please; with two sugar lumps.

(Se sienta cómodamente para tomar el té. JAIMITO la mira cada vez más preocupado, y CHUSA canturrea desde la cocina mientras calienta el agua.)

JAIMITO	¿Y por qué vas a llevarla? Quieres que nos cojan, ¿no?
CHUSA	*(Desde la cocina.)* Será que me cojan a mí, porque a tí, ahí sentado...
JAIMITO	Oye, no sé a qué viene eso. Sabes muy bien que no voy por lo de la cara sospechoso. Pero yo vendo, ¿no? ¿O me echas algo en cara?
CHUSA	Lo único que te digo es que se va a venir conmigo, para sacar pelas. Y ya está.
JAIMITO	Pues que venda aquí si quiere, pero ir, no, Si es una cría.
ELENA	Es que como quiero viajar...
JAIMITO	Pues hazte un crucero, tía. ¿Pero tú le has explicado a ésta de qué va el rollo? A ver si se cree que esto es ir de cachondeo con Puente Cultural.
CHUSA	*(De la cocina, con el té.)* Tú no te metas; eso es cosa mía. ¿Con mucho azúcar has dicho, Elena?
ELENA	Dos terrones.
CHUSA	Es que no tenemos terrones aquí.
ELENA	Bueno, pues regular de azúcar. Es que engorda. Trae, me la echo yo. ¿Sacarina no tenéis?
CHUSA	No.
ELENA	¿Y la cucharilla, para darle vueltas?
JAIMITO	Trae, te doy las vueltas con el dedo.
CHUSA	*(Cortándole.)* ¡Venga tú! *(A ELENA.)* Mete la parte de atrás de la cuchara. *(A JAIMITO.)* ¿Tú quieres?
JAIMITO	*(Seco.)* No.

(Beben las dos mientras él, malhumorado, vuelve a su trabajo con las sandalias.)

(She makes herself at home ready for her tea. JAIMITO looks at her in an increasingly concerned manner, and CHUSA hums from the kitchen whilst the water boils.)

JAIMITO	And why are you taking her? You want them to catch us? Is that it?
CHUSA	*(From the kitchen.)* Or, rather, catch me; because you, just sitting there…
JAIMITO	Listen, I don't know what you are getting at. You know I don't come cos my face looks dodge. But I sell, don't I? Or, do you wanna have something to throw in my face?
CHUSA	All I'm saying is she's going to come with me, to make some dosh. And that's that.
JAIMITO	Let her shift stuff here if she wants, but not go there. She's just a little girl.
ELENA	The thing is I like to travel…
JAIMITO	Well take yourself on a cruise, love. But have you told her what this is all about? I bet she thinks this is about having a jolly with Thomas Cook.
CHUSA	*(From the kitchen, with the tea.)* Don't you interfere; this is my business. Did you say with a lot of sugar, Elena?
ELENA	Two sugar cubes.
CHUSA	The thing is we don't have sugar cubes here.
ELENA	Okay, well with a bit of sugar then. The thing is it's fattening. Bring it here, I'll put it in. You don't have sweetener, do you?
CHUSA	No.
ELENA	And the teaspoon for stirring it in?
JAIMITO	Bring it here, I'll mix it in with my finger.
CHUSA	*(Stopping him.)* Come here, you! *(To ELENA.)* Use the handle-bit of the spoon. *(To JAIMITO.)* You want any?
JAIMITO	*(Dryly.)* No.

(The two of them drink whilst he, annoyed, returns to his work with the sandals.)

ELENA	¿Saco las cosas?
CHUSA	Sí. No las pongas ahí. Ese es el rincón de Alberto; no le gusta que le desordenen ni le toquen nada. Ya le conocerás luego. Está chachi, te va a gustar. Es muy alto, fuerte, moreno, con una pinta que te caes. ¡Ah! Ese es Humphrey, el hámster. Le encanta la lechuga.
ELENA	(*Al mirar al rincón de* ALBERTO *ve una porra sobre un mueble.*) Parece una porra. (*Se acerca y la coge.*) Oye, es igualita que la que llevan los…
JAIMITO	(*A* CHUSA, *que está llevando lo del té a la cocina.*) Me vas a acabar metiendo en un mal rollo por tu alma de monja recogetodo que tienes. Bueno, ¿y las pelas para el billete?
CHUSA	(*Desde la cocina.*) Las pones tú, que para eso te quedas dándole a las sandalias, mientras yo ando de safari jugándomela.
JAIMITO	A ti hoy la goma de la olla no te cierra. ¿Quién organiza aquí, eh? ¿Y quién controla para que todo salga bien?
CHUSA	(*Volviendo de la cocina.*) Santa Rita. (*A* ELENA *ahora, al verla con la porra en la mano.*) No toques eso; es de Alberto. Se mosquea rápido en cuanto nota que alguien ha andado ahí. Mete tus cosas aquí, en mi armario.
ELENA	Es que es igualita. ¿Os habéis fijado cómo se parece a las que lleva la…?
JAIMITO	(*Cortándola.*) ¿Qué es eso?
ELENA	¿Esto? Pues ya he dicho, estaba aquí, que se parece a las…
JAIMITO	No, eso. Eso que llevas debajo del brazo.
ELENA	¿Esto? «El País». «El País» de hoy. ¿Por qué?
JAIMITO	Tú eres una tía tela de rara. ¿Por qué compras tú el periódico, a ver? ¿Estas buscando piso?

ELENA	Shall I get my stuff out?
CHUSA	Yes. Don't put them there. That's Alberto's corner; he doesn't like anyone to mess with or even touch his stuff. You'll get to know him soon enough. He's a cutie, you'll like him. He is tall, dark, strong – drop dead gorgeous. Ah! That's Humphrey, the hamster. He loves lettuce.
ELENA	(*On looking at* ALBERTO'*s corner, she sees a truncheon on top of some furniture.*) It looks like a truncheon. (*She goes nearer and picks it up.*) Listen, it's exactly the same as those carried by the...
JAIMITO	(*To* CHUSA *who is carrying the stuff to make the tea into the kitchen.*) Your Saint Teresa habit of picking everything and everyone up is going to end in tears for me. And, in any case, the dosh for the ticket?
CHUSA	(*From the kitchen.*) You'll provide it. That's why you stay here fiddling with your sandals whilst I'm on safari putting my neck on the line.
JAIMITO	You just can't keep your trap shut today. Who organises everything this end, eh? And who makes sure that everything runs smoothly?
CHUSA	(*Returning from the kitchen.*) Speak to the hand. (*On seeing* ELENA, *now with the truncheon in hand, she turns to her.*) Don't touch that; it's Alberto's. He gets angry real quick as soon as he clicks someone's been mooching round there. Put your things here, in my wardrobe.
ELENA	The thing is, it's exactly the same. Have you noticed how it looks just like those carried by...?
JAIMITO	(*Interrupting her.*) What's that?
ELENA	This? It was here. Like I said, it was here, and it looks...
JAIMITO	No, what you're carrying under your arm.
ELENA	This? It's the newspaper. Today's El País Why?
JAIMITO	You're one loony tune. Now then, why have you bought the newspaper? You looking for a flat?

ELENA	Es que mi madre, siempre que me escapo, manda una foto a «El País», con un anuncio para que me encuentren. A ver si he salido... (*Hojea el periódico ante la mirada sorprendida de los otros dos.*) Sí, mira, aquí está.
JAIMITO	¿Esta eres tú? Pues si te tienen que encontrar por la foto...
CHUSA	La verdad, no te pareces en nada.
ELENA	Es de cuando era pequeña. Hace mucho que no me hago fotos. Salgo muy mal yo en las fotos.
JAIMITO	Sí sales mal, sí. Tienes cara de loca.
ELENA	Como estoy de frente... y luego el papel.
CHUSA	(*Leyendo el pie de la foto.*) «Vuelve a casa hija, que te perdono. Tu madre.»
ELENA	(*Recortando el trozo de periódico.*) Hago colección.
JAIMITO	¿Y no tienes padre, o ése no te busca?
ELENA	No, padre no tengo.
CHUSA	Yo tampoco tengo padre. Es mejor.

(Se abre de pronto la puerta de la calle y entra a todo correr ALBERTO, el otro habitante del piso vestido de policía nacional. Tiene unos veinticinco años, alto, y buena presencia. ELENA se queda blanca al verle.)

ALBERTO	¡La policía! ¡La policía, tíos! ¡Rápido, que vienen! ¡Tirar al water lo que tengáis! ¡Han salido de mi comisaría a hacer un registro, no vaya a ser aquí, que venían para esta zona! (*Esconde el tiesto de «maría». En este momento se da cuenta de la presencia de ELENA.*)
CHUSA	Es una amiga. Oye, no sé qué vamos a tirar, si no tenemos nada. (*A JAIMITO.*) ¿Te queda algo?

ELENA	The thing is that every-time I run away, my mother sends in a photo of me, along with an ad, to El País in order to track me down. Let's see if I'm in here… (*She flicks through the paper to the bemusement of the other two.*) Yes, look, here it is.
JAIMITO	Is that you? Well if they have to track you down by the photo…
CHUSA	Honestly, it doesn't look anything like you.
ELENA	It's from when I was young. It's been a long time since I've had photos taken. I'm not at all photogenic.
JAIMITO	Yes, it's true, you don't come out well. You've got a crazed look.
ELENA	As it's just my face… and then with that kind of paper.
CHUSA	(*Reading underneath the photo.*) "Come home, my daughter, all is forgiven. Your mother."
ELENA	(*Ripping the cutting out of the newspaper.*) I've got a collection.
JAIMITO	And you don't have a father, or doesn't he go looking for you?
ELENA	No, I don't have a father.
CHUSA	Me neither. Better that way.

(*The front door suddenly opens and* ALBERTO, *the flat's other resident, comes running in as fast as he can wearing the national police uniform. He is about twenty-five years old, tall, and with a smart appearance.* ELENA *turns white on seeing him.*)

ALBERTO	The police! Guys, the police! Quick, they're on their way! Flush whatever you've got down the toilet! They've come out of my station to carry out searches and they could well wind up here, they're coming round this area. (*He hides the flowerpot with the 'ganja'. At that point, he becomes aware of* ELENA's *presence.*)
CHUSA	She's a friend. Listen, I don't know what we're going to throw out, if we don't have anything. (*To* JAIMITO.) Have you got anything left?

JAIMITO   Una china grande, pero no la tiro, que es lo único que
                   nos queda. Rápido, tú. (*A ELENA.*) A practicar. Toma,
                   métetela donde no te la encuentren…
ELENA   (*Retrocede asustada sin atreverse a cogerlo.*) ¡Yo no
                   sé!
CHUSA   ¡Trae! (Coge la china y se mete en el lavabo.)
JAIMITO   (*A ALBERTO, señalando a ELENA.*) Se la ha
                   encontrado.
ELENA   (*Ofreciendo, educada, su mano a ALBERTO.*) Elena,
                   mucho gusto. Anda que si te pillan… ¿Por qué tienes
                   puesto ese uniforme?
ALBERTO   Pues porque estoy de guardia, por qué va a ser.

(Va a la ventana, la abre y mira fuera. Luego cierra.)

                   No se ve nada raro. Yo me largo de todas formas, no
                   sea que… ¿Qué hay de comer?
JAIMITO   Ahora iba a bajar a la compra. Se largó la Chusa
                   anoche y me dejó sin un clavo.
ALBERTO   Salgo a las tres, así que a y cuarto o así estoy aquí.

*(Va hacia la puerta, mientras CHUSA sale del lavabo. En este momento
llaman con golpes fuertes. Todos se esconden donde pueden en un
movimiento reflejo. Vuelven a golpear más fuerte aún.)*

VOZ FUERTE DE MUJER   ¡Abrir de una vez! ¡Alberto! ¡Abre!
ALBERTO   Parece mi madre.

*(Abre la puerta y entra la señora ANTONIA, madre de ALBERTO, gorda y
dicharachera. Nada más entrar, empieza a dar golpes con el bolso a su
hijo.)*

DOÑA ANTONIA   ¿Se puede saber qué haces aquí, golfo, más que
                   golfo? ¡Ya estás otra vez con toda esta panda! ¡He
                   ido a llevarte el bocadillo a la comisaría y nada! ¡La

JAIMITO	I've got just under a gram wrapped up but I'm not throwing that away; it's all we've got left. Quick, you (*To ELENA*), let's practice. Take it and put it where they won't find it.
ELENA	(*Moving back nervously, and without daring to take it.*) I don't know!
CHUSA	Give it here! (*She takes the package and puts it down the toilet.*)
JAIMITO	(*Addressing ALBERTO and pointing at ELENA.*) She's picked this one up.
ELENA	(*Politely holding out her hand to ALBERTO.*) Elena, pleased to meet you. And what if they were to catch you? Why have you got that uniform on?
ALBERTO	Because I'm on duty. Why else would it be?

(*He goes towards the window, opens it and looks outside. He then closes it.*)

	I can't see anything out of the ordinary. I'm gonna get out of here anyway; that is, unless… What is there to eat?
JAIMITO	I was just about to do the shopping. Chusa went off last night leaving me broke.
ALBERTO	I finish at three, so I'll be here at 'bout quarter past.

(*He heads towards the door whilst CHUSA comes out of the bathroom. At that moment, there are loud knocks on the door. As a reflex action, they all hide as best they can. There are even louder knocks.*)

A STRONG FEMALE VOICE	Open this door now! Alberto! Open!
ALBERTO	It looks like my mum's here.

(*He opens the door and ANTONIA, ALBERTO's mother, comes in. Fat and foul-mouthed, she starts hitting her son with her handbag the second she's through the door.*)

DOÑA ANTONIA	Might I ask what you are doing here, you waster? You're worse than a waster. Back with this motley crew once again! I went to take your sandwich to the police station and the entrance empty, nobody, not a

puerta de la comisaría vacía, sin nadie, y tú aquí! ¡Ya te voy a dar yo a ti...!

ALBERTO   (*Tratando de sujetarle el bolso.*) Pero mamá, sólo he venido a por la porra, de verdad, que se me había olvidado.

JAIMITO   No se ponga así, señora, que no nos comemos a nadie, ni tenemos la lepra.

DOÑA ANTONIA   ¿Y por qué no abríais, eh, degeneraos? Seguro que os estabais drogando bien a gusto, ahí, con las jeringuillas. ¡Si estuviera aquí tu padre ya te ibas a enterar tú, sinvergüenza! ¡Eso es lo que eres!

CHUSA   Señora, no es para tanto. Aquí no hay jeringuillas ni nada de eso. Puede mirar lo que quiera.

JAIMITO   La ha tomado con nosotros.

ALBERTO   Mamá, que no. No te enteras. No abríamos porque creíamos que era la policía. Por eso.

DOÑA ANTONIA   ¿La policía? (*Esconde el bolso en medio de un gran sofoco que le entra.*) ¡La policía! ¡Que viene la policía!

ALBERTO   ¡Que no! Que creíamos que era, pero que no era... (*Se da cuenta entonces de la reacción de su madre.*) ¿Qué esconde ahí?... A ver... Seguro que ya ha estado otra vez con lo mismo. ¡Traiga aquí!

(*Le quita el bolso de un tirón, muy en policía y ella trata de impedir que vea lo que hay dentro.*)

DOÑA ANTONIA   ¡No, no, de verdad que no...! ¡Dámelo ahora mismo, que es mío!

(*Abre* ALBERTO *el bolso y empieza a sacar montones de baberos de niño ante la mirada divertida de los demás.*)

ALBERTO   ¡Madre! No ve que me va a comprometer si la cogen.

DOÑA ANTONIA   Es una enfermedad, hijo, ya te lo dijo el médico. Es como el que tiene gripe, qué le vamos a hacer. Pruebas que nos manda Dios. Peor es lo tuyo de las drogas. Eso además es pecado mortal.

	soul in sight, and you, here! I'll make you wish you hadn't been born...!
ALBERTO	(*Trying to keep her handbag at bay.*) But, mother, I'm only here to pick up my truncheon that I left behind. Honestly.
JAIMITO	There's no need to get like that, madam. We don't eat people and neither do we have the plague.
DOÑA ANTONIA	So why don't you open the door then, eh? You bunch of degenerates. I'd bet my bottom dollar that you were getting drugged up, happy as Larry there with your syringes. If your father was here, then you'd know. Shameless! That is what you are!
CHUSA	Madam, it's not that serious. There are no needles here or anything of the kind. Feel free to look all you like.
JAIMITO	He's taken it with us.
ALBERTO	It's not true mother. We didn't open up because we thought you were the police. That's the reason.
DOÑA ANTONIA	The police? (*She hides her handbag whilst she suddenly comes over all breathless.*) The police! The police are on their way!
ALBERTO	No! We thought they were but they're not. (*He then becomes aware of his mother's reaction.*) What are you hiding there?... Let's see... You've been up to your old tricks again, without a doubt. Give it here!

(He snatches the handbag off her with one fell swoop in full-on police mode. She tries to stop him from seeing what's inside.)

DOÑA ANTONIA	No, no. Honestly, no! Give it to me, now – it's mine.

(ALBERTO opens the handbag and starts to take out a whole load of baby's bibs much to everyone's amusement.)

ALBERTO	Mother! Don't you see that you'll put me in a very compromising position if they catch you.
DOÑA ANTONIA	It's an illness, son, the doctor's told you that. It's like someone who's got the flu, what's to be done? Tests sent from the Lord to try us. What you get up to with drugs is far worse. That's also a mortal sin!

ALBERTO	(*Muy duro.*) ¡Qué enfermedad ni qué leches!
CHUSA	Deja a tu madre, que haga lo que le dé la gana, que ya es mayorcita. No te pongas en policía con ella.
ALBERTO	Es que me va a meter en un follón. Cualquier día me toca ir a detenerla, fíjate el numerito. Vamos a salir en los periódicos.
JAIMITO	Como ésta. (*Por ELENA*) Le pone la madre anuncios para que vuelva. Enséñales la foto, anda.
ALBERTO	Además roba cosas que no valen para nada. Ahora le ha dado por los baberos. ¿Por qué ha cogido todos esos baberos, eh? ¿Es que no tenemos ya bastantes en casa? Toda la casa llena de baberos, montones de baberos. Debajo de la cama, baberos. En la cocina, baberos. En el frigorífico, baberos.
JAIMITO	Podíais poner una babería.
ELENA	¿Y eso qué es?
CHUSA	Está de coña. (*A ALBERTO, que mira ahora de mala manera a JAIMITO por la broma.*) Venga, no le des importancia, que no es para tanto. Y vamos a guardarlos, a ver si van a venir y nos detienen por lo que no hemos hecho.
JAIMITO	O también podíamos poner una guardería.

(*Coge un babero y se lo pone. ALBERTO se lo quita de un tirón. CHUSA ayuda mientras tanto a DOÑA ANTONIA a guardar los que se le han caído por el suelo.*)

DOÑA ANTONIA	¿Quién es? (*Por ELENA.*)
JAIMITO	Se la ha encontrado ésta. Como usted los baberos.
ALBERTO	Bueno, ya, ¿eh? ¡Basta de cachondeos con mi madre, que saco la porra!
JAIMITO	¡A ver si te vas a mosquear ahora conmigo, madero, que eres un madero!

(*Mira ALBERTO con tristeza a su amigo, acusando el golpe. Luego mira su reloj.*)

ALBERTO	(*Very harshly.*) An illness, don't make me laugh!
CHUSA	Leave your mother alone to do what she wants to do, she's a grown adult. Don't give her your whole police routine.
ALBERTO	It's that she's going to get me in a bloody fix. It'll fall to me to arrest her any day now; imagine the hoo-ha. We'll be in all the papers.
JAIMITO	Like this one. (*About ELENA.*) Her mother puts adverts in the paper so she'll go back. Show them the photos, go on.
ALBERTO	Worse still, she robs worthless things. Now she's gone for bibs! Why have you picked up all these bibs, eh? Don't we have enough at home? The whole place full of bibs, piles of bibs. Under the bed, bibs. In the kitchen, bibs. In the fridge, bibs.
JAIMITO	You could open a bib boutique.
ELENA	And what's one of those?
CHUSA	He's taking the piss. (*To ALBERTO, who's now giving JAIMITO a dirty look because of the joke.*) Don't get stressed about it, it's no big deal. And we'll look after them – let's see if they'll come and arrest us for something we haven't done.
JAIMITO	Or, alternatively, we could set up a nursery.

(*He picks up a bib and puts it on ALBERTO who whips it off. At the same time, CHUSA helps DOÑA ANTONIA gather together the bibs that have fallen on the floor.*)

DOÑA ANTONIA	Who's she? (*About ELENA.*)
JAIMITO	This one picked her up. Like you with the bibs.
ALBERTO	All right, eh. Enough of winding up my mother; I'll get the truncheon out.
JAIMITO	Ah, so the copper is going to take a pop at me now; a copper, you're a right copper.

(*ALBERTO looks at his friend sadly, taking the knock to heart. He then looks at his watch.*)

ALBERTO   Me tengo que ir, no se den cuenta. Ya no creo que
               vengan, no sería aquí. Cualquier día me vais a meter
               en un lío entre todos... (*Mira a* JAIMITO.) «¡Madero!»
               Encima.

JAIMITO   Espera, bajo contigo, así me tomo un café, que estoy
               en ayunas. (*Le da un golpe amistoso en el hombro.*)
               Y no te mosquees, que te mosqueas por nada
               últimamente.

(*ALBERTO reacciona con otro golpe amistoso, y salen los dos dándose
puñetazos en un juego que se adivina viene de muchos años atrás.*)

DOÑA ANTONIA   Un café a la una, qué desbarajuste. (*A su hijo,
               alcanzándole en la puerta.*) Toma el bocadillo, y
               estírate la camisa. (*Le da el bocadillo y le coloca la
               ropa.*) Que vas hecho un cuadro.

ALBERTO   ¡Vale! ¡Vale! Hasta luego.

(*Sale y cierran la puerta. Se oyen las risas perdiéndose escaleras abajo
entre ruidos que indican que siguen jugando a golpearse como dos críos.
Quedan en escena las dos chicas y DOÑA ANTONIA, mirándose sin saber
qué decirse.*)

DOÑA ANTONIA   (*Suspirando.*) ¡Ay, Dios mío! ¡Qué hijos éstos!

ELENA   ¿Tiene usted más? ¿Más hijos?

DOÑA ANTONIA   Te parece poco con este bala perdida. Anda, dadme
               una copa de coñac si tenéis por ahí, a ver si se me
               quita el disgusto que tengo.

CHUSA   Se acabó usted el último día la botella. Sólo hay té.
               ¿Quiere té?

DOÑA ANTONIA   ¿Té? Quita, quita. Yo sólo tomo té cuando me duele
               la tripa. ¿Y tú quién eres? No te conocía.

ELENA   Es que soy nueva. Soy Elena. Mucho gusto.

(*Le da la mano. DOÑA ANTONIA se limpia la suya y se la estrecha encantada,
sorprendida de los buenos modales de alguien en aquella casa.*)

ALBERTO   I have to go now, they can't clock me. I don't think
            they'll come now, not here. Between you, you lot are
            going to get me in a right mess any day now. (*Looking
            at JAIMITO*.) Copper! That takes the biscuit.

JAIMITO   Wait a second, I'll come down with you and have a
            coffee. I haven't had anything, I'm starved. (*He gives
            him a friendly slap on the shoulder*.) And don't get in
            a strop. You've got in a strop over anything recently.

*(ALBERTO reacts with another friendly slap and they leave punching each
other in a game which you can guess goes back many years.)*

DOÑA ANTONIA A coffee at one o'clock, what's the world coming to.
            (*To her son, catching him at the door*.) Here, take the
            sandwich and get that shirt ironed. (*She gives him the
            sandwich and rearranges his clothing*.)

ALBERTO   Alright! Alright! See you later.

*(They go out, closing the door behind them. You can hear, amongst other
sounds which suggest they are still hitting each other like a pair of kids,
their laughter drifting into the distance as they go down the stairs. The
two young women and DOÑA ANTONIA are left on stage looking at each
other not knowing what to say.)*

DOÑA ANTONIA (*Sighing*.) Oh, my lord. What are these kids like!

ELENA   Have you got more? Other kids?

DOÑA ANTONIA Don't you think I've got enough on my plate with
            this loose cannon. Here, give me a glass of brandy
            if you've got any 'bout the place. Let's see if that'll
            help get me over this unpleasantness.

CHUSA   You finished the bottle the other day. Tea's all there
            is. Would you like some tea?

DOÑA ANTONIA Tea? No way. I only have tea when I have belly aches.
            And you, who are you? I didn't recognize you.

ELENA   The thing is I'm new. I'm Elena. A pleasure to meet
            you.

*(She offers her hand. DOÑA ANTONIA cleans her own and holds it out with
pleasure, surprised that someone could have such good manners in that
household.)*

DOÑA ANTONIA	¡Huy! Encantada, hija. Antonia del Campo, calle de la Sal, doce, bajo C. Allí tienes tu casa. ¡Ay, Dios mío! Otra infeliz que cayó en el vicio con la cara de buena que tienes. ¡En fin! (*Se arregla la ropa y coge el bolso.*) Bueno, me voy a echar un bingo. A ver si cojo hoy un par de líneas por lo menos. A esta hora es cuando está mejor y más decente. Como está enfrente del mercado, sólo señoras, amas de casa y alguna criada.
CHUSA	Adiós, doña Antonia, que siga usted bien.
ELENA	Adiós y encantada,
DOÑA ANTONIA	Y a ver si venís algún sábado a las reuniones, que si cae un rayo allí no os pilla, no. Hala, adiós.
CHUSA	No se preocupe, que el sábado vamos sin falta los cuatro. Adiós, adiós. (*Sale DOÑA ANTONIA.*) ¡Puf! Menos mal Si no es por el bingo hoy no nos la quitamos ya de encima.
ELENA	¿Y tenemos que ir el sábado a una reunión? ¿Qué reunión?
CHUSA	Esa es otra. Un sábado nos lió y nos llevó a una reunión de neocatecumenales. Sí, sí: «No estás solo, el Señor te guarda...», y todo eso.
ELENA	Está peor que mi madre.
CHUSA	¿También es neocatecumenal?
ELENA	Era lo que le faltaba.
CHUSA	Pues chica, ésta nos ha metido cada rollo con las catequesis que dan y eso... Además, como es para recuperación de marginales a nosotros nos viene al pelo, como ella dice. (*Ríen las dos.*) Como somos «drogadictos», por cuatro porros, sabes; pero es que para ella todas las drogas son iguales y pecado. Pero el coñac es agua bendita, eso sí.

DOÑA ANTONIA	Oh! The pleasure is all mine, my dear. Antonia del Campo, of 12 Sal Street, number C, basement level. You always have a home there. Oh, My Lord! Another sad soul who's fallen into vice, and with that angelic face of yours. Well, what's to be done. (*She tidies up her clothes and picks up her handbag*). Right, I'm going to have a flutter at the bingo. Let's see if I can get a couple of lines at least. This is the best and most respectable time to go. As it's opposite the market, there's only ladies of leisure, housewives and the odd maid here and there.
CHUSA	Bye, Doña Antonia, and look after yourself.
ELENA	Goodbye, a pleasure to meet you.
DOÑA ANTONIA	And let's see if we'll see you at the meetings one of these Saturdays, though pigs will probably fly before we'll get you there. Alright, bye.
CHUSA	Don't you worry, the four of us will be there on Saturday without fail. Bye, bye. (*DOÑA ANTONIA leaves.*) Phew! That's a relief. If it wasn't for the bingo today, we wouldn't have got her out of our hair.
ELENA	And we have to go to a meeting on Saturday? What meeting?
CHUSA	That's something else. One Saturday she trapped us and took us to a Neocatechumenate meeting.[v] Yes, yes, "You're not alone. The Lord looks after you…", and all of that.
ELENA	She's worse than my mother.
CHUSA	Does she also belong to the Neocatechumate?
ELENA	Everything but.
CHUSA	Well, love, this one has got us mixed up in everything you can imagine with the catechisms they give and all that… Anyway, as it's about saving those who have lost their way, it suits us down to the ground as she says. (*The two of them laugh.*) Because we have the occasional joint, we're all "drug addicts" I'll have you know; but, as far as she's concerned all drugs are the same and a sin. But brandy is holy water, oh yes.

ELENA	¿Y qué hacías allí el día que fuisteis?
CHUSA	Cantábamos. Cantábamos todos muy serios. (*Canta imitando.*) «Cuando el Señor dijo Sión... todos nos fuimos al pantano...», o algo así. (*Ríen las dos.*) Como te coja un día por banda no te vas a reír, no. Es peor que el telediario.
ELENA	¿Y el hijo también es neocatecumenal?
CHUSA	¿Alberto? ¡Qué dices! Alberto es normal, aunque le veas así vestido de policía, es completamente normal. Bueno, también es que lleva poco tiempo. Es muy guapo, ¿no?
ELENA	No está mal, aunque así, con esa ropa, no me hago una idea.
CHUSA	Pues a mí me encanta, chica. Con esa ropa, con cualquier ropa, y sin ropa. Bueno, tenemos que prepararlo bien todo para el viaje. Hay que llevar pocos bultos para que no nos paren, e ir bien vestidas. ¿Sólo tienes eso?, ¿no tienes nada que te dé más pinta de mayor?
ELENA	En casa sí pero aquí... La falda que tengo en la bolsa, sí acaso. (*La saca de la bolsa.*) Me puedo poner ésta y el jersey marrón. Puedo ir a por más ropa si quieres el fin de semana, que no está mi madre; se va a la sierra.
CHUSA	¿El fin de semana? Si nos vamos pasado mañana o al otro como mucho.
ELENA	¿Así? ¿Tan pronto?
CHUSA	Ahora en Semana Santa es mejor. Hay más turistas, más lio, viaja más gente... ¿Te echas atrás?
ELENA	No, no, si quiero ir, pero no sé si sabré así tan pronto. Como no me lo has explicado bien, a lo mejor no sé.

ELENA	And what did you do there the day you went?
CHUSA	We sang. We all sang very solemnly. (*She imitates them singing*): "When the Lord said Zion, we all went to the swamp..." or something along those lines. (*The two of them laugh.*) If they get their hands on you for their flock, you won't be laughing then. It's worse than the news on the television.
ELENA	And her son, does he also belong to the Neocate-chumenate?
CHUSA	Alberto? What are you saying? Alberto is normal even though you see him like that dressed up as a policeman, he's completely normal. Well, also, he's not being doing it for long. He's really handsome. Isn't he?
ELENA	He's not bad though like that, with those clothes, I can't really think of him like that.
CHUSA	Well he does it for me, love. With those clothes, with any clothes and with no clothes. Right, we have to get everything ready for the trip. We can't carry too much luggage otherwise they'll stop up, and go well dressed. Have you only got that? You haven't got anything that makes you look older?
ELENA	At home, yes, but not here... Well, perhaps, the skirt I've got in my bag. (*She takes it out of her bag.*) I could put that on and the maroon jersey. If you want, I could go and get more clothes at the weekend. My mother won't be there, she goes to the mountains.
CHUSA	The weekend? But we're going the day after tomorrow or the day after that at the very latest.
ELENA	Really? So soon?
CHUSA	Now at Easter is the best time. There's more tourists, more confusion, more people travelling... Are you backing out?
ELENA	No, no, I want to go but I don't know if I'll work it out so soon. As you haven't really explained it all that well, perhaps, I don't know.

CHUSA	No hay nada que explicar. Vamos, llegamos, lo compramos y volvemos.
ELENA	¿Dónde cogemos el tren? ¿En Atocha?
CHUSA	Pues sí, en Atocha. ¿Y eso qué mismo da si es en Atocha o no es en Atocha?
ELENA	Nada, mujer, es por saber. En Atocha. Este pantalón es muy bonito, me lo tienes que dejar algún día. (*Saca del armario y se prueba un pantalón de* CHUSA.) En Atocha.
CHUSA	Sí, en Atocha. Montamos en el tren, una detrás de la otra. Antes hay que sacar los billetes. (*ELENA la mira sin entender por qué le dice esa tontería.* CHUSA *le ayuda a hacer un hueco en su armario y a colocar sus ropas probándose algunas que le gustan.*) Bueno, mira: vamos primero a Algeciras, y para eso cogemos el tren en Atocha. Y luego allí, un barco nos cruza en dos horas.
ELENA	En el barco me mareo. Yo enseguida lo echo todo.
CHUSA	Mientras no te dé colitis a la vuelta, te puedes marear y vomitar lo que quieras. Está la barandilla del barco puesta a una altura a propósito, y el mar ni se entera. Te pones en la cola, y hala.
ELENA	Yo me pongo malísima.
CHUSA	Si no es nada. Dos horas. No te das ni cuenta. Es peor el tren, que es un latazo. Tarda como doce horas.
ELENA	¿Tanto?
CHUSA	Es un mogollón de tren; está lleno de moros, huele mal. Seguro que nos encontramos a alguien conocido en él, basquilla. Pero tampoco hay que dar mucho cante, que están los trenes últimamente fatal; a la mínima de cambio, como te fumes un canuto, ya la

CHUSA	There's nothing to explain. We go, we arrive, we buy it and we come back.
ELENA	Where do we catch the train? In Atocha?[vi]
CHUSA	Well, yes, in Atocha. And what's it to you if we do or we don't catch it in Atocha?
ELENA	It doesn't matter at all, just so I know. In Atocha. These trousers are really nice, you'll have to lend them to me one day. (*She takes some of* CHUSA's *trousers out of the wardrobe and tries them on.*) In Atocha.
CHUSA	Yes, in Atocha. We get on the train, one behind the other. We have to get the tickets beforehand. (*ELENA looks at her not understanding why she's saying such a stupid thing. CHUSA helps her make some space in the wardrobe and, on hanging up her clothes, tries on some she likes.*) Right, look: first we go to Algeciras and we catch the train at Atocha to get there. And then a boat will take us across in two hours.[1]
ELENA	I get sea sick on boats. I throw everything up straight away.
CHUSA	As long as you don't get colitis on the way back, you can get sick and vomit to your heart's content. The boat's railings are up high for a reason, and the sea won't even notice. You join the queue and Bob's your uncle.
ELENA	I get really bad.
CHUSA	But, it's nothing. Two hours. You don't even notice. The train's worse, that's a real drag. It takes, like, twelve hours.
ELENA	That long?
CHUSA	The train takes forever; it's full of Moors, it smells bad... No doubt we'll bump into a familiar face there, jammed in like sardines. But we can't play up there either. The trains have been awful recently; you do anything slightly different, like you smoke the tiniest

---

[1]   See José Luis Alonso de Santos's comments in my interview with him on how the details of the journey need to be changed for productions set in the present.

has hecho. Por eso nosotros, suavito. Nos compramos unos bocatas para comer algo en el viaje, y a las diez o así de la mañana llegamos. Sale de aquí a la diez de la noche y llega allí a las diez de la mañana. Doce horas, lo que te digo. Luego, en Algeciras vamos rápido, a ver si podemos pillar el barco de las diez y media o el de las doce, como mucho. Llegamos a Ceuta y nos vamos directamente a la estación de autobuses, y a Tetuán. Allí cogemos otro autobús, y a Chagüe, que es un pueblecito rodeado de tres montañas, muy bonito, como esos que salen en las películas, con los techos así redondos, todo blanco, precioso.

ELENA   ¿Tú lo conoces bien, no? A ver si nos vamos a quedar allí en las montañas, y nos perdemos o nos pasa algo... ¿Y lo de dormir y todo eso?

CHUSA   Allí, en Chagüe, dormimos la primera noche, en una pensión muy bonita que hay, chiquitita. ¡Huy, qué blusa, déjame...! A ver cómo me está.

(Se la prueba.)

ELENA   ¿Y no cogeremos allí piojos... y cosas?

CHUSA   ¡Qué vas a coger, mujer! No. Bueno, a lo mejor, pulgas sí que habrá; pulgas casi seguro.

ELENA   ¡Pulgas!

CHUSA   No pasa nada. Al día siguiente te has acostumbrado. Y si no, nos echamos limón,

ELENA   A mí me da un poco de cosa con los moros.

CHUSA   Conmigo siempre se han enrollado bien, pero hay que tener mucho cuidado. A un amigo mío en Marruecos le pillaron mangando una manzana y le querían cortar la mano. Es la pena para los ladrones.

ELENA   ¿Todavía?

CHUSA   Fíjate. El tío nerviosísimo, figúrate, y todos sus colegas igual, porque es que veían que se la cortaban. Él tiraba para atrás, pero nada, ellos, cabezones, que

of spliffs and you've had it. Cos of that, we take things calmly. We buy some baps to have something to eat on the trip, and then we arrive at around ten in the morning. We leave here at ten in the evening and get there at ten in the morning. Twelve hours, what I was telling you. Then, in Algeciras, we go quickly and see if we can catch the ten-thirty boat or the twelve o'clock one at the latest. We get to Ceuta and go straight to the coach station, and then onto Tetuán. There we catch another coach, and onwards to Xauen, a pretty little town surrounded by three mountains, like those which you see in the movies with the round roofs, everything white, it's lovely.

ELENA   You know it well, don't you? And what if we go up to stay in the mountains and we get lost or something happens to us. And what about sleeping, and all of that?

CHUSA   There, in Xauen, we'll sleep the first night in a pretty guest-house, very cozy. Hey, what a nice blouse, let me…! Let's see how it suits me. (*She tries it on.*)

ELENA   And we won't pick up lice there… or things?

CHUSA   What are you going to pick up, woman? No. Well, perhaps, there might be flees; there will almost certainly be flees.

ELENA   Flees!

CHUSA   It's fine. You get used to them in a day. And if not, we just cover ourselves in lemon.

ELENA   Moors kind of give me the creeps.

CHUSA   They've always been alright with me, but you have to be real careful. They caught a friend of mine nicking an apple in Morocco and they wanted to cut his hand off. It's the punishment for thieves.

ELENA   Still?

CHUSA   Yeah, listen. The guy super-nervous, go figure, and all his mates the same because they got wise to the fact that they'd cut it off. He's knocked for six and all apologetic but, no, those stubborn guys wanted it

	se la cortaban. Fíjate, montando una allí que te cagas. Robas una manzana y te quedas con el muñón.
ELENA	Qué demasiao.
CHUSA	De qué, ¿no? Encima de que vamos allí a darles de comer los europeos. Qué pasa. Pero nosotras en plan tranqui, nos vamos rápido para Chagüe, que allí ya es otra cosa. Y luego como lo veamos. O nos vamos a comprarlo directamente, o si nos apetece nos vamos antes a dar una vuelta por Fez o Marraquech, a ver a los encantadores de serpientes por la calle, que están tocando la flauta, ahí, y salen del cesto...
ELENA	Ay, qué bien, qué bonito. ¿Vivas? ¿Vivas las serpientes?
CHUSA	Si estuvieran muertas y salieran ya sería demasiado, ¿no? Ya verás qué bonito todo allí, y la pensión de Chagüe, con unos arcos que tienen en el patio...
ELENA	Y con las pulgas.
CHUSA	Que no pasa nada, y es cantidad de barata además. Es lo más barato allí. Cuesta diez dirjan la noche; unas doscientas pesetas.
ELENA	¿No podíamos ir a alguna un poco más cara, que no hubiera pulgas?
CHUSA	Allí hay pulgas en todos los sitios. ¿No ves que es África? Luego ya, desde allí, nos subimos a la montaña, a casa del Mójame, que es el que nos lo vende.
ELENA	¿Y vamos a su casa? ¿En una montaña? ¿Y cómo subimos?
CHUSA	Por la carretera, por dónde vamos a subir. Hay carretera. Y ya verás, tía, se enrollan de puta madre. Los moros de la ciudad, ya te digo, manguis que te caes; pero los de la montaña son buena gente.

	cut off. I mean, listen, misbehave there and you'll be shitting yourself. Rob an apple and you're left with a stump.
ELENA	That's way beyond!
CHUSA	Isn't it just? And, on top of that, it's us Europeans going there that puts food on their tables. It happens. But us, all nice and chilled, we'll go quickly to Xauen, a completely different scene. And then we'll see the lay of the land. Either we'll go and buy the stuff straight away or, if we fancy it, we'll go and have a wander round Fez or Marrakesh, to see the charmers in the street, playing the flute, then the snakes come out the basket...
ELENA	Ah, how nice, how sweet. Alive? Are the snakes alive?
CHUSA	If they were dead and they came out of the basket, that'd be too much, wouldn't it? You'll see how nice it all is there, and the guest-house in Xauen with the arches they have in the courtyard.
ELENA	And with the flees.
CHUSA	It's fine, and it's dirt cheap as well. It's the cheapest there is out there. It costs 10 dirjan a night; about two hundred pesetas.[2]
ELENA	Couldn't we go to a slightly more expensive place where there aren't any fleas?
CHUSA	Fleas are everywhere over there? It's Africa, don't you see? Then, from there, we go up the mountain to Moorish Mo's place. He'll sell it to us.
ELENA	And we go to his place? On a mountain? And how do we get up?
CHUSA	By road, that's how we go up. There's a road. You'll see, love, we'll all get on like a house on fire. The moors in the city, you nick anything and, as I say, you're fucked; but, the mountain ones, they're cool.

---

[2] In the 2008 production, Chusa does what even young Spaniards often do, and says the amount in pesetas and converts it into Euros. She calculates six Euros; this in indicative of how much inflation has hit even the most ostensibly basic places for two hundred pesetas is just over one Euro.

ELENA   A mí lo que me da miedo es si no podemos luego
          volver.

CHUSA   Venga ya, no digas cosas raras. Yo he ido y he vuelto,
          ¿no? Dormiremos allí esa segunda noche, en la casa
          del moro. Ya verás qué punto tiene todo.

ELENA   ¡Ay, hija! Me da un poco de miedo dormir ahí con un
          moro.

CHUSA   Por Dios, tía, no vas a dormir con el moro. El moro
          se va a otro sitio, y a ti te deja en un cuartito de esos
          que tienen una cama todo alrededor que parece como
          si fuera un asiento, pegado a la pared, y duermes allí
          tumbada, de lado. Allí duermen así siempre, en hilera
          y de lado. No tienen camas.

ELENA   ¿Y sábanas?

CHUSA   Pijama también si quieres. Allí no usan eso, pero está
          precioso, tapizado, bonito, con unas mesas de esas
          para tomar el té. En cuanto ven que no haces nada
          te traen un té. Se enrollan los moros de la montaña
          de puta madre. Llegamos allí y le decimos al moro:
          «Mójame, tenemos estas pelas, así que a ver lo que
          nos podemos llevar.» ¿Tú puedes conseguir algo de
          dinero para traer más?

ELENA   Si acaso lo que me he traído, o puedo sacar algo de la
          cartilla si quieres. ¿Y cómo nos lo vamos a traer, lo
          que compremos?

CHUSA   En el culo, en el chumi, nos lo comemos, lo que sea.
          Hay que pasarlo.

ELENA   ¿?

CHUSA   Tenemos que convencerlos para que nos fabriquen
          ellos el costo. También nos lo podemos hacer nosotras

ELENA	What scares me is if we can't then get back.
CHUSA	Get a grip, don't say such odd things. I've gone and come back, haven't I? We'll sleep there in the Moor's place the second night. You'll soon see how cool everything is there.
ELENA	Ah, but mate. I'm a bit scared of sleeping there with a Moor.
CHUSA	For God's sake, love, you're not going to sleep with the Moor. The Moor goes off somewhere else and leaves you in one of those little rooms which has a bed all the way round, kinda like a seat, attached to the wall and you sleep there lying down on your side. They sleep like that all the time, in rows and on their sides. They don't have beds.
ELENA	And sheets?
CHUSA	And pyjamas as well if you like. They don't use that stuff but it's lovely, covered with tapestries, beautiful, with those tables for having tea. As soon as they see you're not doing anything, they bring you tea. The mountain Moors are real fucking easy to rub along with. We get there and we say to him: "Moorish Mo, we've got this cash so what can we take with us." Could you get any money so we can bring some more?
ELENA	Yes, I brought some with me just in case, or I could take some out the bank if you like.[3] And how are we going to carry what we buy?
CHUSA	In the ass, in the pussy, we eat it, whatever. It has to get through.
ELENA	?
CHUSA	We have to convince them to prepare the hash for us. We could do it ourselves if we wanted, but it's a lot

---

[3] In the original, Elena uses the word 'cartilla' which refers to the small book that was used to withdraw money from cash-points in Spain in the past. In line with most of the rest of Europe, a credit or debit card is now more often used and so 'tarjeta' is used in the 2008 production. In the UK, cards came in at a much earlier date so I've not employed a direct translation to avoid confusion.

	si queremos, pero es un curre. Yo por saber, sé. A mí me das unas ramas y te hago un doble cero en nada. Pero te pones las manos hechas polvo. Te salen callos de apretar.
ELENA	¿El doble cero es el mejor, no?
CHUSA	El primer polvo que da la rama. La rama está llena de polen, el primer toque que le das cae el polvito blanco; lo coges y se convierte en una bolita de goma negra. Doble cero. Lo mejor.
ELENA	Pero será lo más caro.
CHUSA	Claro. Ten en cuenta que si tienes, qué te digo yo, a lo mejor diez kilos en varas de hachís cortado en ramas, da sólo doscientos gramos o así de doble cero. Si luego le das cien vueltas ya a la varita, pues le sacas dos kilos, qué quieres que te diga, pero ya del malo, morralla.
ELENA	Sí. Yo de eso no sé; es mejor que te ocupes tú. Yo fumo y me gusta, pero no entiendo nunca ni lo que fumo. Como no me trago el humo…
CHUSA	No te preocupes, que está todo controlado.
ELENA	Yo, más que nada, es por ir. Bueno, también por sacar algo, porque luego, al venderlo aquí… ¿cuanto se saca?
CHUSA	Veinte veces lo que nos hemos gastado, si es un negocio. Y una aventura. Te metes allí, dos tías además, nos lo regalan todo. A mí me han regalado cosas muchas veces. Dicen que tengo cara de mora. Como soy morena…
ELENA	A mí lo que más cosa me da es eso de metérnoslo en el culo. ¿Qué miedo no?
CHUSA	Qué va, tía. Si es que luego estás allí, y te entra un punto de tranquilidad y de paz que es que estás en la gloria. Y nada. La noche anterior a venirnos, nos hacen las bolas.

	of work. I know how to do it, that's no problem. You give me two branches and I'll get you a double zero in no time. But your hands get knackered. All that squeezing gives you corns.
ELENA	Double zero is the best, isn't it?
CHUSA	The first powder that comes from the branch. The branch is full of pollen, when you touch it for the first time, the white powder falls off, you gather it up and it turns into a little ball of black rubber. Double zero. The best.
ELENA	But it'll be the most expensive?
CHUSA	Of course. Bear in mind that if you have, and I can tell you, maybe ten kilos in trunks of hash cut into branches, you'll only get about two hundred grams of double zero. If you then shake the little branch a hundred times, well you'll get two kilos but, what can I say, of really bad gear, of worthless crap.
ELENA	Yes. I'm clueless about that stuff; it's better that you deal with it. I smoke and I like it, but I never even understand what I'm smoking. As I don't inhale…
CHUSA	Don't you worry, it's all under control.
ELENA	For me, more than anything, it's just for the sake of going. Well, also to make something, because then, on selling it here… How much can you make?
CHUSA	What we've spent twenty times over, yep it's one good business. And an adventure as well. You get in there, even more so as two girls, and they'll give you everything. They've given me stuff loads of times. They say I've got a Moorish face. As I'm dark-skinned…
ELENA	The thing I'm not so sure about is that thing about putting it in your ass. It's scary isn't it?
CHUSA	Not at all, love. Once you're there, you become so chilled and at one with yourself that you're in heaven. And that's it. The night before coming back, they'll make up the balls for us.

ELENA	¿Y de cuántos gramos es cada bola? Yo no sé si…
CHUSA	Te tienes que procurar meter por lo menos cien gramos en la vagina, y otros cien o doscientos en el culo.
ELENA	¡Ay, Dios! Yo es que estoy estreñida. Si se me queda dentro…
CHUSA	Mejor. Te tomas luego un laxante y lo echas todo.
ELENA	En el barco de vuelta, mareada y con eso dentro, me muero.
CHUSA	Qué aprensiva eres. Las bolitas son molestas al principio, pero luego se suben para arriba y no notas nada.
ELENA	Tú me tienes que ayudar, porque si no, no sé.
CHUSA	A ver si te voy a tener que meter yo las bolas. Te las metes tú como buenamente puedas, con vaselina.
ELENA	Habrá que llevar mucha vaselina entonces.
CHUSA	Un kilo, no te digo. Eso con una gota hay más que de sobra. Si no duele nada. Mira, hay sólo un problema, qué quieres que te diga: si nos cogen. Es de lo único que te tienes que preocupar. Por eso en la frontera nos tenemos que poner monas, nos pintamos bien, tranquis, sonrientes, y ya está. Echándole morro a la vida, que si no te comen. Tú haces todo lo que yo haga. ¡Ah! Y luego muchísimo cuidado en el tren, que es donde cogen a los pardillos. Sacas un porro, se corre el asunto, y ya te has liado. Otras doce horas en la batidora de la Renfe, y a casita.

(ELENA, que lleva un rato intentando hacer una difícil confesión a CHUSA, por fin se atreve al ver que ésta ha llegado al final de su explicación.)

ELENA	And how many grams are in each ball. It's just that I don't know if…
CHUSA	You have to try and put at least a hundred grams in your vagina and another hundred or two hundred up your ass.
ELENA	My God! The thing is that I'm very tight. And if it stays inside.
CHUSA	All the better. You then take a laxative and you'll let it all out.
ELENA	On the boat back, with sea sickness and all that inside, I'll die.
CHUSA	What a nervous little thing you are. The little balls are a pain to start with, but then they work their way up and you don't notice a thing.
ELENA	You will have to help me because, if not, I don't know.
CHUSA	As if I'm going to have to put the balls up you. You're perfectly capable of putting them up yourself with Vaseline.
ELENA	We'll have to take a lot of Vaseline then!
CHUSA	I'd say a kilo should do it! With that stuff, one drop is more than enough. It doesn't hurt in the least. Look, there's only one problem, what can I say: if they catch us. That's the only thing you have to worry about. That's why at the border we have to do ourselves up nicely, with plenty of makeup, chilled out, smiley and that's it. In this life, the meek will go hungry. You follow what I do exactly. Ah! And be extra-careful on the train, that's where they catch the wet behind the ears amateurs. You take out a joint, word gets about and you're in a fix. Another twelve hours in the rocky sardine can that is Spanish National Rail and home, sweet home.

(ELENA, who has for some time been trying to make a difficult confession to CHUSA finally dares to on seeing that she has reached the end of her explanation.)

ELENA	Tengo que decirte una cosa. ¡Yo no puedo! En el culo a lo mejor... pero nada más. Chusa, soy virgen.
CHUSA	¿Que eres qué?
ELENA	Virgen. Que nunca he... Nunca. Ni una vez.
CHUSA	No me estarás hablando en serio.
ELENA	Ha sido sin querer, de verdad. Yo no quería, bueno, quiero decir que sí que quería, pero es que los tíos son... Se lo dices y empiezan que si tal, que si cual. No se atreven. Ya sabes cómo son de cortados para todo. Se aprovechan de ti y luego nada.
CHUSA	Eso hay que arreglarlo enseguida. Se lo decimos esta noche a Alberto y ya está. No me hace gracia, no creas, pero qué le vamos a hacer. No vas a seguir así. ¿Te ha gustado antes, no? Pues mejor para ti.
ELENA	Me da vergüenza.
CHUSA	Venga, no seas tonta, que eso no es nada. No miramos.
ELENA	¿Pero vais a estar aquí mientras?
CHUSA	Pues claro. ¿Qué pasa? ¿Te vamos a comer?
ELENA	Que me da vergüenza, de verdad.
CHUSA	Más vergüenza tenía que darte ser virgen en mil novecientos ochenta y cinco, y tan mayor. Debes quedar tú sola, guapa.
ELENA	Yo y mi madre. También es virgen, ¿sabes?
CHUSA	¿Quién? ¿Tu madre? (*ELENA asiente con la cabeza.*) Sí claro. Y a ti te trajo la cigüeñita.
ELENA	De cesárea. Nací de cesárea. Y se quedó embarazada en una piscina municipal, con el bañador puesto y todo, y eso que era de los antiguos. Bueno, eso dice ella.

ELENA	I have to tell you something. I can't! In the ass, maybe … but nowhere else. Chusa, I'm a virgin.
CHUSA	You're a what?
ELENA	Virgin. I've never… never. Not even once.
CHUSA	You can't be serious.
ELENA	It's not by choice, honestly. I didn't want, well, what I want to say is that yes I did want to, but the thing is that lads are… You say it to them and they start saying this or that. They don't even dare. You know how they can't commit to anything. They take advantage of you and then, nothing.
CHUSA	We need to sort this out right away. We'll tell Alberto tonight and that's that. I'm not too thrilled by the idea, don't think that I am, but what's to be done. You're not going to carry on like this. You liked him earlier, didn't you? Well, all the better for you.
ELENA	It embarrasses me.
CHUSA	Come on, don't be stupid, it's nothing. We won't look.
ELENA	But are you two going to be here while?
CHUSA	Yes, of course. What's the problem? Are we going to eat you?
ELENA	Honestly, it embarrasses me!
CHUSA	You ought to be more embarrassed by being a virgin at your age in 1985.[4] Darling, you must be the only one.
ELENA	Me and my mother. She's also a virgin, I'll have you know.
CHUSA	Who? Your mother? (*ELENA nods.*) Yes, of course. And the stork brought you.
ELENA	By caesarean. I was born by caesarean. And she got pregnant in a council swimming pool. She had on an old-school swimming costume, not like today's bikinis, and everything. Well, that's what she says.

---

[4] Obviously this was changed in the 2008 production but, nevertheless, lost some of its effect as there hadn't been such a radical change in sexual mores in Spain in recent years.

CHUSA	¿En una piscina? ¿En una piscina municipal? Sería al tirarse del trampolín. Habría uno debajo haciendo la plancha, y ¡zas!
ELENA	Es de verdad, no te lo tomes a broma. Yo soy hija de mi madre y de un espermatozoide buceador.
CHUSA	Desde luego es que no te puedes fiar. Quién sería el animal que se puso allí a... ¡Hay que ser burro, y bestia, y...! ¡Ay, perdona, tú! No me había dado cuenta de que era tu padre.
ELENA	No, si como no le conozco me da lo mismo. A mí como si me dicen que soy una niña probeta. Paso de orígenes.
CHUSA	Pues mira, haces bien, qué quieres que te diga. Tampoco creas tú que mi padre era..., para ese padre casi mejor ser hija del Ayuntamiento como tú. Hoy día además no hay que escandalizarse por nada. Hace poco estuvo aquí durmiendo unos cuantos días uno que hacía Biológicas, y estaba todo el día dándole a un libro de un tal Mendel, que hacía unas guarrerías con los guisantes para que tuvieran hijos que no te creas. Venían los dibujos y todo. Por dónde se tenía que meter el guisante, lo que hacía cuando estaba dentro y se hinchaba, se hinchaba... Todo, venía todo. Ya ves; más de uno tendría por padre a un guisante. Claro que se lo callan. No lo van a ir diciendo por ahí como haces tú.
ELENA	Yo no se lo digo a nadie tampoco. A ti porque te conozco, pero a nadie más. Como no conozco a nadie más... Que no intimo yo con nadie, de verdad.
CHUSA	Oye, ¿tú eres un poco rara o me lo parece a mí? Claro, debe ser por lo de virgen. No te regirán bien las neuronas. Esta noche, Alberto te pasa al gremio de las normales, no te preocupes.

CHUSA   In a swimming pool? In a council swimming pool?
             It'll have been from launching off the diving board.
             They'll have been someone diving and, crash.
ELENA   It's true, don't make a joke of it. I'm the offspring of
             my mother and an underwater spermatozoon.
CHUSA   Of course, you can't trust anyone. Who would be the
             animal who could settle there to... You'd have to be
             a beast, a brute, and... I'm sorry! I hadn't realized it
             was your father.
ELENA   Don't worry. I don't know him so it doesn't bother
             me. As far as I'm concerned, it's as if they told me
             I was a test-tube baby. I don't bother about where I
             come from.
CHUSA   You're right there, no doubt about it. Don't you be
             thinking either that my father was... to have that
             father, you'd almost be better being the offspring of
             the city hall like you. There's no need to be scandalized
             by anything these days. A short time ago, there was
             some guy here who was doing Biological Science,
             and he spent all day with a nose in a book by some
             bloke called Mendel who got up to some disgusting
             stuff you wouldn't believe with peas so they'd have
             kids. It came with pictures and all. Where you had
             to put the pea, what you had to do once it was inside
             and it swelled up, and it swelled up... Everything,
             it came with everything. You see; there'll be more
             than one person out there with a pea for a father. But,
             obviously, they keep it quiet. They don't go about
             telling every Tom, Dick and Harry like you do.
ELENA   I don't tell anyone either. I've told you because I
             know you, but nobody else. As I don't know anybody
             else... I don't confide in anyone, honestly.
CHUSA   Listen, is it just me or are you a bit weird? Ah, of
             course, it'll be because of the virgin thing. Your
             neurons won't be working right. Alberto will let
             you join the normal people's club tonight, don't you
             worry.

ELENA	Y yo… ¿Qué tengo que hacer?
CHUSA	¿Tampoco sabes eso? No te preocupes, que él te enseñará. El sí que sabe; ya lo verás. ¿Tomas la pildora?
ELENA	¿Qué pildora? No. Como soy virgen…
CHUSA	Déjalo, no te esfuerces. Vamos a la farmacia a por algo, no te quedes embarazada a la primera de cambio y me toque encima cuidar del niño. Y menos de Alberto, guapa. No me gustaría nada, ¿sabes?
ELENA	Gracias, Chusa. Eres una tía.
CHUSA	Una madre es lo que soy. Es mi cruz, qué le vamos a hacer. Hala, vamos.

(Van a salir. Abren la puerta. CHUSA regresa desde la puerta y apaga el transistor, que estaba sonando muy bajo.)

ELENA	*(Desde la puerta.)* También así, maja, hacerlo. La primera vez con un madero me da no sé qué. A ver si me va a pasar algo. Yo soy muy supersticiosa.
CHUSA	Alberto es un tío fetén. Y lo hace todo bien: si lo sabré yo. Si te lo dejo es porque es de confianza. Y una vez nada más, ¿eh? No te vayas luego a acostumbrar. En la policía también hay tíos normales, como en todos los sitios. ¿Qué te crees, que muerden? Además, como se quitará el uniforme, ni te enteras.
ELENA	Me imagino. Lo que faltaba era que lo hiciera con el uniforme puesto. ¡Qué escalofrío!, ¿no?

(Salen las dos entre risas y cierran la puerta. Oscuro.)

ELENA	And me, what do I have to do?
CHUSA	You don't know that either? Don't you worry, he'll teach you. He knows alright; you'll see. Do you take the pill?
ELENA	What pill? No. As I'm a virgin…
CHUSA	Drop it, come on. We'll go to the chemist or for something. Don't you go getting pregnant at the first opportunity, it'd only fall to me to take care of the kid on top of everything else. And, darling, certainly not with Alberto; I wouldn't like it at all, you know?
ELENA	Thanks Chusa. You're a babe.
CHUSA	A mother is what I am. What can I say, it's the cross I bear. Come on, let's go.

(They go to leave and open the door. CHUSA comes back from the door and puts off the transistor radio which had been on at a very low volume.)

ELENA	*(From the door.)* Even so, sweetie, to do it for the first time with a copper, it makes me feel, I don't know. I wonder if anything will happen to me. I'm very superstitious.
CHUSA	Alberto's a sound guy. And he does everything well; I should know. If I'm lending him to you, it's cos he can be trusted. And only the once, right? Don't go getting used to it. There are normal guys in the police, like everywhere else. Do you think they bite or something? And, as he'll take the uniform off, you won't even realise anyway.
ELENA	But it'll be in my head. What would have topped it all is if he had done it with his uniform on. It sends shivers down your spine, doesn't it?

(The two of them leave, laughing between themselves, and close the door behind them. Blackout.)

Escena Segunda

*Han pasado varias horas. Son ahora las doce de la noche del mismo día.
En escena, ALBERTO y CHUSA discuten acaloradamente. Humphrey, el
hámster, les mira un tanto melancólico, dando vueltas a su rueda.*

ALBERTO	¡Ah, yo no, ni hablar! A mí no me liéis.
CHUSA	Venga, tío, no seas estrecho ¿No te gusta?
ALBERTO	No es eso. Es que una virgen es un lío. Que lo haga Jaimito.
CHUSA	¿Jaimito? Jaimito es un inútil para esas cosas. (*Le besa.*) Además a ella le gustas más tú. No es tonta, no creas.

*(ALBERTO pasea nervioso por la habitación, vestido como siempre con su
nuevecito traje de policía.)*

ALBERTO	Pues no me da a mí la gana, ya ves. Estamos en un país libre últimamente, ¿no? De algo tiene que servir la democracia, digo yo. Que lo haga otro. Te bajas a la calle y coges al primer salido que pase y te lo subes. ¡Tiene que ser así, de golpe, ahora mismo porque me da la gana! ¿Pero tú que te crees que soy yo?
CHUSA	Que nos vamos dentro de nada al moro, te lo he dicho. Y no va a ir así la pobre.
ALBERTO	A mí no me metáis en vuestros líos. Yo de todo eso no quiero saber nada, ni si vais ni si dejáis de ir. Y de esto, tampoco. Somos amigos, pero cada uno su vida, y sus cosas. El que vivamos juntos no quiere decir…
CHUSA	Venga, quítate el uniforme, que va a subir y si te ve así se corta. Y deja de decir chorradas, que últimamente metes cada rollo que no hay quien te aguante.

Scene Two

A few hours later. It's now midnight of the same day. On stage, ALBERTO and CHUSA are in the midst of a heated argument. Humphrey, the hamster, looks at them with a hint of a melancholy as he goes round on his wheel.

ALBERTO	Ah, not me, don't even think about it! You're not gonna get me mixed up in all this.
CHUSA	Come on, man, don't be so straight-laced about it. Don't you fancy her?
ALBERTO	It's not that. It's that virgins are a drag. Let Jaimito do it.
CHUSA	Jaimito? Jaimito's useless at those things. (*She kisses him.*) Anyway, she likes you more. Don't go thinking she's stupid.

(ALBERTO paces nervously about the room, dressed as ever in his brand new police uniform.)

ALBERTO	But, you see, I'm just not up for it. We're in a free country nowadays, aren't we? In my book, democracy's gotta have some purpose. Let someone else do it. Go down onto the street and bring up the first horny guy you come across. It has to be like that, out of the blue, just cos I'm up for it. But what do you take me for?
CHUSA	We'll be going down to Morocco in next to no time, I've already told you. And the poor girl can't go in her current state.
ALBERTO	Don't get me mixed up in your dodgy deals. I don't wanna know anything about all of that, if you go or if you don't end up going. And not about this, either. We're friends but we have our own lives, our own things. Just cos we live together doesn't mean that…
CHUSA	Come on, take the uniform off, she's about to come up and it'll put her off if she sees you in it. And stop going off on one, recently you've become unbearable making a big deal out of everything.

(CHUSA trata ahora de irle quitando la ropa.)

ALBERTO   *(Separándose de ella.)* ¡Quieta! Sin tocar, que tocando
                    vale más dinero. No quiero y no quiero. ¡Cómo sois
                    las tías! Os pensáis que estamos siempre dispuestos.
                    ¡Hala, al catre! Y ya está. Y nosotros tan contentos.
                    ¡Pero bueno!

CHUSA   Pues conmigo no le pones tantas pegas al asunto.

(ALBERTO se pone tenso antes la alusión de CHUSA a sus relaciones.)

ALBERTO   ¿A qué viene eso ahora? Es otra cosa, ¿no? A ella no
                    la conozco de nada. Tú a veces dirás también que no,
                    digo yo. ¿O es que te metes en la cama con todo el
                    que te lo pide?

CHUSA   ¿Y a ti qué te importa con quién me meto yo en la
                    cama?

ALBERTO   ¿A mí? Pero si no es eso. Yo lo digo por lo de esta tía.
                    Que me quieres liar otra vez.

CHUSA   ¿Otra vez, verdad? Mira, vamos a dejarlo.

ALBERTO   Lo único que quería decir, es que tú no te acuestas
                    con todo el que te lo pide, ¿verdad?

CHUSA   Si es así, un favor como éste… Contigo siempre he
                    querido.

ALBERTO   ¿Y ha sido un favor?

CHUSA   No digo eso. Pues sí que nos entendemos hoy bien.

ALBERTO   Yo no necesito que nadie me haga favores de este
                    tipo, ¿entiendes? Ni tampoco me gusta hacerlos. Era
                    ya lo que faltaba.

CHUSA   Eres un estúpido, eso es lo que eres.

(Se oye llegar a ELENA y a JAIMITO por las escaleras. Están abriendo la puerta de la calle.)

CHUSA   Lo único que te digo es que puedes hacer lo que
                    quieras, pero a mí no me vuelvas a hablar.

(CHUSA is now trying to take his clothes off.)

ALBERTO   *(Moving away from her.)* Stop it! Don't touch, you
                   have to pay more if you want to touch! I don't want
                   to, I don't want to. What are you girls like! You think
                   we're always up for it. Come on, off to bed! And
                   that's that. And us, like kids in a candy store. But,
                   really!
CHUSA   Well you've never played so hard to get with me.

(ALBERTO becomes tense on CHUSA referring to their sexual relations.)

ALBERTO   But why are you bringing that up? That's completely
                   different, isn't it? I don't know her from Adam. And
                   I bet you've sometimes said no. Or do you go to bed
                   with anyone who asks?
CHUSA   And what's it to you who I go to bed with?
ALBERTO   What's it to me? That's not the point. I'm saying it
                   because of the thing with the girl. Yet again, you want
                   to get me mixed up in hassle.
CHUSA   Yet again, is that how it is? Fine, let's forget it.
ALBERTO   The only thing I'm trying to say to you is that you
                   wouldn't sleep with just anyone who asked you.
                   That's true, isn't it?
CHUSA   If it was like this, a favour... With you, I've always
                   been up for it.
ALBERTO   And that was a favour?
CHUSA   That's not what I'm saying. Well we're really getting
                   each other today.
ALBERTO   I don't need anyone to do me favours of that kind, get
                   it? Nor do I like giving them. It's just what I needed.
CHUSA   You're a moron, that's what you are.

*(You can hear ELENA and JAIMITO on the stairs. They are opening the
front door.)*

CHUSA   All I'm saying is that you can do what you want, but
                   don't speak to me again.

(Entran los otros dos cargados de cervezas de litro, bolsas de patatas fritas, etc.)

JAIMITO   Ya está todo aquí. Lo que nos ha costado encontrar algo abierto. Todo preparado para la bacanal romana: patatas fritas eróticas marca «La Ríva», foie-gras de cerdo salido «El gorrino de oro», Mahou a tutiplén, y aceitunas rellenas de afrodisiacos «La olivarera malagueña».

(Ha ido colocándolo todo encima de una mesa. Traen vasos de la cocina, abren las cervezas y empiezan a beber.)

ELENA   *(Coqueta.)* Hola, Alberto, ¿qué tal?

ALBERTO   *(Agresivo.)* Yo bien, ¿por qué?

ELENA   *(Más coqueta aún.)* No, por nada. Era sólo por saber cómo estabas, si estabas bien o no.

JAIMITO   *(Poniendo el casette.)* Un poco de musiquita para ir creando ambiente.

(Se escucha a Los Chunguitos en una rumba flamenca apropiada para el momento. Siguen comiendo y bebiendo.)

ELENA   *(Acercándose a* CHUSA *le da con el codo y la habla por lo bajo.)* ¡Tiene el uniforme!

CHUSA   *(Le contesta también por lo bajo.)* Ya se lo quitará. O se lo quita él o se lo quitamos nosotros, no te preocupes. Acércate a él, dile algo.

ELENA   *(Acercándose muy insinuante a* ALBERTO.*)* ¿Bailamos?

ALBERTO   No. Con el uniforme puesto no se puede bailar. Está prohibido.

ELENA   *(Con una risita.)* Pues quítatelo.

JAIMITO   ¿Qué calor, no? *(Se quita el jersey.)* Hace un calor aquí... ¿Tú no tienes calor? *(A* ALBERTO.*)* Quítate algo.

(The other two come in weighed down with litre bottles of beer, packets of crisps etc.)

JAIMITO We've got everything here. You wouldn't believe how difficult it was to find anywhere open.[5] We're all set for a Roman orgy: sexy "La Riva" crisps; "The golden swine", foie gras from a randy pig; Mahou a plenty;[vii] and "Products of Malagan Oils", olives stuffed with aphrodisiacs.

(He starts putting everything out on the table. They bring glasses from the kitchen, open the beer and start to drink.)

ELENA *(Flirtingly.)* Hi, Alberto. How are you?
ALBERTO *(Aggressively.)* Me, fine, why?
ELENA *(Even more flirtingly.)* No reason. I just wanted to know how you were, if you were well or not.
JAIMITO *(Putting the tape player on.)* A bit of music to get things going.

(You can hear Los Chunguitos[viii] and a very fitting flamenco rumba.[6] They continue to eat and drink.)

ELENA *(Moving closing to CHUSA, she nudges her with her elbow and speaks quietly.)* He's got the uniform!
CHUSA *(She replies, also in a quiet voice.)* He'll take it off soon enough. Either he'll take it off or we'll do it for him, don't you worry. Move closer, say something to him.
ELENA *(Moving closer to ALBERTO provocatively.)* Shall we dance?
ALBERTO No. You can't dance with your uniform on. It's forbidden.
ELENA *(With a nervous chuckle.)* Well, take it off.
JAIMITO It's hot, isn't it? *(He takes his sweater off.)* It's really hot in here... Aren't you hot? *(To ALBERTO.)* Take something off.

---

5   In the 2008 version, Jaimito says they got the supplies from the 'chino'; this refers to the number of twenty-four hour grocery stores generally run by the Chinese that have sprung up all around Madrid in recent years.
6   Replaced with Hot Chocolate's *You Sexy Thing* in the 2008 production.

ALBERTO
: Qué manía habéis cogido todos con que me quite la ropa. Quitárosla vosotros si queréis.

CHUSA
: Por lo menos quítate la pistola, a ver si nos vas a dar a uno.

ALBERTO
: (*Se la quita y la pone encima de su armario.*) Sin tocarla, ¿eh? Que da calambre. (*Risita de ELENA.*)

(*JAIMITO sirve cerveza y sigue bebiendo. Luego se pasan unos canutos. La música rumbera va subiendo y el clima se va calentando. Suenan en esto unos golpes muy fuertes en una pared de la habitación.*)

CHUSA
: Ya está ahí el plasta ese incordiando.

JAIMITO
: Pasar de él. Que tire la casa si quiere.

(*Canta ahora JAIMITO la música del casette y taconea al ritmo flamenco.*)

«…Pues me he enamorao
y te quiero y te quiero,
y sólo deseo estar a tu lado,
soñar con tus ojos, besarte los labios,
sentirme en tus brazos,
que soy muy felíz.
Si me das a elegir,
entre tú y la gloria, pa que hable la historia de mí
por los siglos,
ay amor, me quedo contigo…»

(*Se oye ahora una voz desde el otro lado del tabique, hablando a gritos.*)

OFF
: ¡Tengo que dormir! ¡Bajen la música!

ELENA
: Si sólo son las doce. ¿Quién es? ¿Por qué se pone así?

JAIMITO
: Siempre está igual.

CHUSA
: Madruga el hombre, y claro…

ALBERTO You've all become obsessed with me taking my clothes off. Take yours off if you want.

CHUSA At least get rid of your gun, you could wind up shooting one of us.

ALBERTO (*He removes it and places it on top of the wardrobe.*) No touching, eh? It gives you cramp. (*A nervous chuckle from ELENA.*)

(*JAIMITO pours some beer and keeps drinking. Then they pass around some small spliffs. The rumba music gets louder and things begin to hot up. Someone starts banging loudly on one of the bedroom walls.*)

CHUSA Ah, that pain in the neck's making a nuisance of himself again.

JAIMITO Ignore him. He can knock the place down if he wants.

(*JAIMITO now starts to sing along to the music on the cassette player and clicks his heels to the flamenco rhythm.*)

"…Well I've fallen in deep,
and I love you, I love you,
and I only want to be with you,
kiss your lips, dream of your eyes,
feel you in my arms,
I'm so happy.
If I had to choose,
between you and eternal fame, so that my tale'd be
told for centuries to come,
oh, my love, I'm sticking with you…"

(*You can now hear a voice shouting from the other side of the partition wall.*)

VOICE I need to sleep! Put the music down!

ELENA But, it's only twelve. Who is it? Why is he getting so worked up?

JAIMITO He's always the same.

CHUSA The man has to get up at the crack of dawn, and of course…

JAIMITO   Pues que no madruge. (*Sigue con Los Chunguitos.*)
                 «Si me das a elegir,
                 entre tú y ese cielo,
                 donde libre es el vuelo,
                 para ir a otros nidos,
                 ay amor, me quedo contigo.
                 Si me das a elegir,
                 entre tú y mis ideas,
                 que yo sin ellas,
                 soy un hombre perdido,
                 ay amor, me quedo contigo.
                 Pues me he enamorao,
                 y te quiero y te quiero,
                 y sólo deseo estar a tu lado...»

(Canta ahora JAIMITO directamente a ELENA, que le sonríe encantada.)

                 «Soñar con tus ojos, besarte los labios, sentirme en
                 tus brazos que soy muy feliz...»
ALBERTO   (*Metiéndose en medio, un poco molesto de haber
                 pasado a segundo plano.*) Es un cura. Dice misa en
                 las monjitas, ¿verdad? A las cinco de la mañana. Y el
                 hombre no pega ojo.
CHUSA   Me ha dicho la portera, que es muy maja, que el otro
                 día se fue a quejar, y ella le dijo que en esta casa
                 había libertad religiosa, y que lo que tenía que hacer
                 era trabajar en algo decente, como Dios manda, y no
                 andar con las monjas por ahí a esas horas. (*Risas de
                 los tres.*)

*(JAIMITO sigue intentando canturrearle a ELENA, pero ALBERTO está
delante, descaradamente y le sigue dando su explicación.)*

ALBERTO   Que diga la misa por la tarde. Ahora ya dejan. O por
                 la noche. Se tendría que perder la película de la tele,
                 claro. Todo el día con la tele puesta, y nos tenemos
                 que aguantar. Y luego nosotros ponemos la música, y
                 jaleo.

JAIMITO   Well, he shouldn't get up so early. (*He keeps going
                  with Los Chinguitos.*)
                  "If I had to choose,
                  between you and that sky,
                  where you can fly,
                  to other nests, free as a bird,
                  oh, my love, I'm sticking with you.
                  If I had to choose,
                  between you and my ideas,
                  without which,
                  I'd be a broken man,
                  oh, my love, I'm sticking with you.
                  Well I've fallen in deep,
                  and I love you, I love you,
                  and I only want to be with you,

(JAIMITO now sings directly to ELENA who gives him a warm smile.)

                  kiss your lips, dream of your eyes,
                  feel you in my arms,
                  I'm so happy…"

ALBERTO   (*Nudging between them, a little put out at no longer
                  being the centre of attention.*) He's a priest. He says
                  mass for the little sisters, doesn't he? At five in the
                  morning. And the man doesn't get a wink of sleep.

CHUSA   The porter, she's a really top girl, told me he went
                  to complain the other day and she told him there's
                  religious freedom in this establishment, and what he
                  needed to do was follow God's will, find a respectable
                  job and stop hanging out with those nuns at all hours.
                  (*Laughs from the three of them.*)

*(JAIMITO is still trying to sing softly to ELENA, but ALBERTO shamelessly
pushes him out the way as he continues to give his explanation.)*

ALBERTO   He should say mass in the late afternoon. They're
                  allowed to now. Or in the evening. He'd have to miss
                  the film on the telly mind. We have to put up with him
                  having the telly on all day. And then all hell breaks
                  loose when we put the music on.

JAIMITO	El otro día me lo encuentro en la escalera y empieza a decir gilipolleces. Le dije que se mudara, y me dice el prenda que el que se tenía que mudar era yo, que huelo mal. No te jode. Están fastidiados porque están todos ahora medio en el paro. Se les está acabando el chollo. Alguna misa en las monjitas, y vale. Así está, medio ido.
CHUSA	Eso es de no dormir.
JAIMITO	Pues que duerma, hombre. (*A gritos hacia la pared.*) ¡Que se eche la siesta! «Pues me he enamorao, y te quiero y te quiero, y sólo deseo, estar a tu lado…»

(*Canta ahora* JAIMITO *mucho más alto. Se vuelven a oír más altos también, los golpes en la pared. Y de pronto traspasa el tabique el palo de una escoba.*)

JAIMITO	(*Parando el casette.*) ¡Huy, la hostia! ¡Que nos tira la casa!

(*Agarra el palo y tira. El otro tira desde el otro lado. Finalmente el otro suelta y* JAIMITO *se cae del tirón quedándose con el palo.*)

CHUSA	(*Se acerca al agujero y mira por él.*) A ver…
JAIMITO	¿Qué ves?
CHUSA	(*Mirando.*) Un ojo. (*Habla a voces por el agujero.*) ¡Qué pasa! ¡Que ha roto la pared! ¡A ver ahora, qué va a pasar! (*Se oyen gritos al otro lado.*) Dice que va a llamar a la policía. Encima. (*A gritos otra vez.*) ¡A quien tiene que llamar es a un albañil, a que arregle esto! ¡Y a un psiquiatra, tío loco!
ALBERTO	Esperar, que voy. (*Se ajusta la pistola y la gorra y va hacia la puerta. Echa una mirada a* ELENA *y ésta le amaga una despedida con la mano, como si se fuese a la guerra. Sale.*)

JAIMITO   I bumped into him on the stairs the other day, and he started going off on one talking shit. I told him he should move out and he said the one who needed a change was me, that I smelt bad. Would you believe it? They're all fucked at present because they're all winding their way to the dole office. Time's up on the con. The occasional mass with the little sisters, and that's your lot. That's it, on its way out.

CHUSA   It'll be cos he's not sleeping.

JAIMITO   Well the man should sleep then (*Shouting towards the wall.*) Have a siesta!
"Well I've fallen in deep,
and I love you, I love you,
and I only want to be with you…"

(*JAIMITO is now singing much louder. The banging on the wall, also much louder this time round, starts up again. And suddenly a broomstick comes through the partition wall.*)

JAIMITO   (*Stopping the cassette player.*) Christ! He's gonna trash the place!

(*He grabs hold of the broomstick and starts to pull. The other man pulls from the other side but eventually lets go causing JAIMITO, left holding the broomstick, to fall over from pulling so hard.*)

CHUSA   (*She moves towards the hole in the wall and looks through it.*) Let's see…

JAIMITO   What can you see?

CHUSA   (*Looking.*) An eye. (*She speaks loudly through the hole.*) What's up! The wall's broken! Let's see what's going to happen now! (*You can hear shouts from the other side.*) He says he's going to phone the police. That takes the biscuit. (*Shouting again.*) It's a builder you need to ring, to sort all this out! And a psychiatrist, mentalist!

ALBERTO   Wait, I'll go. (*Putting his gun and hat in place, he heads for the door. He glances at ELENA who gestures goodbye with her hand as if he were heading out to war. He leaves.*)

JAIMITO   Cuando abra y le vea se caga.

(Se oye sonar el timbre de la otra casa.)

ELENA   Pensará que ha llegado volando; nada más descolgar
                      el teléfono y...
CHUSA   A ver si da más golpes ahora.

*(Vuelve a mirar por el agujero y va contando a los otros dos lo que ve
pasar en la casa de al lado.)*

                      Ya va a abrir. Ahora no se le ve... Ya, ya... Vuelve.
                      Está blanco. Ahora mira el agujero, coge un tapón de
                      una botella, se acerca, lo pone y... fin.

(Retirándose.)

ALBERTO   *(Entrando triunfal.)* Mañana viene el albañil. Ya de
                      paso que nos arregle la cocina. *(Se ríen todos.)*
CHUSA   *(A ELENA.)* ¿Has visto lo bien que viene tener la bofia
                      en casa?

*(ALBERTO mira a ELENA. Está ahora en plan héroe de película. Y le sale
el ramalazo conquistador. Por otro lado. ELENA cada vez le gusta más,
sobre todo desde que intentó acercarse a ella JAIMITO. Esta se acerca a
él y le pone orgullosa la mano en el brazo. Se miran.)*

CHUSA   Si queréis podéis meteros en el cuarto. No sea que ése
                      quite el tapón y le dé algo.
ELENA   Bueno, lo que tú digas.
ALBERTO   Al fin y al cabo la policía está al servicio del ciudadano,
                      y esto es un servicio público. *(Van hacia la habitación.
                      Se vuelve desde la puerta.)* ¡Qué liantes sois! ¡Sí, los
                      dos! No bajéis la música. Altita. *(Se quita la gorra y
                      la tira al aire muy chulo, en brindis torero.)* Allá va,
                      y que sea lo que Dios quiera. Va por vosotros.
ELENA   Bueno, adiós.

JAIMITO   He'll shit himself when he opens up and sees who it
                 is.

(You can hear the bell ring from next door.)

ELENA   He'll think he's flown there; the second he puts the
                 phone down and...
CHUSA   Let's see if he bangs the walls again now.

*(She looks through the hole in the wall again and reports back to the
others as to what is happening next door.)*

                 He's about to open. Now you can't see him... Ha,
                 ha... He's coming back. He's gone pale. Now he's
                 looking at the hole, he's taken the cork from a bottle,
                 he's getting closer, he's putting it in and... that's it.

(Moving away.)

ALBERTO   (*Coming in triumphantly.*) The builder's coming
                 tomorrow. While he's here, he can sort the kitchen
                 out for us. (*They all laugh.*)
CHUSA   (*To ELENA.*) Have you seen how good it is to have a
                 rozzer about the place?

*(ALBERTO is looking at ELENA. He's now in movie hero mode. And it
suddenly brings out the Casanova in him. On the other hand, ELENA
fancies him more and more especially since JAIMITO tried to move in on
her. She moves towards him and proudly puts her hand on his arm. They
look at each other.)*

CHUSA   You can go into the room if you want. Just in case that
                 one takes the cork out and it gives him I don't know.
ELENA   Fine, whatever you say.
ALBERTO   At the end of the day, the police are there to help
                 people, and this is a public service. (*They go towards
                 the bedroom. He turns round at the door.*) What
                 smooth operators you are! Yes, the two of you! Don't
                 put the music down. Nice and loud. (*He takes his hat
                 off and punches the air triumphantly as if he were a
                 bullfighter.*)
ELENA   Well, bye, bye.

(Al desaparecer los dos dentro del cuarto y cerrar la puerta, JAIMITO y CHUSA se quedan con la mirada perdida en el vacío. Lo que era un juego se ha convertido en soledad.)

JAIMITO	Qué suerte tiene el tío para todo. Y encima se queja. Es maja, ¿verdad?
CHUSA	Creí que no te gustaba.
JAIMITO	¿A mí? Sólo digo que es muy guapa, y que está muy buena. Encima se meten ahí los dos...
CHUSA	A ver. Si se mete uno solo la cosa es más difícil.
JAIMITO	Yo creí que tú y Alberto..., vamos, que tú y él...
CHUSA	¿Quieres dejarlo ya?

(CHUSA se pasea nerviosa por la habitación y trata de distraerse haciendo algo. Coloca la mesa, mueve las sillas de sitio, y hace dos o tres cosas raras más. Va a la ventana y se queda mirando al infinito.)

CHUSA	*(Tratando de convencerse a sí misma ante la creciente angustia que le está entrando de pronto.)* Esto no tiene importancia. Es una amiga. A ver si vamos a ponernos nosotros antiguos con esta bobada.
JAIMITO	*(Baja el casette.)* No se oye nada... ¿Qué estarán haciendo?
CHUSA	Crucigramas.

(Llega hasta el casette y lo sube otra vez. Va al baño.)

Hay que llamar al fontanero para que arregle de una maldita vez esa cisterna, que se sale. Me da la noche con ese ruidito. *(Pausa.)*

(Llaman en esto a la puerta de la calle. Va JAIMITO a abrir. Lo hace, y entra DOÑA ANTONIA, medio llorando, con un gran disgusto encima.)

(When the other two disappear into the room, closing the door behind them, JAIMITO and CHUSA are left staring into space. What was a game has turned into loneliness.)

JAIMITO   If the guy fell in a bucket of shit, he'd come out smelling of roses. And yet he still complains. She's nice, isn't she?

CHUSA   I thought you didn't like her.

JAIMITO   Me? I'm just saying that she's very pretty, and she's really hot. On top of that, the two of them hide themselves away in there...

CHUSA   Come on. If just one of them went in, the whole thing would be a bit difficult.

JAIMITO   I thought that you and Alberto..., well that you and him...

CHUSA   Can you just let it drop?

(CHUSA paces the room nervously, and tries to distract herself by doing something. She sets the table, moves the chairs about, and does two or three more odd things. She goes over to the window, and just stares into space.)

CHUSA   *(Trying to convince herself in the face of a growing anxiety that suddenly descends upon her.)* All of this doesn't mean a thing. She's a friend. As if we're going to go all old-fashioned over something this stupid.

JAIMITO   *(Lowering the volume of the cassette player.)* You can't hear a thing... What can they be doing?

CHUSA   Crosswords.

(She goes over to the cassette player and turns it up again. She goes to the bathroom.)

We have to phone the plumber so that he fixes this bloody tank once and for all. That annoying little noise is there all night long. *(Pause.)*

(A knock comes to the front door at this point. JAIMITO goes to open it. When he does, a tearful, clearly distraught, DOÑA ANTONIA comes in.)

DOÑA ANTONIA	¡Ay, Dios mío, Dios mío! ¿Está mi hijo aquí...?
CHUSA	(*Intentando ocultarle.*) No..., me parece que no ha venido, ¿Ha venido? (*A JAIMITO.*)
JAIMITO	Yo desde luego no le he visto. ¿Qué ha pasado? ¿Se encuentra usted mal? Siéntese, mujer. Y cálmese.
DOÑA ANTONIA	¡Ay, Dios mío, Dios mío qué desgracia tan grande!
CHUSA	(*A JAIMITO.*) Tráele agua, o algo...
DOÑA ANTONIA	(*Ve la gorra de ALBERTO.*) ¿Y esto? ¡Está aquí! ¿Dónde está? ¡Alberto, hijo...! ¡Hijo...!

(*Se miran JAIMITO y CHUSA. Como la cosa parece seria deciden llamarle.*)

JAIMITO	(*Llamando a la puerta del cuarto.*) ¡Alberto! Oye, sal. ¡Sal un momento, anda. Es tu madre!

(*Se abre la puerta del cuarto y aparece ALBERTO a medio vestir. Se acerca a su madre que sigue ahogada del disgusto en una butaca. Todos alrededor.*)

ALBERTO	Madre, ¿qué pasa?
DOÑA ANTONIA	¡Ay, qué disgusto, hijo mío de mi alma! ¡Dios mío, Dios mío!
ALBERTO	¿Pero qué pasa, madre? ¿Quiere hablar de una vez? ¿Qué pasa?
DOÑA ANTONIA	¡Tu padre, hijo, tu padre! ¡Que ha salido de la cárcel!

(*Cara estupefacta de todos ante la noticia. Y oscuro.*)

DOÑA ANTONIA	Oh, my Lord, my Lord! Is my son here…?
CHUSA	(*Trying to hide him.*) No… I don't think he's come. Has he come? (*To JAIMITO.*)
JAIMITO	Obviously I haven't seen him. What's happened? Are you unwell? Sit yourself down and calm down woman.
DOÑA ANTONIA	Oh, my Lord, my Lord what a terrible misfortune!
CHUSA	(*To JAIMITO.*) Bring her some water, or some…
DOÑA ANTONIA	(*She sees ALBERTO's hat.*) And that? He's here. Where is he? Alberto, son…! Son…!

(JAIMITO and CHUSA look at each other. They decide to call him because whatever's up seems so serious.)

JAIMITO	(*Calling at the bedroom door.*) Alberto! Listen, come out! Come out for a second, come on! It's your mother.

(The bedroom door opens and ALBERTO appears half naked. He moves towards his mother who, sitting in an armchair, is still overcome with tears from whatever it is that is upsetting her. They all stand around her.)

ALBERTO	Mother, what's going on?
DOÑA ANTONIA	Oh, how horrible, my dear son! My Lord, my Lord!
ALBERTO	But what's going on, mother? Can't you just spit it out once and for all? What's going on?
DOÑA ANTONIA	Your father, my son, your father! He's come out of prison!

(Everyone's faces register shock on hearing the news. And blackout.)

Escena Tercera

Al día siguiente, mediodía. ELENA *está leyendo.* JAIMITO *viene de la cocina con una lata abierta comiendo. Se le acerca.*

JAIMITO	¿Quieres?
ELENA	No, gracias. Ya he comido.
JAIMITO	(*Se sienta a su lado. Sigue comiendo.*) Vaya lío ayer, ¿eh? ¿Has visto hoy a Alberto?
ELENA	No, no ha venido. (*Sigue leyendo.*)
JAIMITO	Vaya corte que te llevarías, llegar ahí la madre, en ese momento… (*Pausa, silencio. Sigue comiendo y ella leyendo.*) Y luego el jaleo ese de su padre. Le habían echado un montón de años, y de pronto a la calle. Ahora es muy difícil que te dejen estar en la cárcel Hay que estar muy recomendado. Un amigo mío que está allí metido, come en casa, y luego duerme allí. Cuando no puede ir algún día llama por teléfono. (*Ve que sus intentos de ser gracioso no van por buen camino y cambia de estrategia.*) Vete tú a saber…, las cosas que pasan… Oye, así que tú sigues igual. Qué mala suerte.
ELENA	¿De qué?
JAIMITO	De lo de virgen.
ELENA	Ah, no importa. Otro día.

(JAIMITO *se quiere ofrecer, pero no sabe por dónde empezar. Está violento, tartamudea. Se levanta y se sienta varias veces. Va al lavabo y se peina.*)

JAIMITO	Sí que es una lata eso de ser virgen. Yo que tú, en la primera ocasión que se me presentara… Estamos solos.
ELENA	(*Distraída con la lectura.*) Sí, Chusa dijo que vendría luego.
JAIMITO	(*Se acerca. Mira el libro que ella lee.*) «Apocalípticos e Integrados». ¿Es buena?

Scene Three

Midday on the following day. ELENA *is reading.* JAIMITO *comes from the kitchen eating something out of a tin. He moves towards her.*

JAIMITO   Do you want a bit?

ELENA   No, thanks. I've already eaten.

JAIMITO   (*He sits next to her. He carries on eating.*) One hell of a kerfuffle yesterday, eh? Have you seen Alberto today?

ELENA   No, he's not been over. (*She carries on reading.*)

JAIMITO   All rather awkward for you, the mother showing up at that precise moment ... (*Pause, silence. He carries on eating and she keeps on reading.*) And then all that commotion about his father. He went down for years and years and then, suddenly, back on the street again. It's real difficult to be allowed to stay in prison these days. You need to come very highly recommended. A friend of mine who's in there, eats at home, and then sleeps there. If he can't go one day, he gives them a ring. (*He sees that his attempts to be funny are not going down well and changes strategy.*) Go figure, things that happen... so, listen, you're still the same. What bad luck.

ELENA   About what?

JAIMITO   The whole virgin thing.

ELENA   Ah, it's no problem. Another day.

(JAIMITO *wants to volunteer himself, but doesn't know where to start, He's agitated and stammers. He gets up and sits back down again on various occasions. He goes to the toilet and combs his hair.*)

JAIMITO   Yes, that whole virgin thing is a real drag. If I were you, the first opportunity that came up... We're on our own.

ELENA   (*Distracted in her reading.*) Yes, Chusa said she'd come later.

JAIMITO   (*He moves closer. He looks at the book she's reading.*) Apocalyptic and Integrated Intellectuals. Any good?

ELENA	Es de Umberto Eco. Está muy bien. Es un ensayo sobre nuestra civilización actual. La crítica literaria, el consumo…, esas cosas.
JAIMITO	Tú has estudiado, ¿no?
ELENA	Sí. Ciencias de la Educación, lo que antes era Filosofía y Letras. Sólo he hecho hasta tercero. Bueno, tengo alguna de segundo. Este año es que no he aparecido por la Facultad. Es un rollo, no aprendes nada. Yo leo y estudio más por mi cuenta. Y con apuntes que me dejan los que van. Luego me examino, y lo voy sacando. Aprendes más. Los profesores no enseñan nada.
JAIMITO	¿Y cómo te puedes examinar si te escapas de casa?
ELENA	Para los exámenes vuelvo.
JAIMITO	¡Ah!
ELENA	¿Y tú, no estudias nada?
JAIMITO	¿Yo? Yo no. Yo soy un ignorante, de verdad. No leo nada… La verdad es que para vender costo y hacer sandalias… A mí lo que me gusta mucho es el cine.
ELENA	La cultura nunca viene mal. Además, es por distraerse. ¿Novelas tampoco lees?
JAIMITO	Novelas tampoco. Algunas de pequeño, pero ahora… Revistas si acaso. Bueno, alguna vez leo algo, pero poco.
ELENA	Claro. Será también por lo del ojo.
JAIMITO	¿El ojo? Qué va. Yo veo igual que tú o que cualquiera. Ver, veo muy bien. Sólo de un lado, pero perfectamente.
ELENA	(*Tapándose un ojo.*) Pues yo si miro con un ojo sólo, veo mal.
JAIMITO	Tú porque no estás acostumbrada.

(Pausa. Ella vuelve a su lectura. De vez en cuando prueba tapándose un ojo. Él, a su alrededor, no sabe por dónde entrarle.)

¿Te vienes al cine?

ELENA	It's by Umberto Eco. It's very good. It's an essay about modern-day civilization. Literary criticism, consumerism…, those things.
JAIMITO	You've studied, haven't you?
ELENA	Yes, Educational Science, what they used to call Literature and Philosophy. I've only got as far as my third year. Well, I've passed some of my second year.[ix] The thing is I haven't been into the department this year. It's such a bore, you don't learn a thing. I read and study more on my own. And, with the notes I get given by those who go. Then I sit the exam, and I'm getting there. You learn more. The lecturers don't teach you anything.
JAIMITO	And how can you sit the exams if you run away from home?
ELENA	I go back for the exams.
JAIMITO	Ah!
ELENA	And you don't study anything?
JAIMITO	Me? I don't. I'm a total ignoramus, honestly, I don't read a thing… To tell the truth, to sell hash and make sandals… What I do like a lot is the cinema.
ELENA	Culture's never a bad thing. Anyway, it's good escapism. You don't read novels either?
JAIMITO	No novels either. Some small ones, but well… perhaps magazines. Well, sometimes I read something, but not much.
ELENA	Of course. It'll be because of your eye.
JAIMITO	The eye. Get away. I see the same as you or anyone else does. Seeing, I see very well. Only on the one side, but perfectly.
ELENA	(*Covering one of her eyes.*) But if I look with just one eye, I can't see very well.
JAIMITO	You don't because you're not used to it.

(Pause. ELENA *goes back to her reading. From time to time, she tries covering an eye. He hovers around her not knowing how to make a move.)*

You wanna come to the cinema?

ELENA	¿Al cine? ¿Al cine a esta hora? ¿A qué cine, qué ponen?
JAIMITO	No sé, es igual. A cualquiera. Es por salir un rato. Nos tomamos unas cervezas y luego nos vemos una que esté bien. Compramos la Guía del Ocio.
ELENA	No, de verdad. Gracias, pero no. Estoy enrollada con esto. Díselo a Chusa cuando venga, y vete con ella.
JAIMITO	(*Atreviéndose.*) Es que yo quiero ir contigo.
ELENA	(*Sin enterarse de nada.*) ¿Conmigo? ¿Por qué?
JAIMITO	No sé, me apetece. Yo soy un tío muy raro. Me dan bascas, así, de pronto. Hay momentos en que una persona me gusta, ¿no?, y entonces, pues al cine.

(Ella sigue leyendo, siguiéndole con automáticos movimientos de cabeza.)

Una vez me enrollé yo con una chica, una vecina mía, cuando vivía en el Puente de Vallecas, antes de venirme aquí a Lavapiés. Trabajaba ella en Simago, allí en la Avenida de la Albufera. Era muy maja. Alta, con el pelo largo... muy maja. Yo la iba a buscar a la salida del trabajo. Nos juntábamos allí un montón de tíos todos los días. Parecía la mili. Esperando, allí, a la salida, todos tan serios. Luego ya salían ellas, y hala, cogía yo a la Merche y nos íbamos al cine. Todos los días al cine. Sin faltar uno. Al cine. Estuvimos un año y pico saliendo y nos vimos todos los programas dobles de Madrid. Nos conocían hasta los acomodadores. Luego ya lo dejamos. Bueno, la verdad es que fue ella la que lo dejó. Se largó con un rockero, de los de las discotecas y chaqueta de cuero. Un fantasma de ésos. La vi después, al año o así. Una noche. Iba con el tío ese y unos cuantos más. Me

ELENA	To the cinema? The cinema at this time? To what cinema? What's on?
JAIMITO	I don't know, it doesn't matter, any film will do. It's just to get some fresh air. We'll have a few beers and then see one that looks good. We'll buy the Guía de Ocio.[x]
ELENA	No, honestly. Thanks, but no. I'm tied up with this. Ask Chusa when she comes back, and go with her.
JAIMITO	(*Plucking up the courage.*) The thing is I want to go with you.
ELENA	(*Completely oblivious to everything.*) With me? Why?
JAIMITO	I don't know, I fancy it. I'm an odd guy. Out of the blue, things suddenly take my fancy. There are times when I like someone, right? And then, well, off to the cinema.

(*She carries on reading, nodding as he speaks without paying any attention to what he's saying.*)

One time, I hooked up with a girl, a neighbour of mine when I was living on the edges of Vallecas, before coming here to Lavapiés. She worked in Simago,[xi] the supermarket over there on Albufera Avenue. She was very nice. Tall with long hair…, very nice. I'd go and wait for her when she came out of work. There'd be a load of guys there, everyday. It was like military service. Waiting there, at the exit, all of us dead serious. Then they'd come out and, hey, I'd pick Merche up and we'd go to the cinema. Every day in the cinema. We didn't miss a day. In the cinema. We went out for just over a year and we saw all the double-bills in Madrid. Even the ushers knew us. Then we split. Well, truth be told, she was the one who left me. She went off with a rocker, one of those who hangs round the clubs with a leather jacket. One of those ghouls. I saw her a year or so later. One night. She was with that guy and a few others.

dijo que estaba harta de ir al cine. A gritos, desde la otra acera de la calle: «¡Estoy harta de cine!» Al año y pico, fíjate. Era de noche, me acuerdo muy bien. Me lo podía haber dicho entonces, cuando salíamos. Yo iba porque creía que a ella le gustaba. A mí tanto cine, la verdad... (*Se da cuenta de que ella hace rato que no le escucha.*) Bueno, te dejo estudiar. Ya me iba. Daré una vuelta por ahí. (*Llega hasta la puerta.*) Hasta luego, ¿Sabes una cosa, Elena? ¿Elena?

ELENA   (*Dejando el libro.*) ¿Sí, qué?

JAIMITO   Que estás hoy muy guapa. Muy guapa, de verdad.

ELENA   Anda, guasón, que eres un guasón.

(*Ella vuelve a su libro. Él abre la puerta y va a salir. En ese momento llega corriendo por las escaleras ALBERTO. Entra como un vendaval.*)

ALBERTO   ¿Está Elena? (*Entra, la ve y se acerca y le da un beso. Ella deja el libro automáticamente. JAIMITO lo mira todo desde la puerta.*) Oye, me he escapado un momento. Tengo que volver rápido a la comisaría. (*Coge la porra que está encima de su armario.*) Otra vez me la he dejado aquí. Cualquier día tengo un lío por esto. (*Se la pone.*) Menudo jaleo con mi padre, chica. Está rarísimo. Serio, formal... Estuvo una hora anoche preguntándome por todo. Yo no sé qué decirle. Menudo mogollón. Bueno, que a la noche vengo. Me tengo que ir a comer con él, no tengo más remedio. Hasta luego, adiós.

She told me she was fed up of going to the cinema. Shouting, from the pavement on the other side of the road: "I'm fed up of the cinema!" A year and a bit, go figure. It was nighttime, I remember very well. She could have said something to me before, when we were going out. I went because I thought she liked it. Truth be told, I find all that cinema… (*He realises she hasn't been listening to him for a good while.*) Right, I'll leave you to study. I was on my way out. I'll go for a wander about the place… (*He gets as far as the door.*) Catch you later. Do you know something, Elena? Elena?

ELENA   (*Leaving the book.*) Yes, what?

JAIMITO   That you look really beautiful today? Honestly, really beautiful.

ELENA   What are you like? A joker, that's what you are, a joker.

(*She goes back to her book. He opens the door and is about to leave. At that moment, ALBERTO arrives running up the stairs. He comes in like a tornado.*)

ALBERTO   Is Elena in? (*He comes in, sees her, moves towards her and gives her a kiss. She stops reading automatically. JAIMITO watches everything from the door.*) Listen, I've just escaped for a moment. I have to be quick getting back to the police station. (*He picks up the truncheon from on top of the wardrobe.*) I've left it here again. Any day now, I'm going to get into trouble because of this. (*He straps it in.*) Girl, I tell you, it's been one hell of a commotion with my father. He's gone super-weird. Responsible, formal… He spent an hour last night asking me about everything. I don't know what to say to him. One hell of a lot of things going on. Right, I'll be here tonight. I'll have to go eat with him, I haven't any choice. See you later, bye.

(Sale otra vez como un torbellino. Vuelve y habla a ELENA *desde la puerta, al lado de* JAIMITO *que sigue allí clavado.)*

Luego seguimos donde lo dejamos anoche, ¿eh? (*Le tira un beso.*) Tú (*A* JAIMITO.) Guárdamela bien hasta que vuelva. (*Le amenaza jugando con la pistola en la funda, le da los puñetazos cariñosos de siempre en el hombro y sale. Ella queda encantada mirando hacia la puerta.* JAIMITO *sigue allí, violento, sin saber si irse o quedarse.*)

JAIMITO   ¿Cómo es, eh? Bueno, yo también me iba. Luego vuelvo para la fiesta. No me la quiero perder. Adiós. ¡Que adiós!

ELENA   Adiós.

(Sale JAIMITO. *Ella suspira, los ojos perdidos a lo lejos, Y vuelve a su libro. Oscuro.)*

(He leaves, again like a tornado. He goes back and speaks to ELENA from the door, next to JAIMITO who is glued there.)

> Later, we'll carry on where we left off last night, eh? (*He blows her a kiss.*) You (*To JAIMITO.*) Look after her well for me until I get back. (*He threatens him playing with the gun in its holster, gives him the standard affectionate punches on the shoulder and leaves. She is left on cloud nine looking towards the door. JAIMITO, agitated, is still there, not sure whether to stay or go.*)

JAIMITO   What's he like, eh? Well, I was also heading out. I'll come back for the party later. I don't want to miss it. Bye! I said, bye!

ELENA   Bye.

(JAIMITO leaves. She sighs, her eyes lost in the distance. And she returns to her book. Blackout.)

Escena Cuarta

Noche del mismo día. En escena, CHUSA *cortándose las uñas y de muy mal humor. Se abre la puerta de la calle y entra* JAIMITO *cargado de nuevo con cervezas de litro, ginebra, patatas fritas etc.*

JAIMITO	Ya estoy aquí. ¿Qué? ¿He tardado mucho?
CHUSA	Dos horas. Te lo puedes volver a llevar por donde lo has traído todo, si quieres. Aquí ya no hace falta.
JAIMITO	¿Dónde están? ¿Se han ido?
CHUSA	*(De mala uva.)* Ahí. *(Señala con la cabeza el cuarto.)*
JAIMITO	*(Se queda un momento en silencio, mirando la puerta cerrada.)* ¡Joder! ¡También! Encima de que voy a por... ¿Y qué hacen?
CHUSA	¿Tú que crees?
JAIMITO	*(Sigue mirando descorazonado a la puerta.)* ¿Hace mucho que...?
CHUSA	Un rato.
JAIMITO	No se oye nada.
CHUSA	No. *(Se quedan los dos en silencio. Sólo se oye el cortauñas con el que* CHUSA *sigue cortándose las uñas, ahora de los pies, haciéndose todo el daño que puede.)* No corta. Seguro que lo has estado usando con las sandalias.
JAIMITO	¿Antes tampoco se ha oído nada?
CHUSA	No, antes tampoco se ha oído nada.
JAIMITO	Haberles dicho que esperaran, ¿no?
CHUSA	Se lo he dicho.
JAIMITO	¿Y qué?
CHUSA	Ya lo ves.
JAIMITO	*(Acercándose más a la puerta, intentando escuchar.)* ¿Y no has oído nada, nada, nada?
CHUSA	Te crees que lo radian o qué. *(Se fija en que sigue con todo en sus brazos como un pasmarote. Le coge las bolsas y las pone sobre la mesa.)* Ginebra y todo.

Scene Four

Nighttime of the same day. On stage, CHUSA, in a very bad mood, cutting her nails. The front door opens and JAIMITO comes in weighed down once again with litre bottles of beer, gin, crisps, etc.

JAIMITO	I'm here now. What? Did I take a long time?
CHUSA	Two hours. You can take it all back from where you brought it if you want. There's no need for it here now.
JAIMITO	Where are they? Have they gone?
CHUSA	(*Moodily.*) There. (*She signals towards the room with her head.*)
JAIMITO	(*He stays in silence for a moment looking at the closed door.*) Fuck! As well! On top of the fact I've gone for… And what are they doing?
CHUSA	What do you think?
JAIMITO	(*Still looking downheartedly at the door.*) How long have…?
CHUSA	A while.
JAIMITO	You can't hear anything.
CHUSA	No. (*The two of them remain in silence. The only sound to be heard is the nail clippers which CHUSA continues to use, having now moved onto her toenails, doing as much damage as possible.*) It doesn't cut. I bet you've been using them on your sandals.
JAIMITO	You couldn't hear anything before, either?
CHUSA	No, you couldn't hear anything before either.
JAIMITO	And you told them to hold off for a bit, right?
CHUSA	That's what I said.
JAIMITO	And what?
CHUSA	Well, you can see.
JAIMITO	(*Moving closer to the door and trying to listen.*) And you haven't heard anything? Not a thing?
CHUSA	You think they broadcast it or what? (*She notices that he's still holding everything like a dummy. She takes the carrier bags off him and puts them on the table.*) Gin and everything.

JAIMITO	Era para animar esto un poco.
CHUSA	No les ha hecho falta. Se la beberá su madre cuando venga.
JAIMITO	(*Reaccionando.*) Ese Alberto es que es un cabronazo. Me tiene ya hasta la… Se mete ahí, con ella, y ¡hala! Ni cerveza, ni ginebra, ni nada. (*Gritando.*) ¿Para eso he traído yo las patatas fritas?
CHUSA	No grites.
JAIMITO	A mí, como un gilipollas, me manda a por patatas fritas. Y a ti, que eres su novia, te pone aquí de guardia.
CHUSA	No soy su novia, y no estoy de guardia.
JAIMITO	¿Se ha quitado el uniforme?
CHUSA	Ha entrado con él, pero supongo que se lo habrá quitado.
JAIMITO	(*Merodea alrededor de la puerta, intentando adivinar cómo va lo de dentro.*) No se lo quita ni para mear. Decía que no se iba a acostumbrar a llevarlo, ¿te acuerdas? Fíjate ahora. Todo el día de madero.

(Sigue al lado de la puerta. Parece que va a llamar.)

CHUSA	¿Te quieres quitar de ahí y dejarlos en paz?
JAIMITO	¡Que no me da la gana! ¿Qué pasa, eh? Se mete ahí el tío que te gusta con otra chorva y tú aquí, tan tranquilamente. Es que eres, tía, como la sábana de abajo. ¡Qué pachorra, y qué…!
CHUSA	¿Quieres que me ponga a llorar o que llame a los bomberos? Además, ayer se lo pedimos nosotros, ¿no?
JAIMITO	Ayer era ayer, y hoy es hoy. Estábamos los cuatro…, era otra cosa. ¡Así no me da la gana!
CHUSA	Tú no tienes nada que ver en esto, ni yo tampoco. No sé cómo no te das cuenta.

(Coge un jersey grandón de su armario, se lo pone y va hacia la puerta de la calle.)

JAIMITO	¿A dónde vas?

JAIMITO	It was to get things going a bit.
CHUSA	They didn't need it. His mother will drink it when she comes over.
JAIMITO	(*Reacting.*) That Alberto is a bastard. I'm up to... with him. He hides himself away in there with her and, hey. No beer or gin or anything. (*Shouting.*) Is this what I bought crisps for?
CHUSA	Don't shout.
JAIMITO	Dickhead here got sent for crisps. And you, the girlfriend, are put here on security patrol.
CHUSA	I'm not his girlfriend, and I'm not on patrol.
JAIMITO	Has he taken the uniform off?
CHUSA	He had it on when he went in, but I imagine he'll have taken it off.
JAIMITO	(*He prowls around the door, trying to work out how it's going inside.*) He doesn't take it off, not even to piss. He said he wouldn't get used to wearing it, you remember? Look at him now. One hundred percent copper, twenty-four seven.

(*He stays next to the door. It looks as though he's going to knock.*)

CHUSA	Do you want to come away and leave them be?
JAIMITO	I don't want to! What's going on, eh? The guy you like locks himself away there with another bird and you, here, quiet as a mouse. So passive and so...!
CHUSA	What do you want? For me to start crying or phone the fire brigade? Anyway, wasn't it us who asked them yesterday?
JAIMITO	Yesterday was yesterday, and today is today. The four of us were... it was something else. I don't know how you don't click.

(*She gets an oversized sweater from the wardrobe, and heads for the front door.*)

JAIMITO	Where are you going?

CHUSA   Por ahí, a dar una vuelta hasta que acabe el numerito. (*Dolida.*) No me importa nada, ¿sabes?, pero no me apetece estar aquí de guardia, como tú dices.

JAIMITO   Es un mariconazo. Siempre hace lo que le da la gana, y cuando le da la gana.

CHUSA   Pues ella tampoco es manca. Ha sido la que menos ha querido esperar, qué te crees. (*Mira hacia la puerta.*) Al fin y al cabo fue idea mía. Prepárales la cerveza y las patatas fritas para cuando salgan que tomen algo. Estarán cansados.

(Llegan a la puerta de la calle. Se miran.)

JAIMITO   Abre, a ver si hay suerte y es otra vez su madre, y se les jode el plan.

(Al abrir CHUSA, vemos en el descansillo a dos chicos jóvenes, el pelo muy corto, buena ropa y evidentemente de clase social alta.)

ABEL   (*Desde fuera.*) Venimos de parte de Sebas (*Cara de CHUSA de no saber quién es*), el camarero del Pub Valentín, que os conoce; uno alto, con bigote...

CHUSA   No sé quién es. (*A JAIMITO.*) ¿Tú sabes quién es? ¿Lo conoces?

JAIMITO   De vista. Es amigo de Ricardo, me parece.

(Entran, ABEL delante, y de detrás el otro, NANCHO, con pinta muy nerviosa y algo extraño en la cara.)

ABEL   Nos ha dicho que vosotros a lo mejor teníais algo para vendernos.

JAIMITO   No nos queda casi nada. (*A CHUSA.*) ¿Verdad?

ABEL   Lo que sea... unos gramos... Lo necesitamos, aunque sólo sea para un pico.

CHUSA   De eso no tenemos, tú. No tenemos nada.

CHUSA   Out and about, to have a wander before the big event comes to an end. (*Hurt.*) It doesn't bother me in the least, you know? But I don't fancy being here on patrol as you call it.

JAIMITO   He's a wanker. He always does whatever he wants whenever he wants.

CHUSA   Well she's not backwards in coming forwards either. It was her, I'll have you know, who least wanted to wait. (*She looks towards the door.*) At the end of the day, it was my idea. Get the beer and crisps ready for them so they have something for when they come out. They'll be tired.

(Someone knocks on the front door. They look at each other.)

JAIMITO   Open up, we might hit lucky if it's mother again who'll fuck up their plan.

(When CHUSA opens the door, we see two young lads on the landing with very short hair, good clothes and clearly from a high social class.)

ABEL   (*From outside.*) Sebas sent us (*CHUSA looks as if she doesn't know who that is*), the barman from Pub Valentín who knows you; a tall guy with a moustache…

CHUSA   I don't know who he is. (*To JAIMITO.*) You know who he is? Is he an acquaintance of yours?

JAIMITO   I know him by sight. I think he's a friend of Ricardo.

(They come in. ABEL first, and then the other guy, NANCHO, who has something strange on his face and gives the impression of being very nervous.)

ABEL   He told us you guys might have something to sell us.

JAIMITO   We've hardly got anything left. (*To CHUSA.*) Right?

ABEL   Whatever you've got. We need it even if it's only enough for one hit.

CHUSA   Listen you, we've got nothing of that sort. We don't have anything.

ABEL (*A JAIMITO.*) Has dicho antes que tenías un poco. Pues lo que sea, ya. No jodas ahora. A ver si te vas a volver atrás.

JAIMITO Oye, no, te he dicho que teníamos un poco, pero de chocolate, nada más. Nosotros a eso no le damos.

ABEL ¿Chocolate? Vamos, no jodas. (*Al otro, que está con el mono cada vez más nervioso.*) Este se cree que somos gilipollas. ¡Saca la navaja, mecagüen su puta madre!

(Saca de pronto NANCHO una navaja y amenaza, nerviosísimo, a JAIMITO y CHUSA, que retroceden asustados.)

ABEL ¡Venga! ¡Tráelo aquí ahora mismo, todo lo que tengáis! Si no (*A NANCHO*) le metes un navajazo a ese muerto de hambre de mierda. (*Se oyen en este momento ruidos y jadeos en la habitación. ABEL retrocede asustado al oírlo. Coge luego de un rincón una especie de barra de hierro que se encuentra. Va hacia JAIMITO, hablando a NANCHO.*) ¡Coge a ésa, que no grite! (*NANCHO lo hace, poniendo amenazador el cuchillo en el cuello de CHUSA, tapándole la boca con la otra mano. ABEL amenaza con el hierro a JAIMITO.*) ¡Di al que esté ahí que salga! ¡Con cuidado! ¡Vamos!

JAIMITO (*Golpeando la puerta tratando de aparentar normalidad, quedando muy falso en su intento.*) ¿Alberto? ¿Estás ahí? Oye, Alberto, a ver si puedes salir un momento. Sal si puedes. No pasa nada, pero sal. (*Se oye la voz de ALBERTO dentro refunfuñando, y las risas de ELENA. NANCHO acerca más el cuchillo a la garganta de CHUSA.*) ¡Alberto! (*Golpea ahora mas fuerte.*) ¡Sal, joder! ¡Sal de una vez! (*Se oye dentro a ALBERTO protestar, y ruidos confusos.*)

ALBERTO (*Apareciendo en calzoncillos por detrás de la puerta.*) A ver qué coño pasa ahora...

ABEL   (*To* JAIMITO.) You said, before, you had a little. Whatever it is, hand it over. Don't fuck about now. Let's see if you're gonna backtrack.

JAIMITO   No. Listen, I said we had a little, but of weed, nothing else. We don't give out that stuff.

ABEL   Weed. Come on, don't fuck about. (*The other guy, who's in withdrawal, is becoming increasingly nervous.*). This guy thinks we're pricks. Get the knife out! Fuck you and fuck your mother!

(*NANCHO suddenly takes a knife out and nervously threatens* JAIMITO *and* CHUSA, *who both move back in fear.*)

ABEL   Come on! Bring it here right now, everything you've got! If not (*to* NANCHO), shank this miserable sack of shit. (*At this point, they hear noises and heavy breathing in the bedroom.* ABEL *moves back, scared on hearing this. He then picks up an iron crowbar of sorts which he finds in a corner of the room. He moves towards* JAIMITO, *speaking to* NANCHO.) Take hold of the girl, make sure she doesn't scream! (*NANCHO does as instructed, and holds the knife to* CHUSA's *neck, covering her mouth with his other hand.* ABEL *threatens* JAIMITO *with the crowbar.*) Tell whoever's in there to come out. Be careful what you do! Come on!

JAIMITO   (*Banging on the door, trying to feign normality and, in the process, coming over very unnaturally.*) Alberto? Are you there? Listen, Alberto, come out if you can for a moment. Come out if you can. Everything's fine, but come out. (*You can hear* ALBERTO *grunting inside and* ELENA's *laughs.* NANCHO *moves the knife closer to* CHUSA's *throat.*) Alberto! (*He now bangs harder.*) Come out, for fuck's sake. Come out. (*You can hear* ALBERTO *protesting inside, and confused noises.*)

ALBERTO   (*Appearing in his boxers from behind the door.*) All right, what the hell's going on now.

(ABEL llega hasta él con la barra en alto, y le empuja contra la pared.)

ABEL   ¡Quieto ahí! *(Da una patada a la puerta abriéndola del todo. Al fondo vemos a ELENA, paralizada y desnuda. Reacciona tapándose con lo primero que pilla.)* Estaban chingando, no te jode. ¡Sal, sal para fuera, no te quedes ahí, que te queremos ver bien!

(Sale ELENA despacio, aterrada. ALBERTO trata de meterse, avanzando.)

ALBERTO   ¿Qué pasa? ¿A qué viene esto...?

ABEL   *(Empujándole otra vez contra la pared, mucho más fuerte ahora, y levantando la barra sobre su cabeza.)* ¡Que te estés quieto, mierda! *(A ELENA.)* ¡Venga, aquí! ¡Y no te tapes tanto, suelta eso! ¿Te da vergüenza? ¡Que lo sueltes, que te doy....! *(A NANCHO, que está mirándola fijamente mientras sigue sujetando a CHUSA.)* ¿Está buena, eh? ¿Te la quieres tirar? ¡Vosotros quietos!

(ALBERTO mira a JAIMITO desconcertado y éste trata de ganar tiempo y bajar un poco el clima de violencia.)

JAIMITO   Han venido a por caballo de parte del Sebas... un amigo; pero ya les hemos dicho que no teníamos... y se han puesto, fíjate. *(A NANCHO.)* ¡Suéltela, que no va a hacer nada!, ¿verdad, Chusa? Cuidado con la navaja... Vamos a hablar... lo que sea... pero suéltala. *(ABEL ha cogido la punta del vestido con que se medio tapa ELENA poniéndoselo delante, y tira, mientras ella trata de retroceder sin soltar la prenda.)*

ALBERTO   Oye... que le vas a hacer daño a la chica... Nos sentamos y hablamos tranquis, tíos, entre colegas,

(ABEL goes right up to him and, holding the crowbar up, pushes him against the wall.)

ABEL   Keep still there! (*He kicks the door, opening it completely. At the far end of the room we can see ELENA still as a statue and naked. She reacts by covering herself with the first thing she can lay her hands on.*) They were shagging, fucking hell. Come out, come on out, don't stand there, we want to be able to see you properly!

(ELENA comes out slowly, terrified. ALBERTO tries to intervene, moving forward.)

ALBERTO   What's going on? What's all this about?

ABEL   (*Pushing him against the wall again, but much more forcefully this time, and raising the crowbar above his head.*) Keep still, you piece of shit. (*To ELENA.*) Come here! Don't cover yourself up so much, let that go! Does it embarrass you? Let it go, I'll give you… (*To NANCHO who's looking intensely at her whilst continuing to restrain CHUSA.*) She's hot isn't she? You wanna fuck her? You lot, keep still.

(ALBERTO, disconcerted, looks at JAIMITO, and tries to buy some time and calm the violent situation down somewhat.)

JAIMITO   They've come for some smack. Sebas… a friend, sent them, but we've already told them we don't have any… and they've got all, well you can see. (*To NANCHO.*) Let her go, she's not going to do anything. Isn't that right, Chusa? Take care with the knife… We can talk about… whatever… but let her go. (*ABEL has grabbed hold of the edge of the dress which ELENA was half covering herself with. He positions himself in front of her and starts tugging at it whilst she tries to move backwards without letting go.*)

ALBERTO   Listen… you're going to hurt the girl… Let's sit down and we can talk guys, all nice and chilled.

¿no? Nos lo hacemos bien... sin jaleos... lo que
queráis.

JAIMITO   ¡Pero suelta! ¡Suéltala! ¡Que la sueltes!

(Se pone en medio. ABEL amaga con la barra y JAIMITO retrocede.)

ABEL   *(A JAIMITO.)* ¡Te parto la cabeza como te metas otra
vez! *(A ELENA.)* ¡Que te doy a ti, gilípollas! Estabas
chingando, ¿eh?

*(Da un fuerte tirón y se queda con la ropa en la mano. Ella se refugia
desnuda detrás de ALBERTO.)*

ALBERTO   *(Cubriéndola, trata de ganar tiempo, y poder hacer
algo.)* Bueno, bueno, ¿qué pasa? Que queréis caballo,
Es eso sólo. ¿Si os lo damos nos dejáis en paz? *(A
JAIMITO.)* Pues dales el caballo de una vez. ¿A que
lo necesitáis? Pues ya está. Yo os lo traigo si queréis,
que sé dónde está, pero sin hacer nada a nadie. No
armar lío por estas cosas. Si necesitáis caballo...

ABEL   *(A JAIMITO, amenazador.)* ¿No teníais, eh? ¡Te voy a
partir a ti...!

JAIMITO   ¡Pero suéltala! ¡Que la sueltes, que la vas a ahogar!

*(JAIMITO retrocede, asustado ante el amago de ABEL.
A una señal de ABEL, NANCHO destapa la boca a
CHUSA. JAIMITO ahora intenta seguir con el plan de
ALBERTO.)* Casi la ahogas. Es que tenemos poco, y no
os conocíamos. Luego, si os ponéis así, a lo bestia...
Dáselo, Alberto...

ALBERTO   A ver, que preparen el dinero.

ABEL   Ahora gratis, ¿está claro? Y sin cachondeos. ¡Todo
lo que tengáis, sácalo! Si no nos tiramos a ésta, y a tí
también...

| | We're amongst mates, aren't we? We'll sort it out fine… no hassle needed… whatever you want. |
| JAIMITO | But let her go…! Let her go! Let her go for Christ's sake. |

(He puts himself between them. ABEL makes a threatening gesture with the crowbar and JAIMITO backs off.)

| ABEL | (*To JAIMITO.*) Interfere again and I'll crack your skull open! (*To ELENA.*) And you, you silly bitch, I'll give you! You were shagging, eh? |

(He gives a forceful tug and is left with the item of clothing in his hand. She takes refuge, naked, behind ALBERTO.)

ALBERTO	(*Covering her, he tries to buy time so as to be able to do something.*) Alright, alright, what's up? You want some smack. That's all. And if we give you some, will you leave us in peace? (*To JAIMITO.*) Well just get it over with and give them the smack. I bet you need it? Well fine, problem solved. I'll bring it for you if you want as I know where it is, but nobody gets hurt. No need to create a ruckus for these things. If you need smack…
ABEL	(*Threateningly to JAIMITO.*) You don't have any, eh? I'm going to split your…!
JAIMITO	But let her go! Let her go, you're going to suffocate her. (*JAIMITO backs off scared by the gesture from ABEL. NANCHO, following a sign from ABEL, removes the gag from CHUSA's mouth. JAIMITO now tries to play along with ALBERTO's plan.*) You nearly suffocated her. The thing is we don't have much, and we didn't know you. Now you get like this, all heavy… Hand it over, Alberto…
ALBERTO	Hang on, let them get the cash ready.
ABEL	It's for free now. Is that clear? And no funny business. Give us everything you've got! If you don't, we'll fuck the girl, and you as well.

JAIMITO	A ti te ha entrado el mono violador hoy. No te lo montes así, tío, de verdad, que así no vas a ningún lado.
ALBERTO	Si quieres pincharte, te pinchas y ya está. Te chutas bien y tranquilo.
JAIMITO	Y si luego quieres follar, pues follamos, y no pasa nada, pero por las buenas, ¿verdad, Chusa?
ALBERTO	Anda, guarda la navaja esa, y vamos a hablar...
ABEL	Lo primero la harina. Venga, traedlo aquí, todo.
ALBERTO	Está ahí dentro. Un momento, que lo saco. (*Va al cuarto.*)
ABEL	¡Quieto! Que lo traiga este gilipollas. Venga, y cuidado.
JAIMITO	(*Va hacia el cuarto y mira a ALBERTO sin saber bien qué hacer. Finalmente decide seguir adelante como sea con lo que cree que pensaba hacer él.*) Bueno, pues voy yo, pero no te enrolles mal. (*Trata de hacer una broma.*) Anda, Elena, sigúeles haciendo un strip-tease aquí a los amigos, mientras yo les traigo la harina: «Tariro, tariro...».

(*Entra en el cuarto canturreando música de strip-tease, y se le oye seguir cantándolo dentro. Como la puerta ha quedado entreabierta y pueden acercarse y mirar lo que pasa dentro, CHUSA trata de llamar la atención para que dejen de estar pendientes de él.*)

CHUSA	(*A ELENA.*) Vas a coger frío, y tú, Alberto, también. Estás guapísimo en calzoncillos. Nos podríamos desnudar todos, y así estábamos todos igual... (*Tararea ahora la misma música de JAIMITO.*) «Tariro, tariro...»

(*De pronto aparece en la puerta del cuarto JAIMITO con la ropa de policía de ALBERTO a medio poner, pistola en mano apuntando nerviosísimo.*)

JAIMITO	¡Manos arriba! ¡Aquí la policía! ¡Os mato si os movéis! ¡Arriba las manos! ¡Arriba las manos

JAIMITO	You've come over all rapist cold-turkey today. Don't get like that, mate, honestly it won't get you anywhere.
ALBERTO	If you want to shoot up, shoot up and that's that. You can get your nice hit, no problem.
JAIMITO	And then, if you want to fuck, well we'll fuck, and that's fine, but with the right vibe. Right, Chusa?
ALBERTO	Come on, put that knife away, and let's talk.
ABEL	First, the powder. Come on, bring it here, all of it.
ALBERTO	It's inside. Hang on a minute, I'll get it. (*He goes towards the bedroom.*)
ABEL	Keep still! Let this prick get it! Come on, and be careful what you do.
JAIMITO	(*He goes towards the bedroom and looks at ALBERTO without really knowing what to do. He eventually decides to keep going, by whatever means possible, and do what he thinks ALBERTO was going to.*) Fine, I'll go, but don't make things any more complicated. (*He tries to crack a joke.*) Come on, Elena, carry on doing a striptease for our friends whilst I bring the powder. "Da, da, da, da da."ˣⁱⁱ

(*He goes into the bedroom humming the music for a striptease, and you can hear him continuing to sing inside. As the door has been left ajar, and they could potentially move towards it and see what is happening inside, CHUSA tries to make a scene to stop them observing what he's up to.*)

CHUSA	(*To ELENA.*) You'll catch a cold and you as well Alberto. You look really handsome in boxers. We could all take our clothes off, and then we'd all be the same. (*She now hums the same music as JAIMITO.*) "Da, da, da, da, da…"

(*JAIMITO suddenly appears at the bedroom door with ALBERTO's police clothes half on and a gun in his hand nervously taking aim.*)

JAIMITO	Hands in the air! The police are here! If you move, I'll kill you! Hands in the air! Hands in the air right now,

ahora mismo, y suelta eso! ¡Y tú! ¡Drogadictos, a la comisaría los dos, y a la cárcel! ¿Es que no oís? Cuento tres y disparo: ¡Una, dos y tres!

(De pronto se le escapa un tiro, que hace que todos reaccionen: ALBERTO y las dos mujeres tirándose al suelo, y ABEL y NANCHO abriendo la puerta y desapareciendo escaleras abajo a toda velocidad. ALBERTO se levanta, va hacia JAIMITO, que se ha quedado paralizado mirando la pistola, se la quita, va a la puerta y sale detrás de ellos en calzoncillos. Se le oye fuera hablar con alguien.)

OFF ALBERTO   No, no es nada, padre. No se preocupe. Es que se me ha disparado al limpiarla, sin querer. ¿Un agujero en la pared? Ponga usted otro tapón.

(Entra y cierra. Coge su ropa que se está quitando JAIMITO, y se la pone. ELENA se viste también.)

ALBERTO   Era el cura. Esos están ya a diez kilómetros. *(Mira a JAIMITO.)* Tú estás pirao Si nos das a uno, ¿qué? pero ¿has visto dónde has apuntado?

JAIMITO   Se me ha escapado, Alberto, de verdad. No sé lo que ha pasado.

ALBERTO   Ha pasado que has quitado el seguro, y casi matas a alguien. Has apretado el gatillo, si no no se dispara sola. Eso es lo que ha pasado. ¡La madre que le…! Trae la gorra, anda… Inútil.

CHUSA   Ya está bien. Gracias a él no nos ha pasado nada, con tiro o sin tiro.

ELENA   Voy a devolver,

CHUSA   Pues échalo en el water, guapa, a ver si nos colocas aquí el zumo.

JAIMITO   *(Sorprendidísimo aún de su propia heroicidad.)* Anda que… *(A CHUSA.)* ¿Te has fijado? *(Simula con la mano la pistola y hace el tiro con la boca, soplando después el cañón.)* ¡Pum…! *(Le da la risa.)*

CHUSA   *(Siguiéndole.)* Muy bien, pistonudo. ¿Has visto cómo

and drop that! And you! Druggies, the police station and prison for the pair of you. Can't you hear me? I'll count to three and shoot: one, two and three!

(He suddenly lets a shot go off accidentally, making everyone react: ALBERTO and the two women throw themselves onto the floor, and ABEL and NANCHO open the door and disappear down the stairs as fast as they can. ALBERTO gets up and goes towards JAIMITO, who's stopped in his tracks staring at the gun; he takes it off him and goes to the door pursuing them in his boxers. You can hear him talking to somebody outside.)

ALBERTO'S VOICE No, it's nothing, Father, Don't you worry. The thing is I fired a shot when cleaning it without meaning to. A hole in the wall? Fill it with another cork.

(He comes in and closes the door. He picks up his clothes that JAIMITO is in the process of taking off. ELENA also gets dressed.)

ALBERTO   It was the priest. They'll be miles away by now. (*He looks at JAIMITO.*) You've gone nuts. What would have happened if you'd hit one of us? But, did you look where you were aiming?

JAIMITO   It just went off. Alberto, honestly. I don't know what happened.

ALBERTO   What happened was you took the safety valve off, and nearly killed someone. You pulled the trigger, if not it wouldn't have fired on its own. Christ above. Give me the hat, and get out of my sight you moron.

CHUSA   That's enough. With or without the bullet, it's thanks to him that nothing happened to us.

ELENA   I'm going to wretch.

CHUSA   Well go and bring it up in the toilet, darling, or you'll end up spilling your juice up here.

JAIMITO   (*Still flabbergasted by his own heroic behaviour.*) I mean… (*To CHUSA.*) Did you see? (*He mimics the gun with his hand and the sound of the shot with his mouth, and then blows to make the sound of the barrel.*) Pam… (*It makes him laugh.*)

CHUSA   (*Following on from him.*) Great, top dollar. Did you

corrían? Y la cara que han puesto cuando te han visto salir con la pinta esa y la pistola. Es que parecías del Oeste. (*Se ríe también.*)

ALBERTO   (*Acabando de vestirse.*) Eso, reíros. Casi matas a alguien, me puedo buscar un follón por tu culpa, y os reís.

JAIMITO   Como vi que ibas tú a..., pues yo...

ALBERTO   No es lo mismo. ¿Pero tú te crees que se puede manejar una pistola sin saber? Y yo no iba a disparar, ni mucho menos. ¡A quién se le ocurre liarse a tiros! Si estaban ya medio convencidos. Dos minutos más, y tan amigos. Como mucho ponerte el uniforme, o coger la pistola y darles un susto en último extremo, pero no ponerse a disparar, que estás loco.

CHUSA   Y dale.

ALBERTO   No se te ocurra volver a tocarla. ¿Me oyes?, que no tienes ni puta idea de nada. Una pistola es muy peligrosa, las carga el diablo. (*Se ha acabado de vestir, y ahora ilustra, pistola en mano, su disertación.*) Si no sabes, se te disparan por nada.

(*Como para mostrar lo que dice, maneja la pistola, apunta, y dispara, metiendo un tiro a JAIMITO en el brazo izquierdo. Se quedan todos de piedra.*)

JAIMITO   ¡Huy, la...! ¡Que me ha dado un tiro éste...!

ALBERTO   Perdona. Se me ha disparado. Joder...

JAIMITO   (*Intentando sentarse.*) Me parece que me mareo. Sí, me mareo. Me voy a desmayar... ¡Ay!

(*ELENA, que ha salido del lavabo al oír el tiro, al ver así a JAIMITO, le dan de nuevo arcadas y vuelve a entrar.*)

CHUSA   (*Sujetando a JAIMITO.*) ¡A un hospital! (*Habla a ALBERTO, que sigue mirando sin reaccionar.*) ¡Hay que llevarle a un hospital, o a la Casa de Socorro...!

	see how they ran? And their faces when they saw you run out looking like that, and with the gun. You looked like you'd come straight out of the Wild West. (*She also laughs.*)
ALBERTO	(*Finishing getting dressed.*) That's it, laugh. You nearly kill someone, I might find myself in a bloody mess because of you and you laugh.
JAIMITO	When I saw that you were going to... well I...
ALBERTO	It's not the same. But do you think you can operate a gun without having the know-how? I wasn't going to shoot or anything of the kind. Who thinks of getting mixed up in a shoot-out! They were already half-convinced. Two minutes more, and everyone would have been getting on great guns. At the most, you could have put on the uniform or, as a last resort, picked up the gun to scare them but not get ready to shoot, you're crazy.
CHUSA	And hand it over to him.
ALBERTO	Don't even think about touching it again. You hear me? You don't have a fucking idea about anything. Guns are very dangerous, they're loaded by the devil. (*He's finished getting dressed and now, gun in hand, illustrates his point.*) If you weren't aware, they go off just like that.

(*As if to demonstrate what he's saying, he holds the gun, points and fires, putting a bullet into JAIMITO's left arm. They all freeze.*)

JAIMITO	Hey, the...! The guy's shot me...!
ALBERTO	I'm so sorry. It went off on me... Fuck...
JAIMITO	(*Trying to sit down.*) I'm coming over all nauseous, I think. Yes, I'm nauseous. I'm going to faint... Ay!

(*ELENA, who has come out of the loo on hearing the shot, needs to vomit again after seeing the state of JAIMITO and goes back in.*)

CHUSA	(*Holding JAIMITO up.*) To a hospital! (*She's speaking to ALBERTO who carries on looking without reacting.*) We have to take him to a hospital, or to the charity ward.

ALBERTO	(*A JAIMITO.*) Has quitado el seguro, no me dices nada, y te pones ahí delante.
CHUSA	Deja de decir memeces. Hay que llevarle a algún sitio. ¡Una ambulancia!
JAIMITO	¡No, en una ambulancia no, que me da mucha aprensión! Mejor en un taxi. Me mareo, me estoy..., se me va la...
CHUSA	(*A ALBERTO.*) Sujeta, que se cae. ¡Que se cae!

(Le cogen entre los dos, medio desmayado y van hacia la puerta. Abren y van a salir, cruzándose en ese momento con DOÑA ANTONIA que llega.)

DOÑA ANTONIA	¿Pero qué hacéis? ¡Anda que...! Luego decís que fumar eso no es malo, ¡Virgen Santísima!
CHUSA	Que no, señora. Que no es eso. Es que su hijo le ha pegado un tiro.
DOÑA ANTONIA	Algo habrá hecho. Todo esto os pasa por lo que os pasa. Verás cuando se entere tu padre, con lo formal que se ha vuelto desde que ha salido de la cárcel.
ALBERTO	Así no le podemos bajar. Agua, dale agua.
DOÑA ANTONIA	Una copa de coñac es lo que hay que darle a este chico.
CHUSA	(*Va a por agua a la cocina.*) Que aquí no tenemos coñac, señora.
DOÑA ANTONIA	Lo digo por la tensión, que es muy bueno. Si hubierais estado en la reunión, conmigo, no os pasarían estas cosas.
CHUSA	(*Dándole agua a JAIMITO, que se recupera un poco.*) ¿Qué? ¿Estás mejor? ¿Te duele?
JAIMITO	Estoy bien, sólo un poco mareado.
ALBERTO	Me va a costar esto un lío en la jefatura de no te menees.
CHUSA	Venga, deja eso ya y agarra. (*A JAIMITO.*) Vamos a bajar para llevarte a algún sitio, a que te curen. ¿Puedes?

ALBERTO	(*To JAIMITO.*) You take the safety catch off, don't tell me anything, and stand there right in front of me.
CHUSA	Stop talking nonsense. We have to take him somewhere. An ambulance!
JAIMITO	No, not in an ambulance, that'd make me very anxious. Better in a taxi. I'm feeling nauseous, I am… I'm losing…
CHUSA	(*To ALBERTO.*) Hold him up, he's going to fall down. He'll fall down!

(The two of them support JAIMITO, semi-collapsed, and head for the door. They open it and, as they are leaving, cross paths with DOÑA ANTONIA who's arriving.)

DOÑA ANTONIA	But what are you up to? Come, now… And then you say there's nothing wrong with smoking. Oh, most holy Virgin!
CHUSA	No, madam, it's not like that. What's happened is that your son has shot him.
DOÑA ANTONIA	He'll have done something. What comes around goes around. Wait till your father, who's turned so respectable since coming out of prison, hears.
ALBERTO	We can't take him down like this. Water, give him water.
DOÑA ANTONIA	A glass of brandy is what this lad needs.
CHUSA	(*She goes to the kitchen for water.*) We don't have brandy here, madam.
DOÑA ANTONIA	I only said it because it's good for stress. These things wouldn't happen if you'd all been in the meeting with me.
CHUSA	(*Giving water to JAIMITO who's making a slight recovery.*) What? Are you feeling better? Does it hurt?
JAIMITO	I'm fine, just a bit nauseous.
ALBERTO	The bosses are going to make mince meat out of me for this.
CHUSA	Come on, forget about that and hold tight (*To JAIMITO.*) We're going to take you downstairs to take you somewhere, so they can fix you up. Are you able?

JAIMITO	Sí, pero en una ambulancia no.
CHUSA	Vamos en un taxi.
JAIMITO	Me ha dado en el brazo, aquí arriba. No lo puedo casi mover... ¡Ay!
DOÑA ANTONIA	Pues te ha salvado Dios, porque si te da en la cabeza, o en el corazón... Has tenido suerte.
JAIMITO	(*Mientras le sacan por la puerta entre los dos.*) Sí, suerte, yo siempre tengo mucha suerte. (*Salen.*)
ELENA	(*Saliendo del lavabo.*) ¿Se han ido? ¡Ay, Dios mío!
DOÑA ANTONIA	¡Ginebra! (*Descubre la botella encima de la mesa.*) ¡Hay ginebra! Mira, si te encuentras mal, te tomas una copa de esto y se te pasa, ya verás. (*Trae de la cocina dos vasos y echa ginebra después de abrir la botella.*) Bebe, para la tensión. ¡Ay, Dios, qué hijos éstos! ¡Qué disgustos dan! (*Beben las dos.*) Mira cómo lo han puesto todo de sangre. Hay que quitarla, que si se seca no hay quien la saque.

(*ELENA, entre la ginebra que le cae fatal, y ver la sangre, tiene que ir corriendo otra vez al lavabo.*)

DOÑA ANTONIA	Oye, ¿no estarás embarazada? Estos, cualquier guarrería. ¡Ay Señor, Señor!

(*Se sirve una nueva copa, se la bebe de un trago y se limpia cuidadosamente la boca con un babero que saca del bolso. Oscuro, y fin del primer acto.*)

JAIMITO	Yes, but not in an ambulance.
CHUSA	We'll go by taxi.
JAIMITO	He got me in the arm, here at the top. I can hardly move it... Ay!
DOÑA ANTONIA	Well God has saved you, because if it hits you in the head or the heart... You've had a lucky escape.
JAIMITO	(*As he's being carried through the door by the two of them.*) Yes, luck, I'm always really lucky. (*They leave.*)
ELENA	(*Coming out of the toilet.*) Have they gone? Oh, my Lord!
DOÑA ANTONIA	Gin! (*She finds the bottle on top of the table.*) There's gin! Look, if you're feeling rough, have a glass of this and it'll go away, you'll see. (*She brings two glasses from the kitchen, opens the bottle, and pours the gin.*) Drink, it calms the nerves. Oh, my Lord, the state of these kids! What upset they cause! (*The two of them drink.*) Look how they've got blood everywhere. We have to clean it up; if it dries, it's impossible to get it out.

(*Between the gin, which doesn't agree with her in the least, and seeing the blood,* ELENA *has to run to the toilet again.*)

DOÑA ANTONIA	Listen, you're not pregnant are you? There's nothing so deprived I wouldn't put it past this lot. Oh God, God in Almighty Heaven!

(*She serves herself another glass, and downs it in one. She carefully cleans her mouth with a bib that she takes out of her handbag. Blackout, and the end of the First Act.*)

ACTO SEGUNDO

Escena Primera

Han pasado varios días. El mismo escenario que en el acto primero, aunque las cosas están ordenadas de forma distinta – más convencionalmente. ALBERTO ha ido a recoger a JAIMITO al Hospital. CHUSA anda por tierras del moro. DOÑA ANTONIA toma una copa tras otra de la botella de ginebra, ya casi vacía, mientras plancha la ropa. ELENA la escucha sentada a su lado cosiendo.

DOÑA ANTONIA Lo peor fue el disgusto que se llevó su padre al enterarse. Es que ha salido de la cárcel hecho otra persona: serio, honrado, trabajador... Ha estudiado y todo. Ahora es universitario de carrera, como tú, Ha acabado cuarto de Económicas, así que en un año lo termina. ¿A ti cuánto te queda?

ELENA A mí más. Dos años más, por lo menos.

DOÑA ANTONIA Fíjate. Pues muy formal ha salido, y muy educado. El sábado pasado vino conmigo a la reunión neocatecumenal, y habló. Daba gusto oírle, hija. Qué labia. Dijo que en estos nuevos tiempos hace falta que cambiemos todos, como está cambiando el país, y como él ha cambiado. Y que había que trabajar mucho, mucho para levantar España entre todos. Así, como te lo digo. Dijo que él, antes, con Franco, robaba porque robaba todo el mundo, pero que ahora, con los socialistas, es diferente. Huy, habló muy bien de Felipe González, de Guerra, del Boyer, de todos. Él se va a hacer del partido. A mí me quiere hacer también, y a los de la reunión a lo mejor. Es que hay que ver cómo se ha vuelto: serio, formal, trabajador... ¡Y la suerte que ha tenido con el trabajo! Conoció

ACT TWO

Scene One

A few days have passed. The same stage as in Act One, although things have been arranged differently – more conventionally. ALBERTO has gone to pick JAIMITO up at the hospital. CHUSA is away travelling through Moorish lands. DOÑA ANTONIA has glass after glass from the bottle of gin, which is now nearly empty, whilst she does the ironing. ELENA, at her side, listens whilst sewing.

DOÑA ANTONIA   The worst bit was how upset his father got when he found out. The thing is he's come out of prison a different person: responsible, honourable, hard-working... He's studied and everything. Now he's doing a university degree, like you. He's got through the fourth year of an Economics degree, so he'll finish in a year. How long have you got left?

ELENA   Me, longer. Two years at the least.

DOÑA ANTONIA   See, he's come out very formal and well-mannered. Last Saturday he came with me and spoke at the Neocatechumenate meeting. It was a pleasure to hear him. What a way with words. He said that in these new times, everything needs changing, like the country's changed and he's changed. And that there's a lot of work to be done, that between us we need to make Spain great again. Exactly as I'm saying it to you now. He said he used to steal under Franco because everyone stole but that now, with the Socialists, it's different. Hey, he spoke very well of Felipe González, of Guerra, of Boyer, of all of them.[7] He's going to become a party member. He wants me, and maybe those from the meeting, to do the same. It's that what he's become beggars belief: responsible, formal, hard-working... And the luck

---

[7]   These references to the (in)famously corrupt PSOE government of the 1980s were cut in the 2008 version, presumably because they were no longer topical.

allí en la cárcel a un director de un banco que había hecho un desfalco de un montón de millones. Bueno, pues este señor fue el que le animó a estudiar, y el que le daba las clases allí. Ahora, como ha salido ya y es otra vez director de otro banco, pues fíjate un puestazo que le ha dado a mi marido. Gerente o algo así. Bueno, pues a lo que íbamos, él, encantado de que Alberto trabajara en algo tan decente, ahora al enterarse del escándalo del tiro, lo del hospital, y lo de las drogas de los que vinieron, pues le ha dicho al chico que si sigue por el buen camino, que le paga los estudios para que haga el ingreso y oposiciones al Cuerpo Superior de Policía, pero que si se queda con esa gentuza, que allá se las entienda y que se vaya de casa. Que ya verá cómo va a acabar, en Carabanchel, o un sitio peor. Perdona, pero las cosas son como son, y tiene razón además.

ELENA   No, si a lo mejor en parte es verdad lo que dice.

DOÑA ANTONIA   No va por ti, hija, que tú eres una chica estupenda, de estudios, y muy formal. Y tu madre, no hay más que verla. Una señora. Y la casa que tiene.

ELENA   (*Dejando de coser.*) ¿Mi madre? ¿Conoce usted a mi madre?

DOÑA ANTONIA   He metido la pata, pero en fin. No importa que lo sepas, aunque quedamos que no te diríamos nada. Hemos ido yo y Alberto a tu casa, y hemos hablado con tu madre. Menudo disgusto tiene la pobre. Es que sois de lo que no hay.

ELENA   Sabe que estoy bien. La llamo por teléfono todos los días.

DOÑA ANTONIA   ¡Por teléfono! ¡Ay, Dios, qué hijos! Pues nada, se llevó un disgusto.

ELENA   ¿Mi madre?

he's had with work! In prison he met the executive of a bank who'd committed a multi-million fraud. Well, it was this gentleman who encouraged him to study, and gave him classes there. Now, as he's out of prison, he's back as an executive in another bank and he's given my husband an amazing job, see. Manager or something like that. Well, back to what we were saying, he was so pleased Alberto was working in something decent. On hearing about the scandal of the shooting, the hospital, the guys who came for the drugs and all that, he's said to the lad that, if he sticks on the right path, he'll pay for his studies so he can enrol and apply for a permanent position as an officer within the police force. But he'll have to leave home if he carries on with this scuz; he can make his bed and lie in it. He'll see how the story will end: in Carabanchel prison or somewhere worse. I'm sorry but that's the way things are and, in any case, he's right.

ELENA   No, perhaps there's an element of truth in what you're saying.

DOÑA ANTONIA   I'm not talking about you, my dear, you're a wonderful girl, educated and very respectable. And you only have to see your mother. A proper lady. And the place she has.

ELENA   (*Stopping sewing.*) My mother? Do you know my mother?

DOÑA ANTONIA   I've put my foot in it, but well. It doesn't matter that you know although we agreed not to say anything to you. Me and Alberto have gone to your place, and we have spoken with your mother. The poor woman is besides herself. The thing is you lot are a law onto yourselves.

ELENA   She knows I'm okay. I phone her every day.

DOÑA ANTONIA   By phone. God above, what are these kids like! Well, anyway, they're very distressed.

ELENA   Who, my mother?

DOÑA ANTONIA   No, no mi marido, con lo del tiro del Jaimito ese, que es un Jaimito de verdad. Él fue el que aconsejó a mi hijo para que dieran el parte de que el tiro se lo había dado Jaimito mismamente, como una imprudencia, sin querer. Que cogió la pistola, y eso. El cabeza dura no quería al principio, no te creas. Es lo que yo me digo, ése, al fin y al cabo, le da igual. No tiene oficio ni beneficio, así que... Pero a mi hijo le podían haber metido un paquete gordísimo. Hasta le podían haber expulsado del cuerpo, fíjate. Y más si se enteran de ésos que venían buscando droga, y todo el escándalo. ¡Dios mío!

ELENA   Yo me puse malísima.

DOÑA ANTONIA   Y cualquiera que tenga buen corazón. Es que eso de las drogas es terrible, hija. Tú ten mucho cuidado. Tú ni porros ni nada, que todos empiezan por poco y fíjate cómo terminan. Hasta niños pequeños de seis años se pinchan, que lo he leído en una revista. Le he dicho yo mil veces que no esté con esta gentuza, pero ya ves, les tiene cariño. A ver si tú lo consigues. Hazme caso, estudia, cásate y forma una familia como Dios manda. Si no queréis casaros por la Iglesia, pues os casáis por lo civil, como dice mi marido, que en eso es muy moderno. A tu madre, Alberto le cayó de maravilla. Tenías que haberlos visto hablando como si fueran suegra y yerno. Qué casa, cómo la tiene puesta de bien. De mucho gusto todo, hija. También yo iba a estar viviendo aquí si tuviera esa casa. Con esta mugre.

ELENA   Es que no sé qué voy a decirle a Chusa cuando vuelva. Encima de que no he querido ir con ella.

DOÑA ANTONIA	No, no, my husband, with Jaimito getting shot. That Jaimito is Dennis the Menace brought to life. It was him who suggested to my son he made sure they put in the report stating that Jaimito had carelessly shot himself without meaning to. That he picked up the gun and all that. He's so pig-headed; at first he didn't want to. It's what I say to myself: in the end, it doesn't matter for him. He doesn't have a job or an income of any kind, so… But, as for my son, they could have really gone for him. See, they could even have thrown him out the force. Especially if they'd found out about them coming to look for drugs, and all that malarkey. My Lord!
ELENA	I got really sick.
DOÑA ANTONIA	As would anyone with a good heart. The thing is, my dear, that all that drugs related stuff is terrible. You be really careful. No joints or anything. They all start off with a little and look how it turns out. Even little six year-old kids are shooting up. I read it in a magazine. I've told him a thousand times not to hang around this pond-life but he's fond of them, see. See if you can make him see sense. Listen to me, study, get married and have a family, that's what God says you should do. If you don't want to get married in a church, well have a civil ceremony, as my husband who is very modern in such matters says. Your mother thought Alberto was brilliant. You should have seen them speaking away as if they were in-laws. What a place, how nicely she's got everything. Oh, my dear, it has such a nice feel. I'd sure come and live here if I had that place. With all this grime.[8]
ELENA	The thing is I don't know what I'm going to say to Chusa when she comes back. On top of the fact that I didn't want to go with her.

---

[8] Possibly as a result of Charo Reina – the actress who played Doña Antonia – being the most famous member of the cast, this scene was extended in the 2008 revival so that the older woman tries, unsuccessfully, to teach Elena to iron whilst becoming increasingly inebriated.

DOÑA ANTONIA	No tienes por qué dar explicaciones a nadie. Y no has ido a eso del moro porque no es decente, y has hecho muy bien.
ELENA	Como le había prometido ir con ella... Si ahora vuelve y...
DOÑA ANTONIA	No le haces caso a tu madre, y le vas a hacer caso a esa pelandusca que se las sabe todas. Andaba tonteando con mi hijo, que lo sé yo. Pero ya le dije que de eso nones, ni hablar. Contigo es otra cosa, porque tú tienes estudios; y por tu madre. Además, ya se lo ha dicho mi marido: «Esa chica te interesa. Los otros, fuera.» ¿La tienda esa de electrodomésticos es entera vuestra?
ELENA	Sí, ¿por qué?
DOÑA ANTONIA	Por nada, hija, por nada. Es muy bonita, y qué grande. Y luego en el sitio que está, en plena Glorieta de Quevedo. A esa tienda si se la trabaja bien se le tiene que sacar mucho.
ELENA	A mí no me gusta la tienda. Sólo he ido por allí dos o tres veces. Es muy hortera.
DOÑA ANTONIA	Tú calla y a estudiar, que es lo que tienes que hacer. De la tienda no te preocupes. Ahí en la glorieta de Quevedo tenía yo una amiga, pero se mudó a Villaverde Alto a un piso nuevo con vistas estupendas, y mucho sol. Bueno, pues lo que yo te estaba diciendo... ¿qué te estaba yo diciendo?
ELENA	Lo de Villaverde Alto, me parece.
DOÑA ANTONIA	... No, no... antes... ¿por qué te estaba yo diciendo eso? No sé dónde tengo la cabeza últimamente, hija.
ELENA	Me estaba diciendo que tenía un piso muy bonito, su amiga, en Villaverde Alto. Que se había ido a vivir...
DOÑA ANTONIA	Allí hay unos pisos estupendos, en Villaverde. Pero mejor en Móstoles. Eso ha dicho mi marido. Y a acabar la carrera, que sin una carrera hoy no se va a ningún sitio. Ya ves mi marido, con cincuenta años y todo el

DOÑA ANTONIA   You don't have to give explanations to anyone. And you haven't gone over there, to Morocco, because it's not decent, and you've done the right thing.

ELENA   As I'd promised to go with her... If now she comes back and...

DOÑA ANTONIA   You don't listen to your mother but you do to that floozie who's no better than she ought to be. She was fooling around with my son, I know that. But I said to him, don't even think about it. With you, it's something different because you've got qualifications; and because of your mother. Anyway, as my husband's already told him: "That girl's right for you. Banish the others from your mind." Does the whole electrical appliances shop belong to you?

ELENA   Yes, why?

DOÑA ANTONIA   No reason, my dear, no reason. It's very nice and so big. And the location, right by Quevedo roundabout.[xiii] If that shop's well run, you must be able to make a packet.

ELENA   I don't like the shop. I've only been there once or twice. It's really tacky.

DOÑA ANTONIA   You keep quiet and study, that's what you've got to do. Don't worry about the shop. There, on Quevedo roundabout, I had a friend but she moved out of town, to Villaverde Alto, to a new flat with amazing views and a lot of sun. Right, well, what I was saying to you... what was I saying to you?

ELENA   About Villaverde Alto, I think.

DOÑA ANTONIA   ... No, no... before that... why was I saying that? Recently, my head's been all over the shop.

ELENA   You were telling me she had a very nice flat, your friend, in Villaverde Alto. That she had gone to live...

DOÑA ANTONIA   There are some amazing flats there, in Villaverde, But even better in Móstoles. That's what my husband says. And finish the degree, you can't get anywhere without a degree these days. You can see my husband, fifty

día estudiando. Llega a casa y se pone con los libros. Quién le ha visto y quién le ve. Cómo cambia todo en España, hija. Antes es que si le ves no le conoces. Pero de eso es mejor no hablar. Ya nos dijo tu madre lo de tu padre. (*ELENA la mira sorprendida de que su madre le haya hablado del oscuro incidente de la piscina.*) Checoslovaquia está lejos, pero no tanto. Hoy en día, con los aviones..., ya verás, cualquier día se os presenta aquí, diga ella lo que diga. ¿No ha vuelto mi marido de la cárcel, que es peor? Y tan ricamente. ¡Ay, Señor, Señor! ¡Qué hombres! ¡Que todo en la vida tenga que ser siempre sufrir! Y que las cosas son como son, y que no le des más vueltas. En las reuniones nuestras neocatecumenales, que lo contamos todo, se escuchan casos que te ponen los pelos de punta. Allí desde luego lo hablamos todo, hija. Todos somos pecadores, y las cosas a la luz, que la mierda, con perdón, si no corre atasca el water. Las cosas claras, y el chocolate, espeso. El que bebe, va allí, y lo cuenta. Y el que le pega una paliza a su mujer, lo cuenta también, y se arrepiente, y se da cuenta de que es un pecador, que eso es lo importante. A veces acabamos todos llorando. Y luego las separaciones, con todo el sufrimiento de los hijos, que se los reparten como si fuesen monedas de a duro: éste para ti, éste para mí; éste me toca los sábados y los domingos, y quince días en agosto. ¡Ay, Dios mío, qué mundo éste! Yo es que enchufo la televisión y me da algo: muertos tirados por todas partes, que siempre te los sacan a la hora de comer, para más inri. Una vez fue uno allí a confesarse, ya sabes que allí nos confesamos en voz alta como te digo, delante de todos. Bueno, pues fue allí, nosotros no le conocíamos de nada, pero va tanta gente que vete tú a saber. Pues llegó allí, y empezó a decir guarrerías que había hecho con otro tío. ¡Qué vergüenza! A mí esas cosas me dan mucho asco, qué quieres que te diga. Hay cosas que no se deberían

years old and spending the whole day studying. He arrives home and gets going with the books. Anyone who looked at him now compared to what he was. Everything's changing so much in Spain, my dear. If you'd seen what he was like before, you wouldn't recognize him. But better not to talk about that. Your mother has already told us about what happened with your father. (*ELENA looks at her, surprised by the fact that her mother has spoken to her about the sinister incident in the swimming pool.*) Czechoslovakia is a long way away, but not so far. These days, with planes... you'll see, any day he'll show up here whatever she might say. My husband has come back from prison, hasn't he? And that's much worse. And done so well for himself. Oh, God above, God. What are these men like! Everything in life has to always make you suffer! And that's the way things are, don't give it a second thought. In our Neocatechumenate meetings, people tell you anything and everything, and you hear of cases that make your hair stand on end. There, of course, we talk no holds barred. We are all sinners and, pardon my French, you can't just flush shit down the toilet; it has a way of coming up again and hitting the fan. Everything in its place, and a place for everything. Those who drink, go there and tell all. Those who beat their wives, talk about it, repent, and realise they are sinners, that's the important thing. Sometimes we all end up crying. And then the separations, it's always the children who wind up suffering, divvied about as if they were loose change: this one for you, this one for me; I have this one on Saturdays and Sundays, and for fifteen days in August. Oh, my Lord, what kind of world are we living in! I just have to put on the television and it does something to me: dead people strewn all over the place and what makes it worse is that they always wheel them out at meal times. A guy once

confesar, o no dar tantos detalles, por lo menos. No eran artistas, ni nada. Era un albañil en paro y un mecánico de un taller de motos. ¡Si llegas a escuchar las cosas que contó que estuvieron haciendo... en un solar en medio de un descampado, como animales! Al final se cayó al suelo, devolvió... un desastre. Yo creo que es que estaba completamente borracho. ¡Lo que no veremos allí! ¿Y las guarradas esas de las revistas, con todas esas marranas poniendo el culo como para que les pongan una inyección? Yo acababa con eso en dos días. Así va todo. Es que pasas por un quiosco y hay que mirar al otro lado. Hay algunas que traen posturas de estar... tú me entiendes. Y el cine, y la televisión, que te meten una teta en la sopa en cuanto te descuidas. Y en color ahora es mucho peor. Parece carne de verdad. Ahora que yo cambio de canal, Alberto es muy serio, y muy buen chico. Ya ves, policía. Así que tú hazme caso, por el buen camino. Ya verás luego la alegría que dan los niños, si, mujer, y el hacerlos, que hablando claro se entiende una mejor, y hay cosas que están muy bien en la vida si se hacen decentemente y como Dios manda. Mi marido ha dicho que os regala el vídeo. Claro que por otro lados teniéndolo vosotros en la tienda es una bobada comprar uno. Y un día te tienes que venir conmigo a la reunión aunque sólo sea para verlo.

came to confess, as you know we all confess out loud
there, in front of everyone, like I say. He was there
and we didn't know him from Adam but, as so many
people come, go figure. Well, he came and started
to talk filth about what he'd done with another man.
What a disgrace! What can I say, those things disgust
me. There are things you shouldn't confess, or at
least not in so much detail. They weren't artists or
anything of the kind. It was an unemployed builder
and a mechanic from a motorcycle workshop. If you
had heard the things that he told us they were doing
in a deserted field, out in the open, like animals. In
the end he fell to the floor and threw up... I think
he must have been blind drunk. What we don't see
there! And those filthy revues, with those flighty girls
putting their buttocks in the air as if they were about
to receive an injection. Give me two days, and I'd
get rid of all that. That's how everything's going.
You pass by a newspaper kiosk and you have to
look the other way. Some of the girls in poses like...
you get what I'm saying. And the cinema, and the
television, take your eye off the ball for a second and
you have a boob in your soup. And now it's in colour,
it's worse. It looks like real flesh. Now what I do
is switch channel. Alberto is very responsible, and a
very good lad. Proof's in the pudding, a policeman.
You listen to me and follow the path of virtue. You'll
see the joy children bring soon enough and, let's be
frank because we'll understand each other better that
way, the happiness in creating them. There are things
that are wonderful in this life if done decently and in
accordance with God's plan. My husband has said
he will give you a video player.[9] Mind you, on the
other hand, it's ridiculous buying you one when you
lot have them in your shop. And you'll have to come
one day with me to the meeting even if it's just to

---

[9]   Changed to DVD player in the 2008 production.

Hay días que está muy bien, no creas que siempre es igual. He cogido un catarrazo... *(Busca un pañuelo en su bolso, y vemos aparecer por él montones de corbatas que lleva dentro.)* ¡Ay, Dios mío, Dios mío! Y que cuando no es una cosa es otra. Qué mona es esa blusa. *(Se da cuenta cómo ELENA mira las corbatas.)* Son para mí marido. Ahora gasta muchas corbatas. Como estaban rebajadas...

(Está guardándolas en el bolso cuando abren la puerta y entran ALBERTO y JAIMITO, el primero vestido de policía, como siempre, y el otro con el brazo izquierdo en cabestrillo. DOÑA ANTONIA cierra el bolso como puede, y recibe al recién llegado del hospital con fría cortesía. ELENA se le acerca con cariño.)

JAIMITO   Hola, buenas. Qué tal, doña Antonia. Hola Elena, cómo estás.

DOÑA ANTONIA   Pues mal, ya ves. Con un catarrazo.

ELENA   Estás muy bien. Se ve que te han cuidado mucho en el hospital. Y el brazo, ¿te duele?

JAIMITO   No, ya nada. Sólo lo tengo que llevar así unos días, por precaución, pero no noto nada. Está ya bien.

ELENA   Siéntate, ¿no?

(JAIMITO capta el cambio operado en la casa en los días que ha estado en el hospital. Y se siente un poco fuera de su territorio.)

JAIMITO   ¿Y qué tal por aquí?

ELENA   Bien, normal, nada de particular, ¿verdad Alberto? Desde que se fue Chusa de viaje... nosotros aquí, solos.

(Se da cuenta de que está tocando un tema delicado. JAIMITO mira enfrente de él a ELENA, ALBERTO y la madre, Y les nota distantes y violentos.)

observe. Some days it's really good, don't go thinking it's always the same. I've picked up a terrible cold. (*She looks for a hankie in her handbag, and we can make out a whole pile of ties she's got inside.*) Oh, my Lord, my Lord! When it's not one thing, it's another. That blouse is really lovely! (*She realises ELENA is looking at the ties.*) They are for my husband. He gets through a lot of ties these days. As they were in the sales.

(*She's stuffing them into her handbag when the door opens and ALBERTO, dressed as always in his police uniform, and JAIMITO, with his left arm in a sling, come in. DOÑA ANTONIA closes the handbag as best she can, and greets the recently discharged patient with cold politeness. ELENA moves towards him affectionately.*)

JAIMITO   Hi, good morning, everyone. Doña Antonia, how are you? Hi, Elena, how you doing?
DOÑA ANTONIA   Not good, as you can see. I've picked up a terrible cold.
ELENA   You look good. You can see they have taken good care of you in the hospital. And your arm, does it hurt?
JAIMITO   No, not at all now. I need to have it like this for a few days, as a precaution, but it doesn't hurt at all. It's fine now.
ELENA   Sit yourself down, won't you?

(*JAIMITO becomes aware of the changes that have taken place in the flat since he's been in hospital. And he doesn't feel completely at home.*)

JAIMITO   And, how's everything here?
ELENA   Fine, as always, nothing special. Isn't that so, Alberto? Since Chusa went off on her travels… us, here, on our own.

(*She realises she's touching on a delicate subject. JAIMITO looks across at ELENA, ALBERTO, and the mother. They look distant and hostile to him.*)

184 José Luis Alonso de Santos

ALBERTO   ¿Quieres tomar algo, un café o cualquier cosa? ¿Has comido?
JAIMITO   Sí, sí. No, no te preocupes. No quiero nada. Ya te he dicho que estoy bien, normal. Pero gracias de todas formas.
ELENA   Te hemos recogido lo de las sandalias. Está en el cuarto. Como no estabas. Además, con el brazo así no podrás trabajar ahora.
JAIMITO   No te preocupes. Está bien.

(Pausa larga y tensa. DOÑA ANTONIA se levanta de su asiento.)

DOÑA ANTONIA   Bueno, yo me voy, que me van a cerrar. (*A ALBERTO y ELENA.*) ¿Venís a cenar a casa, no? Pues hasta luego. No lleguéis tarde, que ya sabes cómo se pone tu padre. (*A JAIMITO.*) Y adiós, tú, que te mejores. (*Sale.*)

(Quedan sólo los tres. Pausa.)

ELENA   ¿Qué tal aquel señor que estaba contigo en la habitación, el de la otra cama?
JAIMITO   Salía también hoy o mañana; le dan el alta ya.
ELENA   ¿Y qué tal ha quedado?
JAIMITO   Bien. Cojo, pero bien. Le han envuelto la pierna que le han cortado en un paquete, se la han dado, y hala, para el pueblo.
ELENA   Qué tonto eres.
JAIMITO   Es la verdad. Le van a poner ahora una a pilas.
ELENA   (*Se ríe.*) Era muy simpático. Y muy gracioso.
JAIMITO   A ver qué iba a hacer. Reírse. Todo el mundo allí se estaba todo el día riendo. ¡Unas carcajadas por los pasillos! (*Pausa.*)
ELENA   Estábamos planchando unas cosas. (*Recogiendo.*)
ALBERTO   Dentro de unos días, cuando estés ya bien, tienes que pasarte por la comisaría, por lo de la declaración.
JAIMITO   Bueno. Cuando tú digas.

ALBERTO	You want to have a coffee or anything else? Have you eaten?
JAIMITO	Yes, yes. Don't worry. I don't want anything. I've already said I'm fine, back to my normal self. But, thanks anyway.
ELENA	We've put all your stuff for making sandals away. It's in the bedroom. As you weren't here. And, anyway you can't work with your arm like that.
JAIMITO	Don't you worry. It's fine.

(A long and awkward pause. DOÑA ANTONIA gets up out of her seat.)

| DOÑA ANTONIA | Right, I'm heading off because, if not, everything will be closed by the time I get out. (*To ALBERTO and ELENA.*) You'll come to have dinner at mine, won't you? Well, see you later. Don't be late, you know how your father gets. (*To JAIMITO.*) And goodbye, I hope you recover soon. (*Exit.*) |

(Only the three of them are left on stage. Pause.)

ELENA	How's the man who was with you in the room, the one in the other bed?
JAIMITO	He'll also be out today or tomorrow; they've already discharged him.
ELENA	And how is he in the end?
JAIMITO	Fine. With a limp, but fine. They have wrapped the leg they amputated up in a packet, given it to him and, hey presto, back to his village.
ELENA	You're so silly.
JAIMITO	It's true. Now he's going to get batteries put in him.
ELENA	(*Laughing.*) He was very nice. And very funny.
JAIMITO	What choice did he have? Laugh or cry. Everyone was laughing all day long there. Hysterics in the corridor! (*Pause.*)
ELENA	We were ironing some things. (*Picking them up.*)
ALBERTO	In the next few days, when you're back on form, you'll have to pop by the police station for the statement and all of that.
JAIMITO	Fine. Whenever you want.

ALBERTO	Tampoco corre tanta prisa. Dentro de dos o tres días.

(Dan golpes en el tabique del vecino. Se oye una voz al otro lado.)

OFF VECINO	¡Oye! ¡Que te llaman por teléfono!
ALBERTO	*(A gritos también.)* ¡Un momento, que voy!

(Sale ALBERTO. JAIMITO mira aquello sin entender nada.)

ELENA	Es el cura. Es muy simpático. Nos hemos hecho amigos. Vino un día a por sal, y empezamos a hablar, a hablar... Nos viene muy bien, sobre todo por el teléfono, como dice Alberto. Ya no dice misa en las monjitas. Ahora le han contratado en un colegio y ya no está enfadado. Nosostros casi no ponemos música tampoco. Dice que en las monjitas le pagaban fatal, y que esos madrugones le estaban volviendo neurótico. Es muy amable y muy educado. Ahora está muy liado con eso de la LODE. El otro día nos dijo que si le acompañábamos a la manifestación pero Alberto no puede ir a manifestaciones. Además le dijo su padre que en eso no hay que meterse. Es joven y majo, aunque sea cura. Es del Atleti, y como Alberto es del Madrid, han tenido cada discusión...

(Acaba de guardar la ropa planchada.)

	No me he acordado de preguntarte si querías que te planchara algo...
JAIMITO	¿Eh? No, no. Gracias, pero no hace falta.
ELENA	Cuando nos llaman por teléfono, nos avisa así por el agujero. Viene bien, ¿no? Quita el tapón y servicio directo. Y si algún día nos entran ganas de confesarnos, nos confesamos por ahí.

ALBERTO   There's no massive hurry or anything. In the next two or three days.

(The neighbour bangs on the partition wall. A voice can be heard from the other side.)

VOICE OF NEIGHBOUR   Listen! They are calling you on the telephone!
ALBERTO   *(Also shouting.)* One moment, I'm on my way!

(ALBERTO leaves. JAIMITO looks at what's going on without understanding a thing.)

ELENA   It's the priest. He's very nice. We've made friends. He came over for sugar one day, and we got talking... It suits us especially, as Alberto says, because of the telephone. He doesn't say mass for the little sisters anymore. They've hired him in a school and he's not angry anymore. And we hardly put music on either. He says that the little sisters paid him a pittance, and that those early mornings were making him neurotic. He's very friendly and well-mannered. He's all mixed up now with the secular education reforms and all of that. He asked us to go with him to the demonstration the other day, but Alberto can't go on demonstrations. Anyway, his father told him you shouldn't get involved in all of that. Although he's a priest, he's young and nice. He's an Atlético fan, and as Alberto supports Real Madrid, they've had all kinds of arguments...

(She finishes putting the ironed clothes away.)

                I forgot to ask you if you wanted me to iron anything for you...
JAIMITO   Eh? No, no. Thanks, but there's no need,
ELENA   When they phone us, he lets us know, like that, through the hole. It's come in handy, hasn't it? He takes the cork out, and it's a direct line. And if someday we decide we want to confess, we can do it through there.

(Entra ALBERTO. *Trae muy mala cara. Cierra la puerta de un portazo.)*

ALBERTO   Han cogido a Chusa. En el tren. Le han pillado con
            todo. La tienen en el cuartelillo de la estación, ¡Qué
            follón, Dios!

JAIMITO   ¿Que la han cogido? ¿Y está en Atocha? ¿Qué más te
            han dicho?

ALBERTO   Eso, nada más.

JAIMITO   ¿La comisaria está allí mismo, en la estación?

ALBERTO   Sí, dentro. La tendrán allí unas horas. Luego la
            pasarán al Juzgado del Guardia, y de ahí, a Yeserías.
            Con todo lo que tenía encima va derecha a la cárcel.
            ¡Vaya un lío!

JAIMITO   ¿Pero cómo, cómo...? ¿Cómo la han cogido?

ALBERTO   Pues cogiéndola. Vosotros os creéis que la policía
            es gilipollas. Hace una hora que está allí. Encima ha
            dado esta dirección. Han llamado a un vecino para
            que nos avisara de que estaba allí, y para comprobar
            si la ha dado bien. Ahora se pueden presentar aquí
            cuando les dé la gana.

*(*JAIMITO *coge una cazadora y se la pone. Mira a ver si lleva dinero y el
carnet de identidad. Va hacia la puerta.)*

JAIMITO   Voy a ir, a ver si puedo verla, o hacer algo... ¿En
            Atocha?

(Sale. ALBERTO *y* ELENA *se miran.)*

ALBERTO   Recoge tus cosas y márchate a casa con tu madre.
            Pueden venir aquí. ¡Esta tía también...! ¡Anda
            que...!

ELENA   *(Empieza a recoger.)* ¿Y cómo la habrán cogido en el
            tren?

(ALBERTO comes in not looking good. He slams the door shut.)

ALBERTO   They've caught Chusa. In the train. They picked her up with everything. They've got her in the duty room in the station. God, what a fuck-up!

JAIMITO   They've caught her? And she's in Atocha? What else have they told you?

ALBERTO   That's all, nothing else.

JAIMITO   The police station is right there, in Atocha itself?

ALBERTO   Yes, inside. They'll hold her there for a few hours. Then they'll take her to the duty court and, from there, to Yeserías,[10] the women's prison. With that much on her, she'll go straight to jail. What a mess!

JAIMITO   But, how, how…? How did they catch her?

ALBERTO   Well, by catching her. You lot think that the police are a bunch of dickheads. She's been there an hour and, on top of that, she's given this address. They've called a neighbour so that he could tell us she was there, and to check she'd given them the right address. Now they can turn up here whenever they fancy.

(JAIMITO picks up a jacket and puts it on. He looks to see if it's got money and his ID card inside. He heads for the door.)

JAIMITO   I'm going to go, to see if I can speak to her or do something… In Atocha?

(Exits. ALBERTO and ELENA look at each other.)

ALBERTO   Get your stuff together, and head off to your mother's place. They could come here. That girl as well…! Would you credit it…!

ELENA   *(Starts to gather her stuff together.)* And how would they have caught her on the train?

---

[10]   As you can see from the original, the name and context was sufficient for a Spanish audience to know what Yeserías was. An infamous prison during the dictatorship, the amnesty laws and release of political prisoners in the transition ensured its notoriety amongst the general public. However, by 2008, it had been replaced simply with the word 'cárcel' [prison].

ALBERTO

Yo qué sé. Porque es tonta del culo. Se habrá puesto a fumar allí, y a dar a la gente... Hay que largarse de aquí rápido. Se lo he dicho veinte veces, que un día les iban a..., pues nada. Yo no sé qué se creen. (*Se pone a ayudarla a recoger.*) Si es que no puede ser. No puede ser...

(Oscuro.)

ALBERTO How do I know? Because she's a stupid arse. She'll have lit up there, or have given people… We need to get out of here smart quick. I said to her time and time again that one day they would…, but to no effect. I don't know what they think. (*He begins to help her gather things together.*) It's that it just isn't on. It isn't on…

(*Blackout.*)

Escena Segunda

Ha pasado casi un hora. En escena ALBERTO, *solo, recogiendo a toda prisa sus cosas y metiéndolas en maletas y cajas de cartón. Se abre la puerta de la calle y aparece* JAIMITO.

JAIMITO	(*Entrando.*) Nada, que no me han dejado verla. Y encima casi me gano un par de hostias. (*Se da cuenta de lo que está haciendo* ALBERTO.) ¿Qué pasa? ¿Qué estás haciendo?
ALBERTO	(*Muy incómodo de que haya vuelto antes de que le diera tiempo a recoger y marcharse.*) Ya lo ves. Recogiendo mis cosas.
JAIMITO	¿Recogiendo? ¿Por qué? ¿Qué ha pasado? ¿Y Elena?
ALBERTO	Se ha ido.
JAIMITO	¿Que se ha ido? ¿Adónde? Para un momento, ¿no? Deja ya eso. ¡Para!
ALBERTO	Oye, me voy. Es en serio.
JAIMITO	¿Que te vas? ¿Dónde te vas?
ALBERTO	(*Sigue recogiendo.*) A casa de mis padres.
JAIMITO	Alberto, no te comprendo, de verdad. Chusa está detenida, ¿no te das cuenta? Tienes que ir tú, que a ti sé que te dejan entrar y hacer lo que puedas…
ALBERTO	Lo siento.
JAIMITO	¿Que lo sientes? Estás aquí, llevándote tus cosas… ¿Y lo sientes? Pues no lo sientas tanto y haz algo.
ALBERTO	¿Qué quieres que haga? No puedo meterme en ese lío, no sé cómo no te das cuenta, y menos después del tiro tuyo ese.
JAIMITO	Dirás del tuyo, el que me diste, ¿no?
ALBERTO	Del que sea, para el caso es lo mismo. No puedo meterme, me la juego.
JAIMITO	¿Y ella? ¿Ella no se la juega? Tú has dicho antes que si no se la saca de ahí la llevan a Yeserías.

Scene Two

Nearly an hour has passed by. ALBERTO is alone on stage gathering his things together as fast as he can, putting them in suitcases and cardboard boxes. The front door opens and JAIMITO appears.

JAIMITO	(*Coming in.*) No joy, they didn't let me see her. And, on top of that, it almost earned me a good beating. (*He realises what ALBERTO is doing.*) What's going on? What are you doing?
ALBERTO	(*Very uncomfortable at the fact that he has come back before he had time to gather everything together and clear off.*) As you can see. Packing my stuff.
JAIMITO	Packing? Why? What's happened? And Elena?
ALBERTO	She's gone.
JAIMITO	She's gone? Where? Hold your horses, won't you? Stop that for a second!
ALBERTO	Listen, I'm going. Seriously.
JAIMITO	You're going? Where are you going?
ALBERTO	(*He continues to pack.*) To my parents' place.
JAIMITO	Alberto, I don't get you, honestly. Don't you realise Chusa's been arrested? You have to go, they'll let you in, and do what you can…
ALBERTO	I'm sorry.
JAIMITO	You're sorry? Here you are, taking your stuff… And, you're sorry? Well stop being so sorry, and do something.
ALBERTO	What do you want me to do? I can't get involved in this mess, I don't know how you can't realise, especially after that bullet wound of yours.
JAIMITO	You mean yours, the one you gave me, don't you?
ALBERTO	Whoever's it is, it makes no difference for the case at hand. I can't get involved, I'd be putting myself in the firing line.
JAIMITO	And her? Isn't she in the firing line? You were the one who said before if she doesn't get out of there, then they'll take her to Yeserías.

ALBERTO   Tú no entiendes de esas cosas, así que cállate.
JAIMITO   Tú sí, ya lo veo. Tú entiendes demasiado.

(Se queda mirándolo fijamente. El otro sigue recogiendo.)

ALBERTO   Os he dicho un millón de veces que no quería saber
             nada de vuestros rollos. Conmigo ya no contéis más.
             Se acabó. Ya está bien. Ella sabía que si iba a por
             hachís la podían coger, ¿o no? Pues la han cogido.
             Hay que atenerse a las consecuencias de lo que se
             hace en la vida, coño, y no andar liando siempre a
             los demás para que le saquen a uno de los jaleos.
             Además, ahora no se puede hacer nada ya.
JAIMITO   Lo mejor es hacer la maleta, ¿verdad?, y largarse.
             Hay que joderse.

(ALBERTO sigue a lo suyo y JAIMITO, haciendo de tripas corazón, intenta entrarle con una nueva estrategia.)

             Por favor, venga, somos amigos, ¿no?, por favor te lo
             pido, aunque sólo sea verla un momento y hablar con
             ella. Luego ya te vas si quieres, pero ahora… Hablas
             con los de allí, por eso no te va a pasar nada, o que
             me dejen entrar a mí si no, que soy su primo… A ver
             si le van a pegar o le hacen algo…
ALBERTO   Venga, no digas idioteces. No le hacen nada. Sólo la
             tienen allí, la interrogan y le quitan lo que sea.
JAIMITO   Vamos un momento, anda, por favor… *(Le sujeta.)*
ALBERTO   Suéltame.
JAIMITO   ¡Qué cabrón eres! Pues de aquí no sales, así si vienen
             te agarran aquí. *(Se pone delante de la puerta.)* Pienso
             decir que eres el que pones el dinero y el que lo hace
             todo, ¡para que te jodas! ¿Me oyes bien?

(Se acerca a él y le agarra.)

ALBERTO   ¡Que me sueltes! ¡Suéltame, que te…!

ALBERTO   You don't understand these things so shut it.
JAIMITO   You, I see, do. You're too wise to everything.

(He looks at ALBERTO, who continues to pack, intensely.)

ALBERTO   I've told you a thousand times I didn't want to know anything about your dodgy dealings. From now on, you can't count on me. And that's that. Fair's fair. She knew they could catch her if she went for hash or didn't she? Well, they've caught her. For Christ's sake, you have to be aware of the consequences of what you do in life and not implicate everyone else by making them get you out of one of your fixes. And, anyway, the time for being able to do anything has passed.
JAIMITO   The best thing to do is pack your suitcase and make a quick exit, right? Fuck me.

(ALBERTO continues doing his thing, and JAIMITO, plucking up the courage, tries to appeal to him with a new strategy.)

            Please, come on, we're mates, aren't we? I'm asking you, please, even if it's just to see her for a moment and to speak to her. Then you can go if you want, but for now... Speak with them there, nothing's going to happen to you for that or, if not, persuade them to let me go in, I'm her cousin... Just to make sure they're not going to hit her or do anything...
ALBERTO   Come on, don't say such idiotic things. They're not going to do anything to her. They'll just have her there, question her and confiscate whatever she's carrying.
JAIMITO   Come on, wait a second, please... *(He restrains him.)*
ALBERTO   Let me go.
JAIMITO   You're such a bastard! Well you're not getting out of here so, if they come, they'll catch you here. *(He stands in front of the door.)* I'm thinking of saying you're the one who provides the money and arranges everything, just to fuck you over! You listening to me? *(He moves closer and grabs hold of him.)*
ALBERTO   Let me go! Let me go, I'm going to...!

(Le da en el brazo herido sin querer al forcejear. JAIMITO se repliega agarrándose con dolor.)

> Lo siento. ¿Te he hecho daño? Perdona. Tienes que entenderlo. Haré lo que pueda, pero más adelante; ahora me voy. Puedo irme cuando quiera, ¿no? ¿O es que me tengo que quedar aquí a vivir con vosotros toda la vida? Tu estás jodido por lo que estás jodido. Pues lo siento, tío, Elena se viene conmigo. Nos vamos juntos, y nos vamos. Y ya está. Qué se va a hacer. La vida es así, no me la he inventado yo. Y Chusa…, tampoco se va a morir por esto. Le pasa a más gente y no se muere. Aquí cada uno hace lo que le conviene, ¿o me ha preguntado ella a mí acaso si me parecía bien que fuera a eso? Yo no me meto, te lo he dicho, así que… ¡Yo no soy el padre de nadie aquí, coño! No sé cómo no te das cuenta de que si me ven ahora con vosotros me la cargo.

JAIMITO   ¿Te lo ha dicho eso también tu padre?

ALBERTO   No metas a mi padre que no tiene nada que ver.

JAIMITO   Anda, tío, pues vete. Vete a tomar por culo de aquí, que no te quiero ni ver. Y llévatelo todo bien. Lo que dejes aquí lo tiro por la ventana.

ALBERTO   Si te pones así mejor.

JAIMITO   Claro, mejor. ¡Qué madero eres y qué cabrón!

(ALBERTO se revuelve echando mano a la porra instintivamente al sentirse insultado.)

JAIMITO   Sí, eso, saca la porra y dame con ella. Así te quedas a gusto. ¡Tu puta madre!

ALBERTO   *(Va hacia él.)* ¡Ya! ¡Vale ya, ¿eh?! ¡Vale!

(JAIMITO le da un golpe fuerte al casette, que está encima de la mesa tirándolo al suelo.)

> ¡Que es mío! ¡Qué pasa! ¡Que te meto una que te…!

(Without meaning to, he hits JAIMITO's wounded arm in the struggle. He staggers back holding onto himself in pain.)

I'm sorry. Have I hurt you? Forgive me. You have to understand how it goes. I'll do what I can, but further down the line; I'm leaving now. I can leave when I want, can't I? Or do I have to stay and live with you two for the rest of my life? Things aren't going the way you wanted them to, fucking deal with it. Mate, I'm sorry, Elena is coming with me. We're leaving together, and that's that. That's life, I didn't make the rules. And Chusa…, she's not going to die because of this. It happens to other people and they don't die. Here everyone does as they please; did she ever ask me if I thought it was okay for her to go off and do that? I don't interfere, I told you that, so… I'm nobody's father here, for fuck's sake! I don't know how you can't click that I'll be in the shit if they see me with you lot now.

JAIMITO   Did your father also tell you that?

ALBERTO   Don't bring my father into this, he's got nothing to do with it.

JAIMITO   Go on then mate, do a runner. Fuck off out of here, get out of my sight. And make sure you take everything. Whatever you leave, I'll throw out the window.

ALBERTO   If you're gonna be like that, it's for the best.

JAIMITO   For the best, of course. You're a cop through and through, and a bastard! (*ALBERTO shudders and, on feeling insulted, instinctively grabs hold of his truncheon.*)

JAIMITO   Yes, that's it, get the truncheon out and hit me with it. That's how you like it. Son of a bitch!

ALBERTO   (*Going towards him.*) Alright! Alright fine! Eh? Fine!

(JAIMITO wallops the cassette player off the table surface causing it to fall onto the floor.)

That's mine! What's the problem? I'll make you wish…

(Le agarra y pelean, arrastrando todo lo que encuentran a su paso en medio de un gran jaleo. En esto se abre la puerta y entra ELENA. Al verla entrar se separan, arreglándose automáticamente la ropa y el pelo. ELENA se queda parada al ver lo que está pasando.)

ELENA   *(Casi sin voz.)* Hola. Está el coche de mi madre abajo. *(A ALBERTO.)* Tienes sangre en el labio.

(ALBERTO entra en el lavabo y ella detrás. JAIMITO, sentado en una silla, mira como un autómata la pared.)

DOÑA ANTONIA   *(Entrando por la puerta que ELENA ha dejado entornada.)* Venga ya, que estamos en doble fila y va a venir la grúa. *(Sin enterarse de nada de lo que está pasando.)* Hola, tú, qué tal el brazo. ¿Nos ayudas a bajar los paquetes? *(Él no se mueve. Habla ahora a los otros que salen del lavabo.)* ¿Todo esto hay que bajar? No va a caber en el coche. *(A ELENA).* Tu madre no puede subir a ayudar; no va a dejar el coche solo para que nos lo roben. Yo cojo esto, que pesa menos.

(Sale cargada con unos paquetes pequeños.)

ALBERTO   *(Con un pañuelo en el labio. A ELENA.)* Coge tú las cajas. Yo llevo las maletas.

(Cargan con todo lo que pueden, sin mirar a JAIMITO, intentando acabar lo antes posible, y salen. Queda la puerta de la calle abierta de par en par. JAIMITO se levanta lentamente, se acerca a ella y la cierra de una patada. Luego se vuelve a sentar. Llaman a la puerta. Se levanta y abre.)

DOÑA ANTONIA   *(Entrando.)* Que se han dejado esto. *(Coge el casette que seguía tirado en el suelo.)* ¿Sabes si hay algo más de ellos por aquí? *(Él no contesta.)* Bueno, pues si acaso ya pasarán a recoger lo que sea otro día. Lo dicho, que te mejores.

(He grabs hold of him and they fight, dragging whatever they happen upon into the violent fray. Whilst this is going on, the door opens and ELENA comes in. They separate on seeing her, automatically putting their clothes and hair back into order. ELENA stops still in her tracks on seeing what is going on.)

ELENA   (*So quietly you can hardly hear her speak.*) Hello. My mother's car is downstairs. (*To ALBERTO.*) You've got blood on your lip.

(ALBERTO goes into the bathroom and she follows. JAIMITO, sitting on the chair, stares at the wall as if he were a zombie.)

DOÑA ANTONIA   (*Coming in through the door that ELENA has left ajar.*) Come on, we're double parked, and we'll get clamped. (*Unaware of anything that's going on around her.*) Hi, you, how's the arm doing? Can you help us take the stuff that's been boxed up down? (*He doesn't move. She then speaks to the other two who are coming out of the bathroom.*) Does all of this need to go down? It won't fit in the car. (*To ELENA.*) Your mother can't come up and help; she's not going to leave the car unattended so that they can come and rob us. I'll take this one, it weighs less. (*She leaves carrying some small packages.*)

ALBERTO   (*With a hanky against his lip. To ELENA.*) You pick up the boxes. I'll take the suitcases.

(They load up everything they can, without looking at JAIMITO, trying to get it over with as soon as possible, and they exit. The front door is left completely open. JAIMITO gets up slowly, goes towards it, and slams it shut with his foot. He then sits back down again. A knock comes to the door. He gets up and opens it.)

DOÑA ANTONIA   (*Coming in.*) They've left that. (*She picks up the cassette player which remains tossed on the floor.*) You know if there's anything else of theirs about the place? (*He doesn't answer*). Well, if there is, they can pass by and pick whatever it is up another day. As I said, get well soon.

(Sale con el casette, volviendo a dejar la puerta abierta. Él se levanta otra vez y está a punto de cerrarla de nuevo con una patada. Luego la cierra despacio con la mano, se recuesta en ella una vez cerrada y mira desde allí la habitación vacía. Va después a la cocina, y vuelve con unas hojas de lechuga en las manos. Llega hasta la jaula del hámster.)

JAIMITO   Toma, Humphrey, lechuga, come. ¿Está buena? A la
                   Chusa le darán la comida también así, por las rejas.
                   ¿Quieres más? Desde luego es que te lo tienen que
                   hacer todo. Te lo tienes montado a lo Onassis. Como
                   un faraón ahí, pasando de todo. Sólo te faltan las
                   pirámides. Si quieres que te diga la verdad, Humphrey,
                   estoy hecho polvo. Tela de chungo estoy. No, no es
                   el brazo, eso no duele ya, un tiro no es nada. Bueno,
                   si te lo dan a ti, que eres un pequeñajo, a lo mejor te
                   espachurran. Lo que duele es lo otro. ¿Qué le habré
                   visto yo a esa gilipollas? ¿Pero tú te has fijado? Si
                   está en los huesos, ni tetas ni nada, y una cara de tonta
                   que no se lame. Cada vez que iba a verme al hospital
                   me sentaba peor que la penicilina. Por cierto, que
                   tú no has aparecido por la cuatrocientos veintidós,
                   sinvergüenza. Hay que ir a visitar a los amigos cuando
                   les dan un tiro. Ya lo sabes, para la próxima vez. En
                   el hospital se estaba bien. Era un poco triste, pero
                   tranquilo. Lo peor eran las vistas. Mi ventana daba
                   justo enfrente del depósito de cadáveres. Un palo, tío.
                   Cada vez que me asomaba me daba un bajón. Pero
                   tranquilo; me iba al pasillo, y paseo va, paseo viene.
                   Allí todos te cuentan la vida. En cuanto te ven se te
                   acercan, y que si la tía, que si el padre, que si yo soy el
                   más enfermo de toda la planta, que no me entienden
                   los médicos… A veces dos, uno de cada brazo a la
                   vez. ¿Tú crees que esto se me pasará? ¡Quieres dejar

(She leaves with the cassette player, once again leaving the door open. He gets up again and is about to slam it shut with his foot for the second time. He then closes it slowly with his hand, and sits against the now closed door, and looks from there at the empty room. He then gets up and goes to the kitchen, and comes back with some lettuce leaves in his hand. He goes up to the hamster's cage.)

JAIMITO   Here, Humphrey, eat some lettuce. Is it nice? They'll also give Chusa her food like this, through bars. Do you want some more? Of course everything has to be done for you. You're all set up there just like Onassis.[xiv] You're like a pharaoh there, oblivious to everything. All you need are the pyramids. Truth be told, Humphrey, I'm done in. Ready for the knackers yard. No, it's not the arm, that doesn't hurt anymore, a bullet is nothing. Well, as you're such a little thing, it might splatter you all over the place if you got hit by one. What hurts is the other thing. What did I see in that stupid bitch? But did you look at her properly? She's all bone, no tits or anything, and a face so stupid you wouldn't believe. Whenever she came to see me in the hospital, it made me feel worse than the penicillin. By the way, you never showed up at room number four-hundred-and-two. Have you no shame? You have to visit your friends when they're shot. Well, you know for next time if there is a next time. I was alright in hospital. A bit sad, but at peace. The worst bit was the views. My window looked right out where they deposited the dead bodies across the way. Mate, that's rough. I got down whenever I looked out. But, don't worry, I went into the corridor and walked up and down. Everyone tells you their life-story there. As soon as they see you, they come up to you and yabber on about their girl, their father, that they are the sickest on the ward, that the doctors don't understand them. Sometimes two at a time, one on each arm. Do you think I'll get over this? For

de dar vueltas de una vez a ese cacharro! No sé cómo no te hartas ya de la rueda esa. No puedo respirar. ¿Has estado enamorado alguna vez, Humphrey? No te lo aconsejo. Claro que tú también, ahí metido, como no te enamores de una mosca que pase. Yo, antes de esto, sólo lo de aquella chica de Simago. No te preocupes, que no te lo cuento otra vez. Pero no era como ahora. Ahora es peor, la otra malo, y ésta peor. ¡Qué cabrón el Alberto, madero, que es un madero! Es ridículo. Esto es ridículo... *(Se suena disimulando las lágrimas.)* Estoy un poco constipado, sabes. Sí, te lo juro. Soy un ridículo, por mucho que te empeñes, lo soy y ya está. Un idiota. ¿Quieres más lechuga? ¡No te comas el dedo, coño! Ahora que porque estaba yo en el hospital, si no, de qué. Ese siempre hace lo mismo. Como sabía que si me quedaba aquí ella se iba conmigo, me da un tiro, y al hospital. Y claro, como estaba triste, y sola. Además, le ha ayudado la madre, la lagarta gorda esa que dice siempre que tú eres una rata. Y la Chusa por ahí, de crucero. Es que se ha juntado todo, Humphrey, te lo juro. ¿Te estás durmiendo? ¿Ahora encima te duermes? Desde luego... No te vuelvo a contar nada, te pongas como te pongas.

(Se aleja de la jaula y hace movimientos por la habitación que recuerdan a los del hámster. Incluso da vueltas a una rueda parecida que hay sobre la mesa, e, inconscientemente, se acaba de comer la lechuga que le queda en la mano.)

Lo peor es lo mal que se respira. Eso es lo peor. ¿Te acuerdas, Humphrey, cuando te dejó a ti la Ingrid?

(Coge la flauta de la pared, se sienta y se pone a tocar muy melancólicamente la canción de la película Casablanca: «Remember always thís a kiss is just a kiss». Oscuro.)

once in your life, can't you stop going round on that thing? I don't know how you haven't got fed up of that wheel yet. I can't breathe. Have you ever been in love, Humphrey? I wouldn't recommend it. Of course, with you being stuck in the there, unless you fall in love with a passing fly. Me, before all that, only with that girl from Simago. Don't worry, I won't tell you the story again. But it wasn't like now. Now it's worse, the other time bad and this time worse. What a bastard Alberto is; a cop, a bona fide cop! This is ridiculous... (*He tries to hide the sound of his tears.*) I've got a bit of a cold, you see. Yes, I swear to you. I'm ridiculous, however much you try to think otherwise, I am and that's that. An idiot. You want some more lettuce? Don't eat my finger, for fuck's sake! It's because I was in the hospital; if not, no way. He always does the same. As he knew she'd go off with me if I'd stayed here, he shot me and that's me straight to the hospital. And, of course, as she was sad and on her own... Anyway, his mother helped him, that fat lizard who's always saying you're a rat. And Chusa, out there, on a cruise. Truth is, it all came together, Humphrey, I swear to you. Are you asleep? On top of everything, are you sleeping? Of course... I'm not gonna tell you anything ever again, whatever you get like.

(He moves away from the cage and does movements about the room reminiscent of the hamster's. He even goes round a similar wheel, which is on top of the table, and, unconsciously, finishes eating the lettuce left in his hand.)

The worst bit is getting breathless. That's the worst. Do you remember,[11] Humphrey, when Ingrid left you?[xv]

(He picks the flute up from the wall and starts to play melancholically the song from the film Casablanca: "Remember always this, a kiss is just a kiss...".[xvi] Blackout.)

---

11   In the 2008 version, a pre-recorded version of the signature tune from the film *Casablanca* accompanied this lament.

Escena Tercera

Han pasado dos días. Es media tarde. La escena, vacía. El hámster en su jaula sigue dándole vueltas a la rueda. Se abre la puerta de la calle y entra CHUSA, con las bolsas en las manos.

CHUSA	¿Hay alguien? ¿No hay nadie?

(Se abre la puerta del lavabo y sale JAIMITO, calado, de la ducha, medio tapándose con una toalla. Sigue con su brazo en cabestrillo.)

JAIMITO	*(Sorprendido.)* ¿Qué haces tú aquí? ¿Pero no estabas en la cárcel?
CHUSA	Me han soltado, ya lo ves.
JAIMITO	¿Que te han soltado? ¿Pero cómo que te han soltado?
CHUSA	Parece que no te gusta. Me han soltado porque me han soltado. ¿O querías que me tuvieran allí toda la vida?
JAIMITO	Después del lío que he armado para que un abogado fuera a verte esta tarde... Ahora irá y no estás allí. No sé qué le voy a decir, después del rollo que le he tenido que meter. Es muy bueno, se llama Alfredo Alonso, y le he estado explicando todo...
CHUSA	Sécate, que vas a coger un trancazo si sigues ahí calado.

(Él se mete en el lavabo. Y con la puerta abierta sigue hablando desde allí. CHUSA empieza a sacar las cosas de las bolsas y a meterlas en su armario.)

JAIMITO	Iba a ir esta tarde, fíjate. Con lo ocupado que está...
CHUSA	Bueno, pues le llamas y le dices que no vaya. ¿Dónde están éstos?
JAIMITO	Se han largado.
CHUSA	¿A dónde?
JAIMITO	*(Sale del lavabo y se le acerca.)* Se han largado del todo; se han abierto tía. Se han llevado sus cosas... Quedan esas cajas de ahí; van a venir luego a por ellas. En eso han quedado.

Scene Three

A few days have passed. It's late afternoon/early evening. The stage, empty. The hamster, in his cage, continues going round the wheel. The front door opens and in comes CHUSA, *bags in hand.*

CHUSA   Anyone in? Nobody home?

(The toilet door opens and out comes JAIMITO, *soaked through from the shower, half covering himself with a towel. His arm is still in a sling.)*

JAIMITO   *(Surprised.)* What you doing, here? Weren't you in jail?

CHUSA   As you can see, they let me go?

JAIMITO   They let you go? But how have they let you go?

CHUSA   It doesn't look like you're too pleased. They let me go because they let me go. Or did you want them to keep me there for the rest of my life?

JAIMITO   After all the hassle I went to so a lawyer would go and see you this afternoon… Now he'll go and you won't be there. I don't know what I'm going to say to him after I've got him mixed up in all this mess. He's very good, he's called Alfredo Alonso and I have been explaining everything to him…

CHUSA   Dry yourself, you'll catch your death soaked through like that.

(He goes into the toilet and, through the open door, keeps talking to CHUSA. *She starts to take things out of the bags and put them in her wardrobe.)*

JAIMITO   He was going to go this afternoon, go figure. When he's so busy and all…

CHUSA   Well, just phone him and tell him not to go. Where are the others?

JAIMITO   They've cleared off.

CHUSA   Where to?

JAIMITO   *(He comes out of the toilet and moves towards her.)* They've left everything behind; they've cleared off for good. They've taken their things… They've left those boxes over there; they'll come for them later. That's how they've left it.

(De pronto ella toma contacto con la realidad. Ve las cajas. Luego las cosas que faltan y el cambio en la habitación.)

CHUSA   *(Deja de guardar la ropa y se sienta muy afectada.)* ¿Pero, cómo? ¿Qué ha pasado?

JAIMITO   *(Acabando de vestirse.)* Se han largado, juntos, los dos. Los dos y sus madres. Los cuatro. Bueno, y el padre. Se van a casar. Han cogido un piso en Móstoles. El día que yo salí del hospital, y te cogieron a ti, fue todo un lío.

CHUSA   ¿Qué tal sigue tu brazo?

JAIMITO   *(Sacandole y metiéndole del pañuelo con que se le sujeta al cuello.)* Bueno, mira. Le puedo mover ya. Mañana o pasado me quito esto. Pues nada, que se han ido.

CHUSA   ¿Alberto también?

JAIMITO   ¿No te digo que se han ido los dos juntos? ¿Y cómo es que te han soltado, así, de pronto?

CHUSA   Me han tenido tres días. Allí no podían tenerme más. Me tenían que soltar o mandar a Yeserías, así que aquí estoy. Tendré un juicio cuando sea. Me pillaron con un montón, trescientos gramos por lo menos, pero la denuncia es por haberme encontrado media bola. Cincuenta gramos. Yo no iba a protestar, claro. Lo demás ha desaparecido por el camino.

JAIMITO   Mejor, ¿no? Por tan poco no te va a pasar nada.

CHUSA   Qué negocio tienen montado algunos. Pensaba pedirle a Alberto que mirara a ver quién se lo ha quedado.

JAIMITO   Olvídate de Alberto. Ya ves cómo ha ido a verte, y lo que se ha preocupado. Pasa de él, de verdad te lo digo. Y de ella, igual.

CHUSA   ¿Te han tratado bien en el hospital?

JAIMITO   Como a un marqués. Las heridas de bala dan mucho prestigio. Y luego, como ha ido varias veces la policía

(Reality suddenly hits her. She sees the boxes. Then the things missing from the room, and the changes.)

CHUSA	*(She stops putting the clothes away and is really taken aback.)* But, how? What happened?
JAIMITO	*(Finishing getting dressed.)* They've cleared off, together, the two of them. The two of them and their mothers. The four of them. Well, and the father. They're gonna get married. They've got their hands on a flat in Móstoles. The day I came out of hospital, and they caught you, it was all a mess.
CHUSA	How's your arm bearing up?
JAIMITO	*(Taking it out and putting it in the cloth sling that holds it in place next to his neck.)* Good, look. I can move it now. They'll take this off tomorrow or the day after. Well, whatever, they've gone.
CHUSA	Alberto as well?
JAIMITO	I told you the two of them had gone off together, didn't I? And how is it they've suddenly let you go?
CHUSA	They held me for three days. They couldn't hold me any longer. They either had to let me go or send me to Yeserías, so here I am. I'll have a trial at some point. They caught me with a load, at least three hundred grams, but the charge is for having found half a ball. Fifty grams. I wasn't going to complain, of course. The rest got lost along the way.[xvii]
JAIMITO	Better that way, right? With such a little amount, you'll be in the clear.
CHUSA	A right nice little business some people have set up. I thought about asking Alberto to see who ended up with it.
JAIMITO	Forget about Alberto. You've seen how he came to see you, and what was worrying him. Get him out of your system, I'm telling you, honestly. And the same goes for her.
CHUSA	Did they treat you well in the hospital?
JAIMITO	Like a marquis. Bullet wounds get a lot of kudos. And

	a interrogarme, allí creían que era de la ETA por lo menos. No veas los platos de comida que me llevaban. Un respeto, tía. La gente, muy maja. Y las enfermeras, de ésas que ya no quedan. ¿Y a ti, en la comisaría?
CHUSA	No me han hecho ni caso. Me han tenido allí tres días, y luego me han soltado.
JAIMITO	Oye, voy un momento a llamar a Alfredo, el abogado, a ver si no se ha ido todavía. Llamo desde la casa del cura, el de al lado. Es que éstos se hicieron amigos suyos cuando no estábamos aquí. Viene muchas veces. Es simpático; y como le gusta cocinar... Ya sabes que a mí eso de la cocina, fatal. Estos días, como estaba solo... Bueno, vengo en seguida y hablamos. Hay té hecho, si quieres. Hasta ahora.

(Sale. Ella se queda sola. Va hasta la jaula del hámster y da unos golpes con los dedos en las rejas. Luego sigue poniendo sus cosas en el armario lentamente. Llaman a la puerta. Va a abrir creyendo que es JAIMITO que vuelve, y se encuentra en la puerta con ELENA. Sorpresa por parte de las dos.)

CHUSA	Bueno, pasa, ¿no? No te quedes ahí parada.
ELENA	Creíamos que estabas...
CHUSA	Me han soltado. Si quieres sentarte... Como si estuvieras en tu casa. Ya sabes dónde está todo.
ELENA	¿Te ha dicho Jaimito...?
CHUSA	Sí, me ha dicho Jaimito. ¿Quieres un té?
ELENA	Sí, gracias.
CHUSA	Pues cógelo, está en la cocina, ¿o te lo tengo que traer yo también? *(ELENA va a la cocina, y vuelve con una taza de té.)*
ELENA	*(Bebiendo.)* He quedado aquí con Alberto para acabar de llevarnos lo que queda. Me alegro de que estés bien.

	then, as the police came to question me a number of times, they all thought I was at least from ETA.[12] You wouldn't believe the food they brought me. Serious respect, love. The people, very nice. And the nurses like those from a bygone age. And, you, in the police station?
CHUSA	They just ignored me. Had me there three days and then let me go.
JAIMITO	Listen, I'm gonna go and ring Alfredo, the lawyer, in case he hasn't gone yet. I'll ring from next-door, the priest's place. The thing is those two made friends with him when we weren't here. He comes round a lot. He's nice and, as he likes to cook… As you know, me and kitchen stuff don't get along. These last few days, as I've been on my own… Right, I'll be back in a second, and then we'll talk. There's tea ready, if you want. See you in a bit.

(He leaves and she's left alone. She goes towards the hamster's cage and taps the bars with her fingers. Then she continues slowly putting her things in the wardrobe. A knock comes to the door. She goes to open it thinking it's JAIMITO who's come back but she finds ELENA at the door. Both of them are surprised.)

CHUSA	Well, come in, won't you? Don't just stand there…
ELENA	We thought you were…
CHUSA	They've let me go. If you want to sit down… Make yourself at home. You already know where everything is.
ELENA	Has Jaimito told you…?
CHUSA	Yes, Jaimito has told me. Do you want a tea?
ELENA	Yes, please.
CHUSA	Well, go get it, it's in the kitchen or do I have to bring that for you as well? (*ELENA goes to the kitchen and comes back with a cup of tea.*)
ELENA	(*Drinking.*) I've arranged to meet Alberto here to pick

---

12   This reference to the Basque separatist terrorist group who were at their most active in the transition period had disappeared from the 2008 production.

CHUSA	Gracias. (*Pausa embarazosa.*) ¿Y qué tal tu madre?
ELENA	Bien. Ahora estoy viviendo allí otra vez, hasta que nos casemos. Ya tenemos el piso, en Móstoles. Si quieres puedes venir un día a verlo.
CHUSA	No, gracias.
ELENA	¿Estás enfadada conmigo?
CHUSA	No, no. Es que Móstoles está muy lejos.
ELENA	Ahora hay metro ya.
CHUSA	Sí, pero no. De verdad. Déjalo.
ELENA	Oye, Chusa, tengo que decirte una cosa... Por las pelas esas no te preocupes ahora. Más adelante, cuando buenamente puedas, me las das, pero ahora me imagino que no tendrás veinticinco mil pesetas aquí... Es que como me las dejó mi madre... Y ahora además, con el piso y eso... Pero vamos, cuando tú puedas, o si puedes ahora algo, y luego poco a poco...
CHUSA	Me cogió la policía. ¿Sabes? Me lo quitaron.
ELENA	Pero yo sólo te lo dejé. Chusa, la verdad.
CHUSA	Ya. Si todo iba bien, y lo vendíamos y ganábamos pelas, para las dos. Y si me lo quitaban, me lo has dejado, ¿verdad? Qué lista eres tú también.
ELENA	Mira, yo no quiero que Alberto se meta en esto, pero él me ha dicho que te lo diga. Una cosa es ser amigos, pero el dinero es el dinero.
CHUSA	Pues no te las voy a dar, para que te enteres. No las tengo, pero si las tuviera tampoco te las daría. Y ya te puedes ir metiendo a Alberto por donde te quepa.
ELENA	No sé por qué te pones así. Somos amigas, ¿no?
CHUSA	Me pongo así porque me da la gana. Y no somos amigas.

up what's left behind. I'm glad you're well.

CHUSA   Thank you. (*An awkward silence.*) And how's your mother?

ELENA   Fine. I'm back living there at the moment, until we get married. We've already got the flat, in Móstoles. If you want, you can come over to see it one day.

CHUSA   No, thank you.

ELENA   Are you angry with me?

CHUSA   No, no. The thing is Móstoles is a long way away.

ELENA   There's a metro stop there now.

CHUSA   Yes, but no. Honestly. Drop it.

ELENA   Listen, Chusa, I've got something to say to you... Don't worry about the cash I gave you, for the moment. Further down the line when you're in a position to do so, you can give me it, but I don't imagine you've got 25,000 pesetas here... It's that my mother gave it to me... And, now, with the flat and all that on top... But, well, let's see, when you're in a position to do so, or if you've got a bit now and then little by little...

CHUSA   The police caught me. Didn't you hear? They took it off me.

ELENA   But, to be frank, I left it in your care.

CHUSA   Yeah. If everything had gone well, and we'd sold it and made some cash, for the two of us. And if they took it off me, I'm left on my own. Very clever on your part.

ELENA   Look, I don't want to bring Alberto into this, but he told me to tell you. Being friends is one thing but money is money.

CHUSA   Well, I'm not going to give it to you, get that into your head. I haven't got it but, even if I had, I wouldn't give it to you either. And you can put Alberto where the sun doesn't shine.

ELENA   I don't know why you're getting like that. We're friends, aren't we?

CHUSA   I'll get like that if I want to. And no, we're not friends.

ELENA	Estás así por lo de Alberto. Pues lo siento.
CHUSA	Pues no lo sientas, y que te aproveche.
ELENA	¿Sabes lo que te digo? Que tiene razón mi madre. Así no se puede vivir. Cualquier día vas a acabar en cualquier sitio. Yo te lo digo por tu bien. Una cosa es pasarlo bien, y la libertad y todo eso, y otra cosa es como tú vives. Mi madre me ha dicho...
CHUSA	(*Cortándola.*) Oye, guapa, no querrás contarme tu vida ahora. Ni la de tu madre, la de la piscina. (*Muy dura. ELENA acusa el golpe. Pausa.*)
ELENA	Entonces, lo del dinero, ¿qué le digo a Alberto?, y a mi madre...
CHUSA	Diles lo que te dé la gana.
ELENA	Anda, que también en qué hora se me ocurriría a mí.
CHUSA	Eso digo yo. En qué hora.

(Se aleja hacia la cocina. Queda ELENA sola. Entra JAIMITO.)

JAIMITO	Ya se había ido... (*Ve a ELENA y se corta.*) Hola. ¿Qué tal?
ELENA	(*Va hacia él y le da dos besos amistosos.*) He venido a por las cosas. Ahora viene Alberto. ¿Qué tal el brazo?
JAIMITO	Bien, muy bien gracias. (*Pausa.*) ¿Quieres un té? (*Ella le muestra la taza que lleva aún en las manos.*) ¿Y qué tal todo? Estás muy guapa, de verdad. Pero siéntate, mujer. A Chusa ya la han soltado, ya ves qué suerte, ¿verdad? ¿Y qué tal la casa?
ELENA	Bien, la estamos amueblando. Ahora vivo con mi madre.
JAIMITO	Ya. ¿Chusa? (*Llama hacia la cocina, y nota algo raro.*) ¿Te pasa algo?
CHUSA	(*Desde la cocina.*) La saliva por la garganta me pasa.
ELENA	Está enfadada. Peor para ella. Dos trabajos tiene.

ELENA	You're like this because of the Alberto thing. Well, I'm sorry.
CHUSA	Well don't be sorry, have your fun with him.
ELENA.	Do you know what? My mother's right. You can't live like this. Any day you're going to wind up god knows where. And I'm saying it for your own good. One thing is having a good time, freedom and all of that, but living like you do is something else. My mother's said to me...
CHUSA	(*Interrupting her.*) Listen, darling, don't you go wanting to tell me your life story now. Or your mother's, with the swimming pool and all. (*Aggressively. ELENA takes it badly. Pause.*)
ELENA	Well, the money issue, what shall I tell Alberto and my mother...?
CHUSA	Tell them whatever you want.
ELENA	Fine, I don't know why I ever thought.
CHUSA	That's exactly what I'm saying. Why I ever thought. (*She moves away towards the kitchen. ELENA's left on her own. In comes JAIMITO.*)
JAIMITO	He'd already gone... (*He sees ELENA and suddenly stops.*) Hi, how are you?
ELENA	(*She goes towards him and gives him a friendly kiss on each cheek.*) I've come to pick the things up. Alberto's on his way. How's the arm?
JAIMITO	Okay, it's fine thanks. (*Pause.*) Would you like a tea? (*She shows him the tea that she's still holding.*) And how's everything? You're looking great, honestly. But sit yourself down. They've let Chusa go; that was a stroke of luck, wasn't it? And how's the flat?
ELENA	Good, we're getting it furnished. I'm living with my mother at the minute.
JAIMITO	Right. Chusa? (*He calls in the direction of the kitchen, and notices something's amiss.*) What's going down?
CHUSA	(*From the kitchen.*) Saliva down my throat.
ELENA	She's annoyed. Her loss. Just makes it harder work for her.

CHUSA	(*Saliendo.*) ¡Eres una estúpida, eso es lo que eres! ¡Una mema, con esa carita de mosquita muerta!
JAIMITO	Bueno, déjalo…
CHUSA	(*Haciéndole burla.*) «Que me he escapado de casa porque no aguanto a mi mamita…»
ELENA	¡Tú lo que tienes que hacer es devolverme el dinero que me debes!
JAIMITO	(*Metiéndose en medio.*) Basta ya, deja… Y tú… Por favor.

(Se abre la puerta de la calle y entran ALBERTO y su madre. Notan el clima, y han oído además los gritos desde fuera. ALBERTO viene de paisano.)

| ALBERTO | Hola, buenas. (*Acercándose.*) ¿Cómo estás? |

(Va a darle un beso y ella se retira.)

CHUSA	Muy bien, ¿y tú?
ALBERTO	Bien. Tienes buena cara.
CHUSA	Regular.
ALBERTO	Ha habido suerte, ¿eh?
CHUSA	Ya ves.
DOÑA ANTONIA	Hala, vamos. Abreviando que es gerundio.

(Empieza a coger los paquetes y cosas que se encuentran junto a la puerta. Coge la flauta de JAIMITO.)

JAIMITO	Oiga, señora, que eso es mío.
DOÑA ANTONIA	Como estaba aquí…
JAIMITO	Lo de ellos es esto, las cajas. No sé si habrá algo más. Yo he metido todo lo que he encontrado.
ALBERTO	No, es igual, de verdad. Está bien.
CHUSA	La mesa camilla es también en parte tuya. Te puedes llevar una pata si quieres. Y tres platos.
DOÑA ANTONIA	Saliendo.
JAIMITO	Yo os bajo el espejo.
ELENA.	A ver si te vas a hacer daño en el brazo.
JAIMITO	No, está ya bien.

CHUSA	(*Coming out.*) You're an imbecile, that's what you are, with that butter wouldn't melt face of yours.
JAIMITO	Alright, drop it...
CHUSA	(*Taking the mickey.*) "I've run away from home because I can't take any more of my mummy..."
ELENA	What you need to do is give me back the money you owe me!
JAIMITO	(*Separating the pair of them.*) That's enough, drop it... And, you... Please.

(*The front door opens and ALBERTO and his mother come in. They sense the atmosphere and have, in any case, heard the shouts from outside. ALBERTO is in civvies.*)

| ALBERTO | Hi, good morning. (*Moving closer.*) How are you? |

(*He goes to give her a kiss and she moves away.*)

CHUSA	Very well, and you?
ALBERTO	Fine, You're looking well.
CHUSA	I'm alright.
ALBERTO	A lucky escape, eh?
CHUSA	As you can see.
DOÑA ANTONIA	Come on, let's get going. We've not got all day.

(*She starts to pick up the boxed-up-stuff. And things she finds by the door. She picks up JAIMITO's flute.*)

JAIMITO	Listen, lady, that's mine.
DOÑA ANTONIA	As it was there.
JAIMITO	That's their stuff, the boxes. I don't know if there's anything else. I've put everything I've found in.
ALBERTO	No, it's fine, honestly. It's fine.
CHUSA	The dining table is yours in part. You can take a leg if you want. And three plates.
DOÑA ANTONIA	Let's be making tracks.
JAIMITO	I'll take the mirror down.
ELENA	Make sure you don't hurt your arm
JAIMITO	No, it's fine now.

(Salen DOÑA ANTONIA, ELENA *y* JAIMITO*. Despedidas frías desde la puerta.*
Se queda el último ALBERTO*, cuando los otros ya han salido.)*

ALBERTO	*(Desde la puerta.)* Bueno, adiós. Chusa. Ya hablaremos otro día más tranquilamente. Hoy está esto...
CHUSA	Alberto.
ALBERTO	¿Qué?
CHUSA	La llave. Tú ya no la necesitas para nada.
ALBERTO	*(Deja el paquete en el suelo. Se busca y encuentra la llave. Se acerca a dársela.)* Toma.
CHUSA	Ahí hay un libro tuyo, el Whitman que te regalé. ¿No lo quieres?
ALBERTO	No, déjalo. O sí, dámelo; lo que tú quieras.
CHUSA	Ese póster también lo trajiste tú. *(Empieza a quitarlo de la pared.)*
ALBERTO	Déjalo, no quiero un póster, Chusa.
CHUSA	*(Ya arrancándolo de mala manera.)* Pues toma, tíralo.
ALBERTO	Bueno, trae.
CHUSA	¿No queda nada?
ALBERTO	Oye, no me voy a la India, ni he muerto. Voy a Móstoles. Hoy no es el momento, pero tenemos que hablar. Siento mucho que te cogieran, y todo lo que ha pasado, de verdad. Me hubiera gustado... Pero déjalo. ¿Qué es lo que te pasó? ¿Cómo te cogieron?
CHUSA	En el tren. Por hacer un favor a uno. Tenía una cara de bueno que se la pisaba, y luego era policía. *(Pausa. Le mira.)* Desde luego es que hoy en día ya no te puedes fiar de nadie.
ALBERTO	Otro día quedamos.
CHUSA	Sí, otro día. El día de los Santos Inocentes. *(Va a salir él.)* ¡Alberto!
ALBERTO	¿Sí, qué?
CHUSA	No, nada. Déjalo. Qué mismo da.

(DOÑA ANTONIA, ELENA and JAIMITO head out. Cold farewells from the door. Once the others have all left, ALBERTO is the last to leave.)

ALBERTO	*(From the door).* Right, bye, Chusa. We'll speak more calmly another day. Today, with all this…
CHUSA	Alberto.
ALBERTO	What?
CHUSA	The key. You won't be needing it for anything now.
ALBERTO	*(He leaves what he's carrying on the floor. He looks and finds the key. He moves closer to give it to her.)* Here.
CHUSA	There's a book of yours over there, the Whitman I gave you.[xviii] Don't you want it?
ALBERTO	No, leave it. Or, yes, give it to me, whatever you prefer.
CHUSA	You also brought that poster. *(She starts to take it off the wall.)*
ALBERTO	Leave it, I don't want a poster, Chusa.
CHUSA	*(Now ripping it off the wall with attitude.)* Well take it, throw it out.
ALBERTO	Fine, give it here,
CHUSA	You haven't left anything?
ALBERTO	Listen, I'm not going to India, nor have I died. I'm going to Móstoles. Now's not the time, but we have to talk. I'm really sorry they caught you, and for all that has happened, honestly. I would have liked to… But, forget it. What happened to you? How did they catch you?
CHUSA	On the train. For doing one of them a favour. His face made him look good-natured, and he turned out to be a policeman. *(Pause. She looks at him.)* Needless to say, you can't trust anybody these days.
ALBERTO	We'll meet up another day.
CHUSA	Yes, another day, the day after the apocalypse. *(He goes to head out.)* Alberto!
ALBERTO	Yes, what?
CHUSA	No, nothing. Forget it. It doesn't matter.

(Él sale. Se cruza en el descansillo con JAIMITO, *que vuelve. Se les ve por la puerta abierta despedirse. Luego* JAIMITO *entra y cierra. Suelta entonces una carcajada, tapándose la boca con la mano para que no le oiga el otro fuera. Viene mojado de la lluvia que cae ahora y que vemos golpea contra los cristales de la ventana. Trae en la mano una corbata chillona de lunares.)*

JAIMITO	¡Se ha caído la gorda! ¡De culo, en un charco! ¡Te meas si la ves! *(Risas.)* Mira, me ha regalado una corbata por ayudarles. Ha abierto el bolso, me ha dado la corbata, y ¡zas!, al charco.

(Se da cuenta de lo triste que está ella y se contagia, quitándosele la risa de golpe. Se acerca a la cabeza del esclavo egipcio y le pone la corbata.)

	Bueno, pues se han ido.
CHUSA	Sí.
JAIMITO	¿Y nosotros qué pintamos aquí?
CHUSA	¿Nosotros? Nada.
JAIMITO	Es que hay que joderse.
CHUSA	Ya ves.

(JAIMITO se deja caer en una butaca, y se revuelve en ella.)

JAIMITO	Me dan ganas de quitarme el ojo y reventar el mundo de un ojazo con él.
CHUSA	Lo único que reventaría sería tu ojo. Déjalo donde está. Estarías muy feo con un ojo sí y otro no. Parecerías un pirata de los de las películas.
JAIMITO	Eso sí que habría sido mejor, haber nacido en la época de los piratas para montarnos en un barco con la bandera negra y la calavera, y a cruzar los mares subido al palo mayor.
CHUSA	Te caerías y te partirías una pierna.
JAIMITO	¡Mejor! Cojo, manco, tuerto... Parecería el terror de los mares, cañonazo va, cañonazo viene, a todos los

(He heads out. He passes JAIMITO, who's heading back in, on the landing. They can be seen making their farewells through the open door. JAIMITO then comes in and closes it. He bursts out laughing, covering his mouth with his hand so that ALBERTO doesn't hear him from outside. He's wet through from the rain that's now falling and we can see hitting against the window glass. He's carrying a garish polka-dot tie in his hand.)

JAIMITO   Fatty's fallen over! Right on her arse, in a puddle! You'd piss yourself if you saw her! (*Laughter.*) Look, she's given me a tie for helping them. She opened her handbag, gave me the tie and, kerplunk, right in the puddle.

(Her sadness is infectious and, on noticing how down she is, he suddenly stops laughing. He moves towards the head of the Egyptian slave and puts the tie on it.)

           Right, well, they've gone.
CHUSA   Yes.
JAIMITO   And what's the point of us being here?
CHUSA   Us? Nothing.
JAIMITO   You can't fucking credit it.
CHUSA   You see.

(JAIMITO slumps into a chair, and curls up into it.)

JAIMITO   They make me want to tear my eye out and blow up the world in the process.
CHUSA   The only thing you'd blow up would be your eye. Leave it where it is. You'd be real ugly with one eye in, and the other one out. You'd look like one of those pirates from the movies.
JAIMITO   That sure would have been better, to have been born in the age of pirates so as to have set sail in a boat, crossed the ocean, black flag and skull hoisted at the mast.
CHUSA   You'd fall over and break a leg.
JAIMITO   All the better! Lame, one-armed, cross-eyed... I'd look like the terror of the sea, cannon-fire here,

cabronazos con dos ojos, dos piernas y porvenir, que se me pusieran por delante. A esos dos los primeros, y a la madre, y al padre... ¡A todos! ¡A todo el que se me pusiera por delante! Ya sabes cómo las gasto yo. Acuérdate el día de la pistola la que armé. Corriendo con el culo colgando que iban esos dos chulos de mierda. Así iban a ir todos.

(Ella se echa a llorar.)

	Venga tía, no te pongas así. ¿Quieres que te cuente el chiste ese tan malo que te hace tanta gracia: «Es que de pequeño estuve muy malito...»? ¡No jodas, Chusa!
CHUSA	Ya estoy mejor. Perdona. Tenía aquí un nudo. Ahora ya estoy bien.
JAIMITO	Venga, ponemos música o lo que sea... Se han llevado el casette. Bueno, pues canto yo: «...Cuando la muerte venga a visitarme, que me lleven al sur donde nací, aquí no queda sitio para nadie, pongamos que hablo de Madrid». ¿Eh, tía? Sí lo vemos mal nos ganamos la vida cantando, dándole al morro. Tú tranquila, de verdad.

(Ella va al lavabo a lavarse la cara. Él, hacia la cocina. Dejan las puertas abiertas y se les ve. Siguen hablando entre ellos desde lejos.)

JAIMITO	Voy a hacer otro té, pero especial, de los que te gustan a ti; un quitapenas moruno a tope. Pero no te pongas chunga, que ya verás cómo no pasa nada. ¿Qué? ¿«Con dos terrones»?
CHUSA	*(Sale del lavabo secándose.)* Sí, dos terrones y cucharilla de plata. *(Pausa.)* Pues nos hemos quedado un poco solos.

cannon-fire there, let all those two-eyed bastards with both legs and a bright future get in my way. Those two would get it first, and the mother, and the father… All of them! Anyone who got in my way! You know how I let rip. Remember the day I picked up the gun. Those two wannabe rude-boys ran out shitting themselves. That's how they're all gonna go down.

(She starts to cry.)

Come on, love, don't get like that. Do you want me to tell you the really bad joke you find so funny?: "The thing is that when I was little, I was really bad…" No, fuck, Chusa!

CHUSA   I'm better now. Sorry. I had a knot in here. I'm fine now.

JAIMITO   Como on, we'll put on some music or whatever… They've taken the cassette player with them… Fine, well I'll sing: "…When death comes to visit me, let them take me back to the south, where I was born, there's no place left for anyone here, let's say I'm talking 'bout Madrid".[13] Eh, love, if things don't go our way, we can always earn a living singing, hand to mouth. Don't you worry, honestly.

(She goes into the bathroom to wash her face. He heads towards the kitchen. They leave the doors open and both of them can be seen. They continue speaking to each other from afar.)

JAIMITO   I'm going to make another cup of tea, but a special one, of that type you like; a pick-me-up with a serious dosage of that Moorish stuff. Don't go getting yourself in a state, you'll see how things will sort themselves out. What? With two sugar lumps?

CHUSA   *(She comes out of the bathroom drying herself.)* Yes, two sugar lumps and a silver spoon. *(Pause.)* Well, we've winded up a bit lonely.

---

[13]   The lyrics are taken from Joaquín Sabina's *Pongamos que hablo de Madrid*. It was not included in the 2008 revival.

JAIMITO	¿Y yo qué? Somos dos, y dos de los que ya no quedan, o sea, que valemos por cuatro, por lo menos.
CHUSA	(*Saca de su armario el álbum de recortes de* ELENA.) Se ha dejado los recortes de su colección. (*Lo hojea.*) «Hija, vuelve, tu madre te necesita.» Ya ha vuelto.
JAIMITO	Esos ya están en el bote. Su pisito, el sueldo al mes, la tele, los niños... Bueno, como todo el mundo; menos tú y yo, y cuatro pirados más de la vida que hay por ahí. Si hacen bien, ¿no? (*Le da el té.*) Toma. Cuidado, que quema. ¿Te has quemado?
CHUSA	No. Ya estoy mejor.
JAIMITO	Voy a liar uno.

(Se sienta y se pone a preparar un canuto.)

CHUSA	Ahora a esperar el juicio encima. No creas que lo mío...
JAIMITO	¿Y yo no? Estoy metido en un fregao también de aquí te espero. Por el tiro. Tuve que firmar que me lo había dado yo; y está muy castigado andar por ahí pegándose uno tiros a lo tonto. ¡Qué follón! ¿Tienes cerillas?

(Ella dice que no con la cabeza. Él va a la cocina. Habla desde allí.)

¡Qué mes! ¡De todo! Sólo nos ha faltado quedarnos embarazados.

(Ella se sonríe tristemente. El vuelve con las cerillas, la mira. Ella le hace señas a la tripa diciendo que sí con la cabeza.)

JAIMITO	¿Qué? ¿Que sí? ¿Que también nos hemos quedado embarazados?

(Ella dice que sí con la cabeza.)

JAIMITO	And what about me? There's two of us, and we're two of a kind like they don't make anymore so we're worth at least four.
CHUSA	(*She takes* ELENA's *album of newspaper clippings out of the wardrobe.*) She's left the newspaper clippings from her collection. (*She flips through it.*) "Child, come back, your mother needs you." She's returned to the fold.
JAIMITO	That lot are all set. Their nice little flat, the steady wage, the television, the kids... Well, like the rest of the world; apart from you and me, and four more nutters out there somewhere. They're doing the right thing, aren't they? (*He gives her the cup of tea*). Here. Careful, it's burning hot. Have you burnt yourself?
CHUSA	No. I'm fine now.
JAIMITO	I'm gonna roll one.

(He sits down and starts to prepare a spliff.)

CHUSA	Now, on top, I've got the trial hanging over me. Don't think that my...
JAIMITO	And what about me? I'm also caught up in a right fix cos of the shooting. I had to sign to say I'd fired the gun; and going around firing shots like a madman gets heavy-duty punishment. What a fuck-up. You have any matches?

(She indicates with her head that she doesn't. He goes to the kitchen and speaks from there.)

> What a month! With everything! All we need now is to wind up pregnant.

(She smiles sadly. He comes back with the matches, and looks at her. She nods, making signs towards her belly.)

JAIMITO	What? You are? We've also wound up pregnant.

(She nods affirmatively.)

	¡Hala! Alegría. Y ahora empezarán a caer las bombas atómicas del Rigan ese. Que no falte nada. (*Se ríen los dos.*) ¿Pero estás segura?
CHUSA	Casi segura. No me he hecho los análisis, pero por los días...
JAIMITO	¿Y de quién es? ¿De Alberto?
CHUSA	De Alberto.
JAIMITO	¿Lo sabe ese desgraciado?
CHUSA	No.
JAIMITO	¿Por qué no se lo has dicho? Ahora mismo me voy a buscarle, y se lo planto en su cara para que se les joda la boda y se les amargue la luna de miel.
CHUSA	No quiero que lo sepa, déjalo.
JAIMITO	¿Pero por qué?
CHUSA	Porque no. Primero no es seguro del todo, y diría que no es fijo que sea de él, que puede ser de cualquiera... Se marcharía igual Y además, no es de él. Bueno, sí es de él, pero como si no lo fuera. Yo me entiendo. Él ya no está aquí. Es un problema mío.
JAIMITO	Y mío también, ¿no? Así que estamos embarazados. Embarazados. Esto no me había pasado a mí nunca, ya ves. ¿Y qué vamos a hacer?

(Ella se levanta, sonríe y al pasar a su lado le acaricia cariñosamente el pelo.)

| CHUSA | No lo sé. Aún tenemos tiempo de pensarlo, en caso de que sea cierto. |
| JAIMITO | Si quieres ir a Inglaterra. Por las libras no te preocupes. Eso es cosa mía. Por otro lado, tampoco estaría mal que tuviéramos un crío; así podíamos bajar juntos al moro. Con el niño en los brazos se me quitaría la cara de sospechoso. |

	Ha! Joy. And now that guy Reagan's atomic bombs will start to fall. Bring it all on; wouldn't want to miss anything out.[14] (*The two of them laugh.*) But are you sure?
CHUSA	Almost certain. I haven't done the test but by the number of days…
JAIMITO	And whose is it? Alberto's?
CHUSA	Alberto's.
JAIMITO	And does that good-for-nothing know?
CHUSA	No.
JAIMITO	Why didn't you tell him? I'm gonna go look for him right now, and say it to his face to screw up their wedding and ruin their honeymoon.
CHUSA	I don't want him to know. Drop it.
JAIMITO	But why?
CHUSA	Because I don't. First, I'm not a hundred percent certain, and he'll say that he can't know it's his, that it could be anyone's… He'll be off, whatever. And, anyway, it's not his. Well, it is his, but as if it weren't. I know what I'm saying. He's not here anymore. It's my problem.
JAIMITO	And mine as well, isn't it? So the two of us are pregnant. Pregnant. This has never happened to me, as you can see. And what are we going to do?

(She gets up, smiles, and, on moving next to him, affectionately caresses his hair.)

CHUSA	I don't know. We've still got time to think about it, if it does turn out to the case.
JAIMITO	If you want to go to England,[xix] don't worry 'bout the pounds.[15] That's for me to deal with. On the other hand, it'd be no bad thing for us to have a little one; that way we could all go down to Morocco. With a kid in my arms, my face would stop looking so dodge.

---

[14] With the Cold War and Ronald Reagan's presidency of the US long finished, this reference was not present in the 2008 production.

[15] This reference to raising the cash to go to the UK for an abortion was absent from the 2008 production (see endnote xix).

CHUSA	Gracias, eres un tío.
JAIMITO	Pues sí, es lo que me parece que voy a ser. (*Se ríen.*) Tío.
CHUSA	Espera, no corras tanto, no sea que se quede en falsa alarma. Además, casi seguro que no lo tendría. ¿Qué íbamos a hacer nosotros con un niño?
JAIMITO	Anda, pues lo que hacen todos. Te imaginas, si naciera un niño ahora, qué cosas pensará luego, cuando sea mayor.
CHUSA	¿Qué va a pensar, de qué?
JAIMITO	De la vida, de las personas, de lo que nos pasa a nosotros, de todo. Para entonces sí que dará gusto vivir, ¿a que sí? Será todo mejor.
CHUSA	Qué optimista eres. O peor. Se liarán a bombazos esos animales, y se acabó,
JAIMITO	Que no tía, que no. Eso es cosa de esta gente de ahora que está podrida. Cuando éste sea mayor será totalmente diferente. Mira, para entonces, ya nadie tendrá que ir a la mili, ni habrá ejército, ni bombas, ni coñas de ésas. Ni habrá Móstoles, ni te meterán en la cárcel, ni nada de nada. Si se te cae un ojo, te pondrán otro enseguida, pero no de cristal, como éste, no, de verdad, de los buenos, de los que se ve. Y si alguien se entera de que va a tener un niño, si no quiere tenerle, todas las facilidades, pero sin irse a Inglaterra ni rollos de esos malos. Aquí a las claras y por la seguridad social. Y si lo quiere tener, pues ningún problema, estupendo, todos encantados. Y nacerán ya de más mayores cada vez, para que no lloren por las noches, ni se caguen, ni se pongan malos. Y nada más nacer, zas, una renta vitalicia, un dinero bien como les

CHUSA	Thanks, you're a dude.
JAIMITO	Well, yes, Uncle Dude, that's who I'm gonna be. (*They laugh.*)
CHUSA	Hold your horses, don't get ahead of yourself, it might be a false alarm. Anyway, I'm almost certain I wouldn't have it. What would we do with a baby?
JAIMITO	Come on, what everyone does. Can you imagine, a baby born now, what it'd think later on when it's grown up.
CHUSA	What it's going to think? About what?
JAIMITO	About life, about people, about what we all go through, about everything. By then, it'll be a pleasure to be alive, won't it? Everything will be better.
CHUSA	You're so optimistic. It could be worse. These animals could blow the shit out of each other, and that'll be that.
JAIMITO	No, love, it won't. That's these people's thing now, they're rotted from the inside. When this one's older, everything will be completely different. Look, by then, nobody will have to do military service,[16] there won't be any army, or bombs, or any of that shit. Móstoles won't exist, they won't put you in prison, nothing of that kind. If your eye falls out, they'll put another one in straight away, not made of glass like this but a real one, the good ones with which you can see. And if someone realises they're going to have a baby, and they don't wanna have it, they'll have every opportunity available to them, without going to England or all that unpleasant muddle. Here, everything out in the open and on social security. And if they want to have it, well no problem, great, everyone happy. And they'll be born older and older so they don't cry at night, shit themselves, or misbehave. And as soon as they're born, zap, riches

---

[16] At least in this respect, Jaimito is correct. Compulsory military service in Spain was abolished in 2001. This, alongside the reference to having to go to England for an abortion, were the only one of his predictions not to feature in the 2008 version.

pasa ahora a los ricos, pues a todos. De entrada naces, y un dinero para que estudies, o viajes, o vivas como quieras, sin tener que estar ahí como un pringao toda la vida; porque todo estará organizado justo al revés de como está ahora, y la gente podrá estar feliz de una vez, y bien. A gusto.

CHUSA   Sí, jauja.

JAIMITO   Ya lo verás, tía, ya lo verás. Oye, ya estoy sin papelillo otra vez, ¿tienes?

CHUSA   No, pero voy a buscarlo a la calle. (*Se levanta.*) Así me da un poco el aire. Enseguida vengo.

JAIMITO   Y no te traigas de paso a todo el que encuentres por ahí, que luego mira.

CHUSA   (*En la puerta.*) A todo el que encuentre, ¿oyes? A todo el que encuentre y no tenga adonde ir. (*Sale.*)

JAIMITO   Eres una tía cojonuda, Chusa, te lo digo yo. (*Se mira los bolsillos.*) Bueno, se llevó otra vez las llaves.

(Mira un momento a su alrededor, da un golpecito cariñoso en la jaula del hámster, saca su material de trabajo, se sienta en el colchón, y se pone de nuevo a hacer sandalias.)

for life, a good wad of cash, what the rich get now but for everyone. You're born and, right away, some money to study, or to travel or to live how you want, without having to be there like some loser all your life; because everything will be organised the reverse of how it is now, and people will finally be able to be happy and well. At ease.

CHUSA Yeah, whatever.

JAIMITO You'll see, love, you'll see. Listen, I'm out of Rizla again. You have any?

CHUSA No, but I'll go down and find some. (*She gets up.*) Some fresh air would do me good. I'll be back right away.

JAIMITO And don't bring whatever you stumble upon out there back with you, cos look at how it turns out.

CHUSA (*At the door.*) Anything I find out there, you hear me? Whatever waifs and strays I stumble upon. (*She leaves.*)

JAIMITO You're a top girl, Chusa, I'm telling you. (*He looks through his pockets.*) Well, she's taken the keys again.

(*He looks for a moment at his surroundings, affectionately punches the hamster's cage, takes out his work materials, sits on the mattress and starts to make sandals once again.*)

Endnotes

i   The late 1970s and early-mid 1980s witnessed an explosion in fanzines throughout Spain, influenced by the amateur DIY ethos of the British punk scene. *Víbora* and *Tótem* were two emblematic titles, which were both sold in the Rastro.

ii   John Lennon (1940–1980), the most outwardly rebellious member of the Beatles, who then pursued a solo career, and was shot by a crazed fan in New York.

iii   A US American jazz pianist, keyboardist and composer (1941–), who, amongst many other achievements, played in Miles Davis' band.

iv   All Spanish citizens have to carry ID cards (DNI) by law. First introduced at the outset of the Franco regime to keep track of ex-Republicans, they were soon extended to the general population and are still required for booking hotel rooms, paying with credit cards *etc.*

v   The Neocatechumenate, also known as The Neocatechumenal Way, NCW or, colloquially, The Way, is a group within the Catholic Church that focuses on the formation of Christian adults. It was formed in Madrid by Kiko Argüello and Carmen Hernández in 1964. Taking its inspiration from the catechumenate of the early Catholic Church, by which converts from paganism were prepared for baptism, it provides post-baptismal educating and training to adults who already belong to the Church. The Neocatechumenate is implemented in small, parish-based groups of between twenty and fifty people. There are around forty thousand communities around the world, with an estimated million members.

vi   Madrid's principal train-station. Another of Joaquín Sabina's most-loved songs about the Spanish capital and its inhabitants is titled *Yo me bajo en Atocha/I get off at Atocha*.

vii A traditional and popular lager brewed in Madrid.

viii A rumba band from Vallecas, formed in the 1970s, who mixed flamenco and romani music. They supplied the music for some of the most emblematic quinqui films of the 1980s such as *Deprisa, deprisa* and *Perros callajeros*.

ix   Most Spanish degree programmes operate differently to those in the UK or US. Students have to pass a series of modules but there is no set time-frame in which they have to do this. As a result, some young people are almost perpetual students.

x   Madrid's leading listings guide that translates literally as 'Leisure Guide', a much cheaper equivalent to London or New York's *Time Out*.

xi   This supermarket chain ceased to exist in the early 1990s but, during the 1980s, was a ubiquitous presence in Spanish towns and cities whose closest UK and US equivalents would probably be ASDA and Wallmart. In Spain, Simago has been superseded by the low-budget Día chain.

xii I have chosen "Da, da, da" because it is the sound that accompanies the song *You can leave your hat on* as heard in the famous strip scenes in *The Full Monty*, a 1997 film whose soundtrack also includes Hot Chocolate's *You Sexy Thing* used at an earlier point in the 2008 production (see footnote 6). Although Tom Jones recorded the arguably definitive version for the film soundtrack, the song was originally written

and recorded by Randy Newman in 1972, and Joe Cocker did a well-known cover version which also appeared in a strip scene in the 1986 film, *Nine and 1/2 Weeks*, so its presence wouldn't necessarily be anachronistic in a production set in 1985.

xiii   Quevedo roundabout is at the other end of Madrid's central area to Lavapiés and is just the other side of Malasaña. Generally respectable and without the social problems of neighbouring areas, the fact that Doña Antonia finds this middle-class area so posh is a sign of her limited social horizons.

xiv   He is referring to Aristotle Sokratis Onassis, the Greek-born Argentine shipping magnate (1906–1975) famous amongst other things for his affair with opera diva, Maria Callas, and his subsequent marriage to Jacqueline, the widow of assassinated US president, John F. Kennedy.

xv   This is a rather melodramatic and hyperbolic comparison with the film, *Casablanca*, set in unoccupied Africa at the outset of World War II. The protagonist, Rick, played by Humphrey Bogart twice loses Ilsa, played by Ingrid Bergman, because both of them place the fight against fascism above their personal desires and safety. As Huw Aled Lewis notes,

> Jaimito may, like Bogart in the film, have just lost the woman he loves, but Jaimito has only known Elena for a very short time, she has never felt anything for him, and she has just run off with his best friend, Alberto. This is not a world of noble sacrifices and the prioritisation of duty over emotion, but a sordid one where self-interest takes precedence over loyalty and where North Africa, far from being the scene of heroic resistance against an oppressive regime, offers an escape of another kind, based on the peddling and consumption of drugs. In *Casablanca*, characters eventually face up to the harsh demands of reality; in *Bajarse al moro*, characters constantly try to run away from it.

(2007, 111)

xvi   He actually sings the lyrics to the song performed by Dooley Wilson incorrectly. The lines should be sung: "You must remember this, a kiss is just as kiss".

xvii   Chusa is clearly implying that the police had taken the drugs for themselves or to sell on. I do not know if it was a mere urban myth, but as late as 2002–3, there were frequent tales of people being able to buy large quantities of drugs from corrupt police officers in Madrid.

xviii   Walt Whitman (1819–1892), an American poet, essayist and journalist renowned for his bohemian lifestyle who was taken up as something of hero by the American beat authors of the 1950s and continues to be a favourite for those leading alternative lifestyles. Alberto renouncing the book that Chusa gave him is therefore symbolic of him leaving her and a certain lifestyle behind.

xix   Abortion has traditionally been almost totally illegal in Spain, New legislation – that remained in force until 2010 – was introduced in 1985 which legalised abortion in very specific cases: when a woman has become pregnant as the result of a rape; when pregnancy is believed by doctors to incur a physical or mental risk for the mother; and in certain cases where the child will be born with specific deformities or disabilities. As a result, many Spanish women have continued well into the twenty-first century to come to England to have abortions.

Printed and bound by CPI Group (UK) Ltd, Croydon, CR0 4YY

09/06/2025

14685809-0001